CAMPER'S GUIDE TO
NORTHERN CALIFORNIA

PARKS, LAKES, FORESTS, AND BEACHES

Where to Go and How to Get There

MICKEY LITTLE

Gulf Publishing Company
Houston, Texas

CAMPER'S GUIDE TO
NORTHERN CALIFORNIA
PARKS, LAKES, FORESTS, AND BEACHES

Where to Go and How to Get There

SECOND EDITION

Library of Congress Cataloging-in-Publication Data

Little, Mildred J.
    Camper's guide to northern California parks, lakes,
forests, and beaches : where to go and how to get there /
Mickey Little. —2nd ed.
        p.   cm.
    Rev. ed. of: Camper's guide to California parks, lakes,
forests, and beaches. Volume 1, Northern California.
c 1988.
    Includes index.
    ISBN 0-88415-245-6
    1. Camp sites, facilities, etc.—California—Directories.
2. California—Guidebooks.   I. Little, Mildred J.
Camper's guide to California parks, lakes, forests, and
beaches.   II. Title.
GV191.42.C2L58   1997
647′.94794′09—dc21   96-40263
                                                            CIP

Photo Credits

All photographs are by the author unless otherwise credited.

I went to the woods because I wished to live
deliberately, to front only the essential facts
of life, and see if I could not learn what it had
to teach, and not, when I came to die,
discover that I had not lived.

                                    —*Henry David Thoreau*

Contents

Introduction —————— 1

Region 1 —————— 18

Region 2 —————— 68

Region 3 ——————125

Resources for Further Information, 178

Index, 179

Acknowledgments ————————

I am grateful to the following for their cooperation in providing information via maps, photographs, brochures, telephone conversations, and personal interviews. Thank you for helping make this guide possible for others to enjoy.

California Department of Forestry
California Department of Parks & Recreation
California Division of Tourism
DESTINET
National Park Service, Western Region
National Recreation Reservation System
U.S. Bureau of Land Management

U.S. Army Corps of Engineers, Sacramento
    District
U.S. Forest Service, Pacific-Southwest Region

While every effort has been made to ensure accuracy of the information in this guide, neither I nor the publisher assume liability arising from the use of this material. Because park facilities and policies are subject to change, campers may want to verify the accuracy of important details before beginning a trip. Happy Camping!

Mickey Little

Introduction

California is truly a land of contrasts. The highest and lowest places in the contiguous United States are within sight of each other: Mt. Whitney rises to 14,495 feet while 85 miles away is Death Valley, whose lowest point is 282 feet below sea level. Extreme temperatures of –45°F and + 135°F have been recorded, as have extreme yearly rainfall accumulations of zero in the desert and 161 inches in a rain forest.

From north to south, and east to west, California abounds with ideal recreation areas: forests of giant trees; high, rugged mountains; alpine meadows and lakes; fertile valleys; inland deserts; and sandy beaches of the south coast. What better way is there to really see and enjoy the California outdoors than by camping?

The purpose of this *Camper's Guide* is to suggest places to go and provide directions to get there. You will discover information about the popular, well-known campgrounds as well as the lesser-used camping areas. The public campgrounds presented in this guide are provided and operated by federal and state agencies. Outdoor enthusiasts will find recreational opportunities at these sites that are as varied as one's imagination. You can swim, skin or scuba dive, sail, windsurf, water ski or jet ski, boat, canoe, raft, fish, picnic, backpack, bicycle, horseback ride, hike, walk along a nature trail, or kick up some dust with an all-terrain vehicle.

In season, you can also cross-country ski, downhill ski, snow shoe, or snowmobile. You can pursue your favorite hobby as a bird watcher, photographer, botanist, geologist, or naturalist. You may choose to rough it in the backcountry or at a primitive campsite, or enjoy all of the comforts of home in a motor home. You can spend a day, a weekend, or an entire vacation doing what you like best, no matter how active, or inactive.

The number of public campgrounds in California's state and federal parks, lakes, and forests is staggering. This *Camper's Guide* and its counterpart for Southern California contain recreational areas with camping facilities that comprise nearly 120 state parks, covering more than 1 million acres of land; 4 state forests; 13 lakes administered by the U.S. Army Corps of Engineers; 16 national parks covering more than 4.6 million acres of land; and 48 campgrounds on 13.8 million acres of Bureau of Land Management lands. There are also 19 national forests encompassing more than 20 million acres, with 4 million of these acres in 52 designated Wilderness Areas.

The state is approximately 800 miles long and 300+ miles wide at its widest point, with an 840-mile coastline. California has less than 300 miles of gently sloping, sandy beaches, with pleasantly warm water, but of these, only half are publicly owned. Approximately 42% of the shoreline is not open to the public.

To acquaint you with the general topography of California, let's take a quick trip around the state (see map) to get an overall picture of the lay-of-the-land and what's available for recreational pursuits. Starting at the Mexico border on the Pacific Ocean, more than 200 miles of sun-washed sandy beaches stretch north to beyond Santa Barbara. These are the famed beaches enjoyed by swimmers and surfers almost year round.

The Coast Range parallels the shore from just north of the Los Angeles Basin to the Oregon border. These mountains rise abruptly from the sea or from a narrow coastal plain. For the most part, the north coast is a wild and rugged place where waves pound against the rocks, and groves of 300-foot-tall redwoods grow. East of the Coast Range is California's rich Central Valley, nearly 500 miles long and averaging 40 miles wide. It is the largest agricultural region west of the Rockies, with some of the world's most productive acreage. The Sacra-

California's Topography

mento/Stockton area has a huge maze of inland waterways.

In the north, the Coast Range merges with the Cascade Range. The Cascades rise to peaks and ridges 5,000 to 10,000 feet high. Massive and white, Mt. Shasta dominates the landscape, rising to a height of 14,161 feet. To the southeast, the Cascades merge with the Sierra Nevadas near Lake Almanor. The Sierra Nevada, the largest mountain mass in the United States, is more than 400 miles long. The range extends through Lake Tahoe, Yosemite, Kings Canyon, and Sequoia, then disappears into the Mojave Desert.

To the west of the Sierras, gently rolling foothills rise gradually from the Central Valley. The west slopes, cut by many rivers and streams, are generally moderate. The deep-blue waters of Lake Tahoe straddle the California-Nevada border. The east slope of the Sierras drop steeply into Owens Valley. The southeast quarter of California is a vast and fascinating area of three deserts—Mojave, Colorado, and Sonoran—extending to the Colorado River. Winter vacationers enjoy the warm winter days of the desert, which comes alive with a colorful spring wildflower bloom in February and March.

Your whirlwind mini-tour of the state is now complete. The only thing that remains is to plan your next camping trip and pack your gear. You will, no doubt, agree that it may take a lifetime to see all that California has to offer. What a challenge! Go for it!

Visitors from other states who drive to California should be aware that there are state information centers located on major highways entering the state. Not only do these centers provide a good rest stop, but they also give up-to-date information, brochures, guides, and maps to visitors. The centers are located at U.S. 199 and I-5 (near SR 96) at the Oregon border, and at 5 locations along the

Nevada border. Listed from north to south, they are: I-80 near Truckee, I-15 near Halloran Springs, I-40 near Fenner, I-10 near Blythe, and I-8 near Felicity. Prior to a trip, you may want to contact the California Division of Tourism for information. The address for the Division of Tourism, as well as for all agencies that provide camping facilities in California, may be found on page 178.

There are rules and regulations encountered at all public campgrounds, whether administered by a national, state, or county agency. Please keep in mind that policies, fees, regulations, and available facilities change from time to time. Campers must stay informed by requesting updated information from the parks they visit, by reading the material posted or distributed at the parks, and by reading newspaper articles reporting policy changes. And while we're on the subject of staying informed— take time to get acquainted with the rest of the information in this introduction. You'll find a variety of related topics. In other words, keep reading, don't stop now!

The north coast of California is a wild and rugged place where waves pound against the rocks. (Photo: Lillian Morava)

How to Use the Camper's Guide

This guide divides Northern California into the three geographic regions shown in the illustration. The parks, lakes, and forests within each region are arranged alphabetically and are cross-listed by name and city in the index. The first page of each region locates the park, lake, or forest on the map and gives the page number where you can find detailed information and maps. (The *Camper's Guide to Southern California* does the same for the lower half of the state. Note: Yosemite National Park appears in both volumes because of its popularity and pivotal position on the somewhat arbitrary north-south dividing line.)

All information in this *Camper's Guide* has been supplied by the respective operating agency, either through literature distributed by them, through verbal communication, or through secondary sources deemed reliable. The information presented is basic; it describes the location and outstanding features of the area, tells you how to get there, and lists the facilities and recreational activities available. Mailing addresses and telephone numbers are given in case you need additional information prior to your trip.

The maps showing the location of facilities within a park should be of considerable help. These maps are usually available to you at the park headquarters, but they can also aid you in planning a trip to an unfamiliar park. Most parks are easily found with the help of a good road map; however, in some instances, vicinity maps have been included. Signs along the way can also be relied upon after you reach the general vicinity of a park.

Because each ranger district within a national forest operates somewhat independently of the national forest as a whole, distributes its own materials, and in many ways has its own "personality" because of terrain, recreational opportunities, etc., information on each national forest is arranged by ranger districts. Visitors who wish to camp off-the-beaten-path should seriously consider purchasing the official national forest map, because even the best road map often does not show the many back roads in the forest.

Backcountry use is so popular in California that a section on "Backcountry Ethics" has been included on pages 16 and 17 as a guide to traveling and camping by the rules of "low impact." Checklists to guide you in planning your camping trips are included on pages 18 and 19. Careful and adequate planning can mean the difference between an enjoyable trip and a miserable trip.

The facilities available at a campground often change, but a change in status usually means the addition of a service rather than a discontinuation. In other words, a camper often finds better and more facilities than those listed in the latest brochure.

May this *Camper's Guide* serve you well in the years ahead, whether you are a beginner or a seasoned camper. Take time to camp, to become *truly* acquainted with nature . . . and with yourself and your family! Don't put off until tomorrow what can be enjoyed today!

Not only will this guide help you find places to camp, it will also show you places to hike. (Photo: Lillian Morava)

State Parks

Recreation! That's what California's State Park System means to millions of Californians and visitors. This guide cites 54 state parks comprising some 265 state park units that are located on over one million acres of land. Each park offers its own unique opportunities for fun and adventure, as illustrated by the range of titles—state park, historic park, recreation area, beach, wilderness, wayside campground, historical monument, and vehicular recreation area. Henceforth, they all will be referred to simply as "state parks."

There are several types of campsites found in California state parks:

Developed campsites—ordinarily have improved roads, restrooms with hot showers, piped drinking water, and campsites with a table, stove, or fire ring.

Primitive campsites—typically have chemical or pit toilets in an informal area containing tables and central water supply, or in a designated area without any facilities.

Trailer hookups—found at only a few parks. Of course, trailers, campers, and motor homes may also use developed or primitive campsites. Maximum lengths that can be accommodated must be considered by the park visitor.

Enroute campsites—day-use parking areas where self-contained trailers, campers, or motor homes can be parked for one-night stays; they cannot be reserved in advance and the campsites must be vacated by 9 a.m.

Environmental campsites—primitive sites that are isolated from each other and from the main campground; you must hike a short distance to reach them and sometimes carry in water and other supplies.

A variety of special park passes is available. They include an annual day-use pass, an annual boat pass, a Golden Bear pass for people 62 years of age or older with limited monthly incomes, a limited-use Golden Bear pass for anyone 62 years or older for use during off-peak-season (Labor Day to Memorial Day), a disabled veteran/prisoner of war pass, and a disabled discount pass. For detailed information on these passes, contact the California State Parks Store. See "Resources," page 178.

Selected information on camping that is basic to state parks in general is cited here rather than repeated for each park:

Each park offers its own unique opportunities for fun and adventure, including spending quality time with one another.

▲ Camping is allowed only in designated campsites.
▲ Family campsites will accommodate up to 8 persons and 2 licensed vehicles, including trailers.
▲ Campsites for groups are available at 54 state parks. Over 40 of them can be reserved through the State Park Reservation System (see page 11). Some of them must be reserved directly with the park.
▲ Environmental campsites are available at many state parks. Maximum stay at any one campsite is 7 days and occupancy is limited to one family or 8 people. Pets are not allowed. Reservations are available for environmental campsites at several parks during peak season (April through October) through the State Park Reservation System.
▲ Other types of campsites available at some state parks include individual trail camps, group trail camps, individual horse campsites, group horse camps, boat-in camps, and hike and bike campsites.
▲ Wheel-chair accessible trails and facilities are available in many state parks, and more are being constructed each year. Many parks have accessible campsites. Phone the park of your choice for specific local information about accessibility.

▲ Length of stay at each campground is limited, with the range usually from 7 to 30 consecutive days, depending on the season. In addition, there is a limit of 30 days in any calendar year in that unit for general occupancy by the same persons, equipment, or vehicles.

▲ Camping fees vary for each classification of campsites, i.e., developed, hookups, developed with coastal access, primitive, enroute, boat-in, and environmental.

▲ Persons 62 years of age or older, verified by identification, will be allowed a discount of $2 at all state park campgrounds; they also will be allowed a $1 discount at all state park units that charge for day use on a per-vehicle basis.

▲ During the peak season, reservations may be made at over two-thirds of the parks through the State Park Reservation System (see page 11). During "non-reservation" periods, campsites are on a first-come, first-served basis; a few campsites at each park remain on this basis even during the reservation period.

▲ Visitors should remember that often a campground that is filled during the summer (or winter for desert parks) will have plenty of room at other times of the year, and even the busiest parks sometimes have vacancies during the week, from Sunday through Thursday nights.

▲ Dogs are welcome in most state parks, although they must be kept on a leash no more than 6 feet long at all times. Dogs are permitted only in the campground and picnic areas; they are not allowed on trails or on most beaches. A fee is charged for each dog entering the park.

▲ Fires are permitted only in park stoves and fireplaces. Gas-type cooking stoves may be used unless the area is otherwise posted. Gathering firewood in the park is not permitted—even down wood. However, you may bring your own firewood or purchase it in the park.

▲ Flowers, rocks, plants, animals, artifacts, and other features of the parks' natural and cultural history are protected by state law and may not be disturbed or collected. However, collection of driftwood and rockhounding is permitted at some beaches.

▲ Special trails for horseback riding and horse camps have been built in some parks. Fourteen parks, some with horse rental facilities, provide equestrian camping.

▲ Hiking trails have been developed in most state parks; many of these trails allow mountain bikes. However, the use of mountain bikes is restricted on some trails because of conflicts with hikers, horseback riders, and potentially hazardous trails.

▲ For the off-highway-vehicle (OHV) enthusiast, there are 5 state vehicular recreation areas that offer vehicular recreation opportunities on primitive dirt roads within their boundaries. A very comprehensive and beneficial brochure entitled "Guide to Off-Highway Vehicle Areas of California" is available. See page 178, "Resources," for ordering information.

▲ A valid fishing license is required to fish in state park units.

▲ Hunting or the possession of loaded firearms is prohibited in all but a few recreation areas; these allow hunting of certain species of game in some areas of the park during specified hunting seasons.

▲ A folder entitled "Guide to California State Parks" is available for $2 from individual parks or from the Sacramento office. See page 178, "Resources," for ordering information.

Most campgrounds can accommodate all types of camping "rigs," but some are limited to specific types. Be sure to check before arriving!

State Forests

There are four state forests in California that permit camping; total acreage is around 67,000 acres. Foresters are involved in a very active program of timber harvest, enhancement of wildlife habitat, and protection of the watershed, along with consideration given to public recreation. Recreational activities available on state forest land include fishing and hunting in season in accordance with state laws and regulations, hiking, horseback riding, picnicking, and camping.

Facilities tend to be rustic; many campgrounds have pit toilets or no toilets, spring or creek water,

or no water. Although camping is free for the rustic facilities, a "campfire and special use permit" is usually required. These are obtainable from the individual forest headquarters. The camping season is normally May/June into November. Three state forests are located in Northern California and are included in this volume: Boggs Mountain State Forest (Region 2, page 73), Jackson State Forest (Region 2, page 86), and LaTour State Forest (Region 1, page 39).

National Parks

There are 20 "parks" in California on 4.6 million acres managed by the National Park Service. These "parks" include monuments, seashores, recreation areas, and historic sites. Sixteen of them provide camping facilities: 1 seashore, 4 recreation areas, 5 monuments, and 6 parks. One of these national recreation areas, Whiskeytown-Shasta-Trinity, consists of three separate units. Whiskeytown Unit is managed by the National Park Service while the Shasta and Trinity units are managed by the U.S. Forest Service. Smith River National Recreation Area is the newest national "park" in California; it is also managed by the U.S. Forest Service. The word "park" is henceforth used as a general term to refer to all of the national areas.

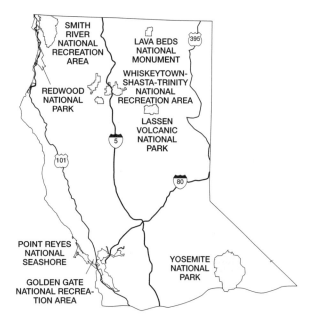

Information on camping that is basic to national parks in general is cited here rather than repeated for each park.

▲ All parks have a visitor/information center containing interpretive displays and, sometimes, museums pertaining to that park. Most sell literature with in-depth explanations of history, geology, flora, and fauna. Often an introductory film or slide show is offered.

▲ The visitor/information center should always be your first stop; brochures, maps, and a schedule of activities are readily available. Many of the larger parks publish a newspaper outlining activities and other pertinent information about the park's services, features, and history.

▲ Both entrance fees and recreation use fees are authorized at many parks. Campsite users are charged recreation use fees at all campgrounds that have certain minimum facilities and services. See page 12 for "Federal Recreation Passport Program."

▲ Fees for concession-operated facilities are charged by the concessionaires and are not federal recreation use fees.

▲ Most individual campsites are available on a first-come, first-served basis and cannot be reserved. Two exceptions are the Whiskeytown Unit of Whiskeytown-Shasta-Trinity National Recreation Area and Yosemite; reservations at both are through DESTINET. Some campsites at Whiskeytown can be reserved from mid-May through Labor Day. Reservation dates at Yosemite National Park are seasonal and are different for each campground. See "Reservation Systems" on page 11.

▲ The length of stay in most parks is 14 days; during the peak season at some parks, it may be 7 days; during the off-season it may be 30 days; at walk-in campsites it ranges from 1 to 3 days.

▲ Areas classified as developed campgrounds have well-defined roads, parking spaces, and campsites. Drinking water, sanitary facilities, and refuse cans are provided. A typical campsite in a campground would include a parking space, fireplace, table and bench combination, and tent/trailer space.

▲ Self-contained recreation vehicles—those requiring no utility connections—can be accommodated at most campgrounds, but size restrictions are imposed at some campgrounds.

▲ A sanitary sewage dump station is provided in some parks for disposal of liquid wastes from recreation vehicles' holding tanks. A fee is sometimes charged.

▲ In a walk-in campground or a walk-in section of a campground, the parking space is provided but is not an integral part of each campsite.

▲ Parks often restrict use of group campgrounds— those designed for large camping parties—to certain kinds of groups, such as educational or youth groups. Fees for group campsites often vary according to the size of the group, but most have a minimum charge. Minimum and maximum group size restrictions may apply. Reservations are usually required for use of group campgrounds.

▲ Primitive camping may be permitted in the remote, roadless areas of the park, but occasionally, backcountry use is prohibited because of emergency conditions, such as high fire danger or severe weather conditions. Check with the rangers at park headquarters to determine current conditions and to secure camping and/or fire permits, if needed.

▲ Backcountry use has been restricted in some areas and a quota system may be in effect. This program requires free permits for overnight use, but limits the number of people permitted in the backcountry at any one time. Contact the appropriate park for information about backcountry restrictions.

▲ Many parks have campgrounds that meet the needs of visitors in wheelchairs. Disabled visitors who have questions about their ability to use a particular campground should contact that park for more information.

▲ The gathering of wood for campfires is always limited to dead material found on the ground;

Point Reyes National Seashore is one of 16 national parks in California that provide camping facilties. There is no car camping at Point Reyes, only hike-in tent camping; reservations are required. (Photo: National Park Service)

sometimes it is prohibited. Campers are encouraged to use liquid-fuel camp stoves or charcoal for cooking. Fires should be confined to fireplaces in established campgrounds and picnic areas.

▲ In many parks, interpretive programs, including nature walks, guided tours, and campfire talks are conducted by park personnel.

▲ Every area of a park is a museum of natural or human history; removal or destruction of any feature is not allowed. The ideal visitor "takes nothing but memories, leaves nothing but footprints."

▲ Do not feed wild animals. Food supplies should be locked up or hung out of reach; such measures are required at some parks.

▲ Hunting is prohibited in national parks and monuments managed by the National Park Service. The use of campgrounds in these areas as base camps for hunting outside park boundaries also is prohibited. Hunting is authorized, in accordance with state laws, in national recreation areas and seashores.

▲ Fishing in all California parks requires a state fishing license.

▲ Pets are allowed in the parks and campgrounds if they are kept on a leash or under other physical restraint at all times. They are generally prohibited in the backcountry areas.

National Forests

California has 18 national forests within its boundaries, plus relatively small portions of Oregon's Rogue River and Siskiyou National Forests, and nearly 695,000 acres of Nevada's Toiyabe National Forest. The portions of the Toiyabe within California are included in this book because they have much to offer in the way of recreational facilities and activities. Shasta and Trinity National Forests, although two forests, were combined into one administrative unit in 1954 and are thus treated as one forest in this book.

In addition, the Lake Tahoe Basin Management Unit is treated as a forest; it is an administrative unit established by the Forest Service in 1973 to manage all national forest lands in the Lake Tahoe Basin, rather than be managed by three different national forests that surround the area.

The Forest Service of the U.S. Department of Agriculture is dedicated to the principles of multiple-use management of the nation's forest resources for sustained yields of water, forage, wildlife, wood, minerals, and . . . *recreation*. Yes, one of the main jobs of the Forest Service is to manage the national forests for recreation—all kinds, for all Americans. You can enjoy just about any kind of recreation on the 20 million acres of national forest land in California. The list of facilities/activities available includes equestrian facilities, marinas, water skiing, boat rentals, swimming beaches, lake/reservoir fishing, stream fishing, hunting, wilderness areas, white-water rafting, OHV trails, snowmobiling, downhill ski areas, cross-country skiing, hiking trails, picnic areas, family and group campgrounds, and dispersed camping.

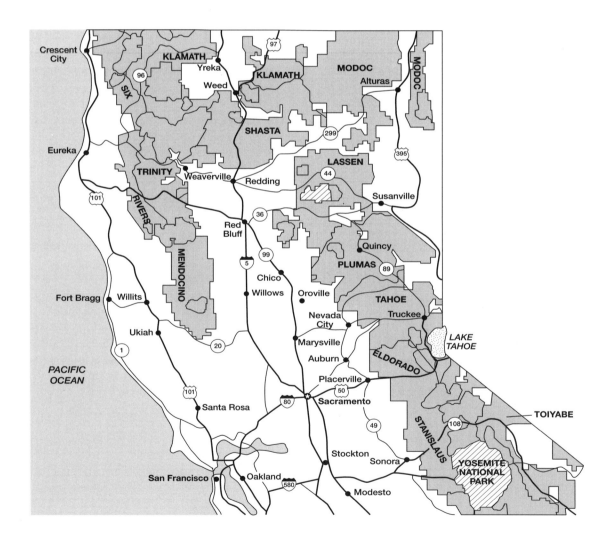

Selected information on camping that is basic to national forests in general is cited here rather than repeated for each forest:

▲ You must pay a fee to use certain developed sites and facilities. Such areas are clearly signed or posted as requiring a fee. Where fees are required, you must pay them before using the site, facility, equipment, or service furnished.

▲ At least one person must occupy a camping area during the first night after the camping equipment has been set up. Camping equipment should not be left unattended for more than 24 hours without permission.

▲ Reservations are required for most group campgrounds through either DESTINET or through the district ranger office; a fee is charged.

▲ Individual family units are for use by one family or a party with a maximum of 6 people. Multiple family units are for use by 2 families or a party with a maximum of 12 people camping together.

▲ Most developed campgrounds have piped drinking water and provide toilet facilities of some type—either flush, vault, pit, or chemical.

▲ Undeveloped campgrounds have very few facilities and many do not have piped drinking water. The water supply is often from a spring, stream, river, or lake. It is recommended that water from such sources be treated by boiling it for 5 minutes.

▲ Golden Age and Golden Access Passports are honored. See "Federal Recreation Passport Program," page 12 for details.

▲ Most campsites are available on a first-come, first-served basis with no reservation accepted. Reservations for some family and group campgrounds can be obtained through DESTINET. See "Reservation Systems," page 11.

▲ Limit of stay at most campsites is 14 days, but may be less in the more popular areas.

▲ In campgrounds, camp only in those places specifically marked or provided.

▲ Dispersed camping is allowed in most forests and is ideal for visitors with self-contained units, or for those who just want to get away from it all. Many areas are available; they have no facilities, are free of charge, but require a campfire permit, obtainable at the ranger district office.

▲ Obey restrictions on fires; they may be limited or prohibited at certain times. Within campgrounds and other recreation sites, build fires only in fire rings, stoves, grills, or fireplaces provided for that purpose.

▲ Barrier-free campgrounds and picnic grounds for physically handicapped visitors are available in most national forests. Inquire about facilities for visitors with handicaps.

▲ The camping season differs from one forest to another and even within a forest. Campgrounds at higher elevations are usually open seasonally, being closed from late fall through spring because of snow conditions.

▲ Many campgrounds do not have garbage pickup, so campers are expected to "pack out what you pack in."

▲ Pets must be restrained or on a leash while in developed recreation sites. Except for guide dogs, they are not allowed in swimming areas.

▲ Saddle or pack animals are allowed in recreation sites only where authorized by posted instructions.

▲ Within campgrounds and other recreation sites, cars, motorbikes, motorcycles, or other motor vehicles should be used only for entering or leaving, unless areas or trails are specifically marked for them.

▲ Obey area and trail restrictions on use of trail bikes and other off-the-road vehicles.

▲ Only travel on foot, horse, or pack animal is permitted in wilderness areas; motor vehicles and motorized equipment are not allowed.

▲ Both fishing and hunting are permitted in season in most forests, but a state license is required and state fish and game laws apply to national forest land.

▲ Indian sites, old cabins, and other structures, along with objects and artifacts associated with them, have historic or archaeological value. Do not damage or remove any such historic or archaeological resource.

▲ Maps of each forest are available for $2 from the national forest offices and ranger stations. The maps show roads not on most road maps, so they are invaluable and necessary for visitors wishing to explore the backcountry.

▲ Visitors to a national forest are encouraged to visit either the office of the forest supervisor or the individual ranger district offices. They are able to supply you with numerous brochures on the various recreational activities, as well as give information on road conditions, weather, campgrounds, dispersed camping areas, and fire conditions. For your convenience, addresses and phone numbers are included for each national forest.

▲ The 18 national forests in California are administered by the U.S. Forest Service's Pacific Southwest Region office in San Francisco. See "Resources for Further Information," page 178, for their address and phone number.

U.S. Army Corps of Engineers' Lakes

Nearly all of the dams constructed in northern and central California by the U.S. Army Corps of Engineers were authorized to provide flood protection and irrigation water. These dams have created lakes, and in addition to accomplishing said objectives, they have created a wide variety of recreational opportunities. Recreation areas are administered by the Corps of Engineers at the 7 lakes/rivers covered in this guide.

Campgrounds are located at all 7 of the lakes/rivers; group campgrounds and boat-in campsites are available at several of the areas. Camping is permitted only at designated sites/areas. There is a 14-day camping limit during any 30-consecutive-day period; Golden Age and Golden Access Passports are honored. Pets are not allowed on swimming beaches and should be penned, caged, physically restrained or on a leash less than 6 feet long in any developed recreation area.

Recreational activities possible at many of the lakes include fishing, boating, waterskiing, jet skiing, sailing, windsurfing, swimming, snorkeling, scuba diving, hiking, horseback riding, and picnicking. The Stanislaus River Parks provide opportunities for rafting, canoeing, and kayaking. Refer to the facility chart for each lake for information regarding availability of piped water, hot showers, boat ramps, marinas, and trailer sanitary station.

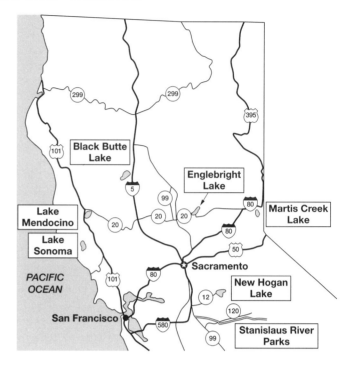

In addition to providing flood protection and irrigation water, dams built by the U. S. Army Corps of Engineers in California have created lakes that offer numerous recreational opportunities. (Photo: California Department of Parks and Recreation)

Reservation Systems

Campground reservations are necessary for popular parks in season, i.e., late spring, summer, and early fall. During the non-reservation periods, family campsites are available on a first-come, first-served basis; this is the same basis for unreserved campsites during the reservation period. The list of parks/campgrounds requiring reservations and their reservation seasons changes from year to year. Even the agency handling the reservations can change so only basic information is given here. Each reservation system charges a fee for the reservation, as well as a cancellation fee. Because these are subject to change, the current fees are not given. As a campground user, the best procedure, each year, is to obtain an up-to-date copy of each brochure (state parks, national parks, national forests) describing the reservation procedure and containing the camping reservation application. The brochure also serves as a valuable source of information on facilities available.

Be familiar with the campground reservation system, especially if you plan to camp at the popular parks in May through September. (Photo: Lillian Morava)

State Parks

For state parks, Ticketron was once used, then MISTIX, now DESTINET. To avoid possible confusion, the phrase "on state park reservation system" is used throughout this book to simply verify that the park/campground is usually on a central reservation system. The reservation system is used extensively for state parks; two-thirds of the park units are presently using it—some seasonally and some year-round. Most of the park units use the reservation system for group campgrounds. Environmental campsites at several parks also can be reserved. Reservations for family campsites and group campsites can be reserved up to 7 months in advance, and as late as 1 day prior to arrival, subject to availability. Reservations may be charged to Visa or MasterCard.

National Parks

Only 5 national parks in California are presently on a reservation system. Death Valley and Sequoia each have one campground on the DESTINET reservation system, Joshua Tree has 2, Whiskeytown has 3, and Yosemite has 9. The reservation period at Joshua Tree and at Lower Pines in Yosemite is year-round; others are seasonal. Reservations for family campsites and group campsites can be reserved up to 5 months in advance, and as late as 1 day prior to arrival, subject to availability. Reservations may be charged to Visa, MasterCard, or Discover.

National Forests

Selected national forest campgrounds in California are reservable during the "peak season" through the U.S. National Forest Reservation Center—which, for most campgrounds is Memorial Day through Labor Day. Reservations may be made up to 12 months in advance of the first night of arrival for group sites and 120 days in advance for family sites, or as late as 10 days prior to arrival. MasterCard and Visa are accepted with phone reservations. Contact the forest supervisor's office of the national forest you plan to visit, to determine which campgrounds are on the reservation system.

For information and reservations, phone the appropriate number listed below. Mailing addresses are cited on page 178 in "Resources."

California State Parks:
DESTINET
1-800-444-7275 (PARK)

National Park Service:
DESTINET
1-800-365-2267 (CAMP)

for Yosemite reservations:
1-800-436-7275 (PARK)

U.S. National Forest Service:
National Recreation Reservation System
1-800-280-2267 (CAMP)
FAX: 301-722-9802

Federal Recreation Passport Program

Some federal parks and facilities can be entered and used free of charge, while other areas and facilities require payment of entrance fees, user fees, and special recreation permit fees. A brochure by the U.S. Department of the Interior entitled *Federal Recreation Passport Program* explains the 5 entrance pass programs. Briefly stated below, these beneficial programs can provide a savings to park visitors.

Golden Eagle Passport—an annual entrance pass to all federally-operated parks, such as national parks, recreation areas, and national wildlife refuges. The passport admits free of charge the permit holder and accompanying persons in a private vehicle; it does not cover use fees, such as fees for camping, parking, and tours. It is valid for entrance fees only. The Golden Eagle Passport costs $25, and is good from date of purchase to one year later; it may be purchased at all national parks where entrance fees are charged. The Golden Eagle Passport is not valid on the national forests or at recreational areas administered by the U.S. Army Corps of Engineers.

Golden Age Passport—for a one-time fee of $10, a lifetime entrance pass for citizens or permanent residents of the United States who are 62 years or older. The passport admits free of charge the permit holder and accompanying persons in a private vehicle plus a 50% discount on federal use fees charged for facilities and services such as camping, boat launching, and parking. The passport does not cover fees charged by private concessionaires at national parks; however, at national forests and at recreational areas administered by the U.S. Army Corps of Engineers, holders of the passport receive a 50% discount even if the facility is operated by a private concessionaire. The passport must be obtained in person, with proof of age; it is available at any of the national parks, U.S. Forest Service offices or ranger stations, or U.S. Army Corps of Engineers' offices.

Golden Access Passport—a free lifetime entrance pass for citizens or permanent residents of the U.S. regardless of age who have been medically determined to be blind or permanently disabled, and, as a result, are eligible to receive benefits under federal law. It offers the same benefits as the Golden Age Passport, and must be obtained in person with proof of eligibility.

Park Pass—an annual entrance permit to a specific park or recreation area. In the National Park System the pass costs $10 or $15, depending upon the area; it is good for one year and permits unlimited entries only to the park unit where it is purchased. An annual pass is now available at Corps of Engineers lakes for $25; it allows use of any Corps-operated boat launching ramp or swimming beach at any project for that calendar year.

Federal Duck Stamp—officially known as the Migratory Bird Hunting and Conservation Stamp and still required of waterfowl hunters, the Federal Duck Stamp now also serves as an annual entrance fee permit to national wildlife refuges. The Duck Stamp is valid for entrance fees only and does not cover user fees. The stamp cost $15, is good from July 1 through June 30 of the following year, and permits unlimited entries to all national wildlife refuges that charge an entrance fee. It can be purchased at most post offices.

Federal parks require payment of entrance fees and user fees, but a view like this is worth the cost!

U.S. Bureau of Land Management Camping Areas –

The Bureau of Land Management (BLM), an agency of the Department of Interior, is responsible for the conservation, management, and development of 13.8 million acres of public land in California. The public lands are characteristic of the diversity that makes the Golden State unique; they are some of the richest and most beautiful in the state.

Public lands offer a variety of recreational uses including camping, hiking, OHV use, hunting and fishing; state licenses are required. Most of the public lands offer numerous opportunities for camping near natural, scenic, and historical resources. Some people prefer developed campsites, with amenities such as tent and recreational vehicle spaces, drinking water, boat ramps, picnic tables, or fireplaces. Others prefer "roughing it" in more primitive camping areas. The public lands have a wide variety of both types of campgrounds.

Reservations are generally not required at BLM campgrounds except for group sites. All others are filled on a first-come, first-served basis. Overnight camping fees are charged at many of these sites. The length of stay is usually limited to 14 days. The Golden Age Passport and the Golden Access Passport entitle the holder to use BLM recreation facilities for half the usual fee.

The public lands are rich in historical and archaeological sites and related artifacts. These fragile resources are protected by federal law, and penalties for unauthorized collection include severe fines and imprisonment. Enjoy, but do not remove or disturb, these remnants of early American cultures. Rocks, minerals, and gemstones as well as berries, nuts, and flowers can usually be collected

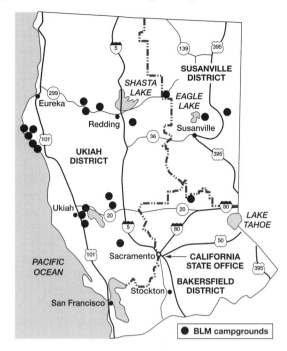

without a permit in reasonable quantities for personal use. A BLM permit is required for collection of large quantities or for commercial use.

Nineteen campgrounds are located in Northern California and their general locations are shown on the accompanying map. For detailed information about these campgrounds, such as campground name, location, available activities and facilities, contact BLM's state office in Sacramento. See page 178 "Resources" for the address and phone number; they have brochures available on camping, trails, and rivers.

Five Bureau of Land Management developed campgrounds are adjacent to the Pacific Ocean. Tidepools are just waiting to be explored. What a thrill to discover this colorful sea star! (Consult Beachcomber's Guide to California *by Tom Niesen, Gulf Publishing Co. for information about shoreline creatures.)*

Wilderness Areas

Nearly 4 million acres of the total 20 million acres of national forest land in California are now designated wilderness. Although many non-wilderness areas in the national forests provide similar opportunities for camping and hiking in an isolated, undeveloped setting, wilderness areas in particular are managed to preserve their natural conditions.

There is no wonder that wilderness areas in California's national forests attract more and more visitors every year as they offer something for everyone: rugged mountain slopes for experienced mountaineers; placid lakes for family campers; and a solitary getaway for people seeking isolation. Visitors are asked to observe no-trace camping practices and to leave areas as undisturbed as possible.

Twenty-two wilderness areas are in the 12 national forests covered in this *Camper's Guide*. Be sure to get a map of the national forest you intend to visit; they are available for $2 for plain paper, and $4 for plastic-covered paper. Large topographic maps (1 inch to the mile) are also available of many of the wilderness areas for $2 each; several cost $4. An informative brochure entitled *A Guide to National Forest Wilderness in California* will also prove helpful to those planning a trip to a wilderness area. All of these items are available from the U.S. Forest Service Office in San Francisco. See page 178 for the address and phone number.

USGS topographic quad maps are available from many camping suppliers or in person from California offices of the U.S. Geological Survey in San Francisco, Menlo Park, and Los Angeles. See page 178 for the locations of these offices. You can obtain a free index map to select the quad map(s) needed for your trip. Mail order sale of USGS quad maps is done only through the Denver office. See page 178.

A visitor permit is no longer required to enter some national forest wilderness areas. However, many areas do require permits, and some have a quota system for peak season use that admits visitors gradually to reduce adverse impact on the wilderness quality of the areas. Contact the forest supervisor's office of the national forest that you plan to visit for information about permit requirements and permit application forms. Group size is limited as very large groups have significantly greater impact on wilderness quality than small

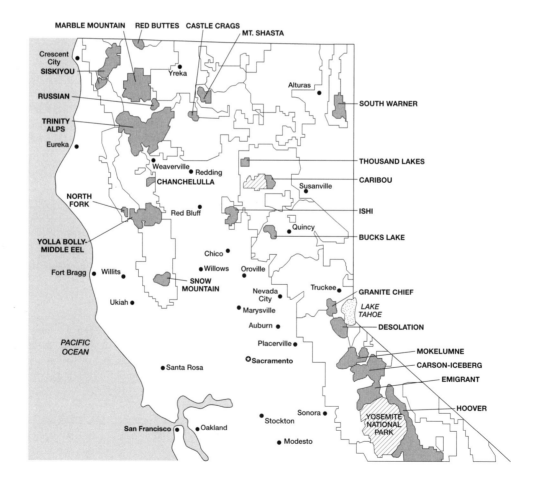

groups. Fishing and hunting are permitted in season in many wildernesses. If you don't want to camp in an area during hunting season, be sure to inquire about the effective dates when you plan your trip.

A campfire permit is required if you plan to use a portable stove or build a campfire during your trip. During periods of severe fire danger, campfires may be prohibited and some areas or parts of areas closed. Be sure to inquire at the forest ranger station at your point of entry for complete information about any fire restrictions in effect.

Generally, a wilderness permit for entry into an area through a national forest is valid for travel through a contiguous area managed by the National Park Service and vice versa. Campfire permits are required in all areas. Specific restrictions regarding use of firewood, stock travel, and group size may vary from area to area.

Pacific Crest Trail

The Pacific Crest National Scenic Trail extends 2,638 miles from Canada to Mexico. In California the trail begins at the California-Oregon border south of Observation Peak in the Siskiyou Mountain Range, and ends at the Mexican border near Campo. It passes through 14 national forests, 6 national parks, 4 state parks, and 16 wilderness areas in California.

The trail was established as part of the National System of Recreational and Scenic Trails by the National Trails System Act of 1968. Although the trail extends along mountain ranges, there are stretches where there is no well-defined "Pacific Crest." Whatever your starting point and however long you plan to spend, the 1,615 miles of the trail in California offer challenge and beauty to match your pace and interest.

The Pacific Crest Trail crosses forests, brushland, mountains, and desert, and the weather and travel conditions differ as much from end to end as the vegetation and landscape. The stretch between Lake Tahoe and the Oregon border is snow-free until late in October. In the Sierra Nevada, snow comes early and stays late, so the best travel time is July through September. This segment of the trail is heavily used. In Southern California, winter and spring are generally the best times to travel.

The trail is designed and intended for travel on foot or with stock. Travel by motorized vehicle is prohibited. You may travel with pets in national forest, national forest wildernesses, and on land administered by the Bureau of Land Management. However, pets are not allowed in national parks and state parks, so if your trip includes sections of either, you should leave your pet at home.

You will want to get detailed maps of the section of the trail you plan to travel, either U.S. Forest maps or USGS quad maps. Many guidebooks, commercially available, have narrative descriptions of the trail and include trip maps. A brochure entitled *Pacific Crest Trail, the California Section* gives basic information you will need to plan a trip. It is available from the Office of Information of the U.S. Forest Service (see page 178 for address).

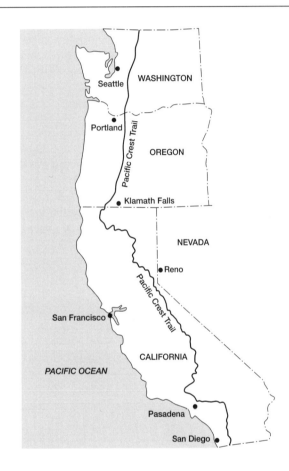

A permit is not required for travel on the Pacific Crest Trail as such, but a permit may be required for travel through wilderness and other special areas. In California, a campfire permit is required for use of stoves and wood campfires outside of developed campgrounds. Prior to your trip, write to the national forest or national park office near your point of entry for a combined permit valid for one continuous trip on all parts of the Pacific Crest Trail in California. Specify when and what segments of the trail you plan to travel. You will then be provided with any special permits that are needed and will be informed of any special restrictions in effect.

Backcountry Ethics

Spectacular areas throughout California await backcountry campers. Rules for backcountry camping are important, common sense rules meant to control actions that may damage natural resources or take away from the enjoyment of an outdoor experience. In recent years, the term "going light" has taken on new meaning. To a backpacker, "going light" is the skill of paring down the load and leaving at home every ounce that can be spared. Today, "going light" also means to spare the land and travel and camp by the rules of "low impact." The U.S. Forest Service suggests the following "low impact" rules. Although these suggestions were written for the hiker and backpacker, they are quite appropriate for anyone camping, whether traveling by foot, canoe, bicycle, or horse.

General Information

▲ Keep noise to a minimum (exceptions may exist for areas inhabited by bears).
▲ Respect other campers' space and privacy.
▲ Do not short-cut trails or cut across switchbacks. Trails are designed and maintained to prevent erosion.
▲ Trampling meadows can create confusion and damage vegetation.
▲ Do not pick flowers, dig up plants, or cut branches from live trees. Leave them for others to enjoy.
▲ Remember, it is unlawful to take, damage or deface any park objects: rocks, plants, and artifacts.
▲ It is unlawful and dangerous to feed animals, large or small.

Planning a Trip

▲ Keep camping groups small.
▲ Take a gas stove to help conserve firewood.
▲ Bring sacks to carry out trash.
▲ Take a light shovel or trowel to help with personal sanitation.
▲ Carry a light basin or collapsible bucket for washing.
▲ Before traveling, study maps of the area, get permits if necessary and learn the terrain.
▲ Check on weather conditions and water availability.

Setting Up Camp

▲ Pick a campsite that does not require clearing away vegetation or leveling a tent site.
▲ Use an existing campsite, if available.
▲ Camp 300 feet from streams or springs. Law prohibits camping within ¼ mile of an only available water source (for wildlife or livestock).
▲ Do not cut trees, limbs or brush to make camp improvements. Carry tent poles.

Whether traveling by foot, canoe, bicycle, or horse, backcountry campers should travel and camp by the rules of "low impact."

Breaking Camp

▲ Before leaving camp, naturalize the area. Replace rocks and scatter needles, leaves, and twigs around the campsite.
▲ Scout the area to be sure nothing is left behind. Everything packed into camp should be packed out. Try to make it appear as if no one has been there.

Campfires

▲ Even when campfires are permitted, use gas stoves when possible to conserve dwindling supplies of firewood.

▲ If a campfire is needed and allowed, use an existing campfire site. Keep it small.

▲ If clearing a new fire site is needed, select a safe spot away from rock ledges that would be blackened by smoke; away from meadows where it would destroy grass and leave a scar; away from dense brush, trees and duff, where it would be a fire hazard.

▲ Clear a circle of all burnable materials. Dig a shallow pit for the fire. Keep the sod intact.

▲ Use only fallen timber for firewood. Even standing dead trees are part of the beauty of wilderness, and are important to wildlife.

▲ Put fires cold out before leaving. Let the fire burn down to ashes, mix the ashes with dirt and water. Feel it with your hand. If it is cold out, cover the ashes in the pit with dirt, replace the sod, and naturalize the disturbed area.

Pack It In—Pack It Out

▲ Bring trash bags to carry out all trash that cannot be completely burned.

▲ Aluminum foil and aluminum-lined packages will not burn completely in a fire. Compact it and pack it out in trash bags.

▲ Cigarette butts, pull-tabs, and gum wrappers are litter too. They can spoil a campsite and trail.

▲ Do not bury trash! Animals dig it up.

▲ Try to pack out trash left by others. A good example may catch on!

Keep The Water Supply Clean

▲ Wash yourself, dishes, and clothes away from any source of water.

▲ Pour wash water on the ground away from streams and springs.

▲ Food scraps, toothpaste, even biodegradable soap will pollute streams and springs. Remember, it is your drinking water too!

▲ Boil water or treat water before drinking it.

Disposing of Human Waste

▲ When nature calls, select a suitable spot at least 100 feet from open water, campsites, and trails. Dig a hole 4 to 6 inches deep. Try to keep the sod intact.

▲ After use, fill in the hole, completely burying waste. Then tramp in the sod.

Emergency Items

▲ According to conditions, carry rain gear, extra warm clothing such as a windbreaker, wool jacket, hat, and gloves. Sunscreen lotion is important to use in warm and cold conditions.

▲ Keep extra high-energy foods like hard candies, chocolate, dried fruits, or liquids accessible. Do not overload yourself, but be prepared.

▲ Travel with a first aid kit, map, compass, and whistle. Know how to use them.

▲ Always leave a trip plan with a family member or a friend. File a trip plan with park rangers.

▲ Mishaps are rare, but they do happen. Should one occur, remain calm. In case of an accident, someone should stay with the injured person. Notify appropriate officials.

These backpackers are wearing their "emergency gear" because there was no snow on the ground when they went to bed.

Camping Equipment Checklist

The following checklists are designed to guide you in planning your next camping trip. Your needs will vary according to the type, length, and destination of your trip, as well as personal preferences, number of persons included, season of the year, and budget limitations.

Obviously, all items on the checklists aren't needed on any one trip. Since using checklists helps you think more methodically in planning, these extensive lists should serve merely as a reminder of items you may need.

When using these checklists to plan a trip, the item may be checked (√) if it needs to be taken. Upon returning, if the item was considered unnecessary, a slash could be used: √. If a needed item was forgotten, a zero could be used (0); if the item has been depleted and needs to be replenished, an encircling of the check could be used:√. This is of particular importance if you camp regularly and keep a camping box packed with staples that can be ready to go on a moment's notice.

Cooking equipment needs are quite dependent on the menu—whether you plan to cook and eat three balanced meals a day or whether you plan to eat non-cooked meals or snacks the entire trip. Many campers find it helpful to jot down the proposed menu for each meal on a 4 × 6″ index card to help determine the grocery list as well as the equipment needed to prepare the meal. By planning this way, you'll avoid taking equipment you'll never use and you won't forget important items.

Typical Menu with Grocery and Equipment Needs

MEAL: Saturday breakfast   Number of Persons: 5

MENU	GROCERY LIST	EQUIPMENT
orange juice	Tang	camp stove
bacon	10 slices bacon	gasoline, funnel
eggs (scrambled)	8 eggs	folding oven
biscuits	1 can biscuits	frying pan
	peach jelly	baking pan
	honey	pitcher
	margarine	mixing bowl
	salt	cooking fork, spoon
	pepper	

Shelter/Sleeping:
_____ Air mattresses
_____ Air mattress pump
_____ Cots, folding
_____ Cot pads
_____ Ground cloth
_____ Hammock
_____ Mosquito netting
_____ Sleeping bag or bed roll
_____ Tarps (plastic & canvas)
_____ Tent
_____ Tent stakes, poles, guy ropes
_____ Tent repair kit
_____ Whisk broom

Extra Comfort:
_____ Camp stool
_____ Catalytic heater
_____ Folding chairs
_____ Folding table
_____ Fuel for lantern & heater
_____ Funnel
_____ Lantern
_____ Mantels for lantern
_____ Toilet, portable
_____ Toilet chemicals
_____ Toilet bags
_____ Wash basin

Clothing/Personal Gear:
_____ Bathing suit
_____ Boots, hiking & rain
_____ Cap/hat
_____ Facial tissues
_____ Flashlight (small), batteries
_____ Jacket/windbreaker
_____ Jeans/trousers
_____ Pajamas
_____ Pocket knife
_____ Poncho
_____ Prescription drugs
_____ Rain suit
_____ Sheath knife
_____ Shirts
_____ Shoes
_____ Shorts
_____ Socks
_____ Sweatshirt/sweater
_____ Thongs (for showering)
_____ Toilet articles (comb, soap, shaving equipment, toothbrush, toothpaste, mirror, etc.)
_____ Toilet paper
_____ Towels
_____ Underwear
_____ Washcloth

Safety/Health:
_____ First-aid kit
_____ First-aid manual
_____ Fire extinguisher
_____ Insect bite remedy
_____ Insect repellant
_____ Insect spray/bomb
_____ Poison ivy lotion
_____ Safety pins
_____ Sewing repair kit
_____ Scissors
_____ Snake bite kit
_____ Sunburn lotion
_____ Suntan cream
_____ Water purifier

Optional:
_____ Binoculars
_____ Camera, film, tripod, light meter

_____ Canteen
_____ Compass
_____ Fishing tackle
_____ Frisbee, horseshoes, washers, etc.
_____ Games for car travel & rainy day
_____ Hobby equipment
_____ Identification books: birds, flowers, rocks, stars, trees, etc.
_____ Knapsack/day pack for hikes
_____ Magnifying glass
_____ Map of area
_____ Notebook & pencil
_____ Sunglasses

Miscellaneous:
_____ Bucket/pail
_____ Candles
_____ Clothesline
_____ Clothespins
_____ Electrical extension cord
_____ Flashlight (large), batteries
_____ Hammer
_____ Hand axe/hatchet
_____ Nails
_____ Newspapers
_____ Pliers
_____ Rope
_____ Saw, bow or folding
_____ Sharpening stone/file
_____ Shovel
_____ Tape, masking or plastic
_____ Twine/cord
_____ Wire
_____ Work gloves

Cooking Equipment Checklist

Food Preparation/Serving/Storing:

_____ Aluminum foil
_____ Bags (large & small, plastic & paper)
_____ Bottle/juice can opener
_____ Bowls, nested with lids for mixing, serving & storing
_____ Can opener
_____ Colander
_____ Fork, long-handled
_____ Ice chest
_____ Ice pick
_____ Knife, large
_____ Knife, paring
_____ Ladle for soups & stews
_____ Measuring cup
_____ Measuring spoon
_____ Pancake turner
_____ Potato & carrot peeler
_____ Recipes
_____ Rotary beater
_____ Spatula
_____ Spoon, large
_____ Tongs
_____ Towels, paper
_____ Water jug
_____ Wax paper/plastic wrap

Cooking:

_____ Baking pans
_____ Charcoal
_____ Charcoal grill (hibachi or small collapsible type)
_____ Charcoal lighter
_____ Coffee pot
_____ Cook kit, nested/pots & pans with lids
_____ Fuel for stove (gasoline/kerosene/liquid propane)
_____ Griddle
_____ Hot pads/asbestos gloves
_____ Matches
Ovens for baking:
_____ Cast iron dutch oven
_____ Folding oven for fuel stoves
_____ Reflector oven
_____ Tote oven
_____ Skewers
_____ Skillet with cover
_____ Stove, portable
_____ Toaster (folding camp type)
_____ Wire grill for open fire

Eating:

_____ Bowls for cereal, salad, soup
_____ Cups, paper, & styrofoam
_____ Forks
_____ Glasses, plastic
_____ Knives
_____ Napkins, paper
_____ Pitcher, plastic
_____ Plates (plastic, aluminum, paper)
_____ Spoons
_____ Table cloth, plastic
_____ _____
_____ _____

Clean-Up:

_____ Detergent (Bio-degradable soap)
_____ Dish pan
_____ Dish rag
_____ Dish towels
_____ Scouring pad
_____ Scouring powder
_____ Sponge

Hiking/Backpacking Checklist

This list is not meant to be all inclusive or necessary for each trip. It is a guide in choosing the proper gear. Although this list was prepared for the hiker/backpacker, it is quite appropriate for anyone using the backcountry, whether they are traveling by foot, canoe, bicycle, or horse. Parentheses indicate those optional items that you may not want to carry depending upon the length of the trip, weather conditions, personal preferences, or necessity.

Ten Essentials for Any Trip:

___ Map
___ Compass
___ First aid kit
___ Pocket knife
___ Signaling device
___ Extra clothing
___ Extra food
___ Small flashlight/extra bulb & batteries
___ Fire starter/candle/waterproof matches
___ Sunglasses

Day Trip (add to the above):

___ Comfortable boots or walking shoes
___ Rain parka or 60/40 parka
___ Day Pack
___ Water bottle/canteen
___ Cup
___ Water purification tablets
___ Insect repellant
___ Sun lotion
___ Chapstick
___ Food
___ Brimmed hat
___ (Guide book)
___ Toilet paper & trowel
___ (Camera & film)
___ (Binoculars)
___ (Book)
___ Wallet & I.D.
___ Car key & coins for phone
___ Moleskin for blisters
___ Whistle

Overnight or Longer Trips (add the following):

___ Backpack
___ Sleeping bag
___ Foam pad
___ (Tent)
___ (Bivouac cover)
___ (Ground cloth/poncho)
___ Stove
___ Extra fuel
___ Cooking pot(s)
___ Pot scrubber
___ Spoon (knife & fork)
___ (Extra cup/bowl)
___ Extra socks
___ Extra shirt(s)
___ Extra pants/shorts
___ Extra underwear
___ Wool shirt/sweater
___ (Camp shoes)
___ Bandana
___ (Gloves)
___ (Extra water container)
___ Nylon cord
___ Extra matches
___ Soap
___ Toothbrush/powder/floss
___ Mirror
___ Medicines
___ (Snakebite kit)
___ (Notebook & pencil)
___ Licenses & permits
___ (Playing cards)
___ (Zip-lock bags)
___ (Rip stop repair tape)
___ Repair kit—wire, rivets, pins, buttons, thread, needle, boot strings

Map Symbols

 BACKCOUNTRY CAMPSITE

 BIKING TRAIL

 BOAT LAUNCH

 CAMPFIRE CENTER

 CAMPGROUND

 ENVIRON-MENTAL CAMPSITE

 FISHING

 FOOD

 GENERAL STORE

 GROUP CAMPING

 GROUP PICNIC AREA

 HIKING/BIKING NO CAMPSITE

 HIKING TRAIL

 HORSEBACK TRAIL

 INFORMATION

 MARINA

PARKING

PICNIC AREA

 PUBLIC RIVER ACCESS

 RANGER STATION/ PARK OFFICE

 RESTROOMS

 SCENIC AREA

 SWIMMING

VC VISITOR CENTER

Who says that camping is a warm-weather, summertime only activity? Try it . . . you may like it . . . see, she's even grinning! (Photo: Rena Koesler)

Crossing a cold mountain stream in the winter requires a little ingenuity and lots of encouragement.

Region 1

1—Ahjumawi Lava Springs State Park, page 22
2—Castle Crags State Park, page 23
3—Del Norte Coast Redwoods State Park, page 24
4—Grizzly Creek Redwoods State Park, page 25
5—Humboldt Lagoons State Park, page 26
6—Humboldt Redwoods State Park, page 27
7—Jedediah Smith Redwoods State Park, page 28
8—Klamath National Forest, page 29
9—Lake Earl State Park, page 32
10—Lassen National Forest, page 33
11—Lassen Volcanic National Park, page 36
12—Latour State Forest, page 39

13—Lava Beds National Monument, page 40
14—McArthur-Burney Falls Memorial State Park, page 42
15—Modoc National Forest, page 43
16—Patrick's Point State Park, page 46
17—Prairie Creek Redwoods State Park, page 47
18—Redwood National and State Parks, page 48
19—Shasta-Trinity National Forests, page 51
20—Six Rivers National Forest, page 56
21—Smith River National Recreation Area, page 59
22—Whiskeytown-Shasta-Trinity National Recreation Area, page 61

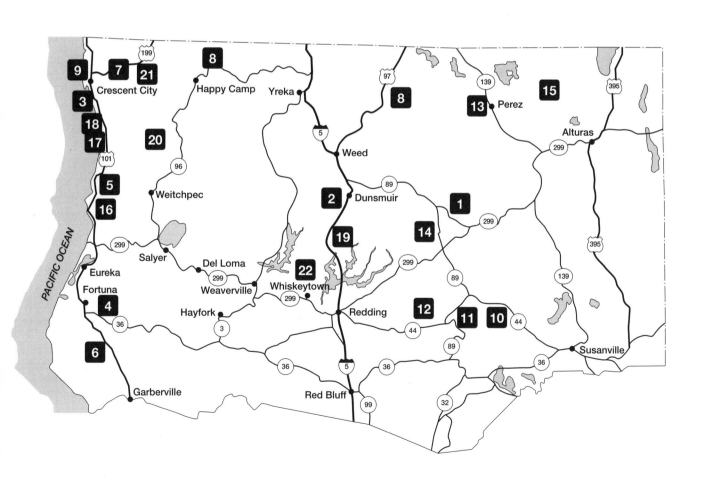

Ahjumawi Lava Springs State Park

For Information

Ahjumawi Lava Springs State Park
24898 Highway 89
Burney, CA 96013
916/335-2777

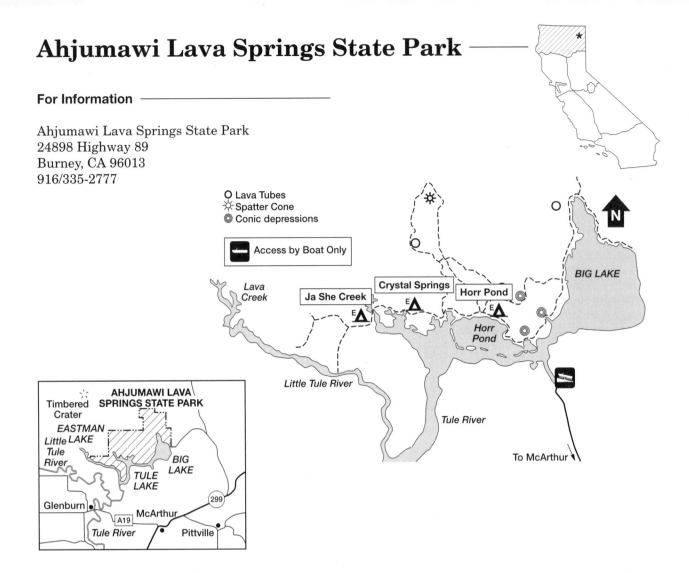

Location

Ahjumawi Lava Springs State Park is accessible only by boat; from the town of McArthur, go to the end of main street past the fair grounds, cross over a canal and proceed 3 miles north on a graded dirt road to Big Lake. Launch at a PG&E public boat launch, locally known as "Rat Farm Landing." The 6,000-acre park is at an elevation of 3,300 feet. There are magnificent views of Mt. Shasta, Mt. Lassen, and other local peaks.

Special Notes

The word "Ahjumawi" means "where the waters come together." The waters that come together at this location are Big Lake, Ja She Creek, Tule River, Fall River, and Pit River. Together, they form one of the largest systems of fresh springs in the world. Preserved within the park are recent black lava flows, lava tubes and caves, abundant fresh springs, wildlife, and prehistoric rock fish traps. Wear sturdy shoes if you plan to hike; the lava is rough. Dress for extreme heat in the summer, or extreme cold in the winter. Mosquitoes are voracious and hikers should watch for rattlesnakes.

Facilities & Activities

primitive camping at 9 environmental campsites*
   3 at Ja She Creek
   3 at Crystal Springs
   3 on the north shore of Horr Pond
pit toilets
water available from springs; must be purified
picnicking
fishing
boating/canoeing
hiking

---

*Camp only in the designated sites; a camping fee is charged.

Castle Crags State Park

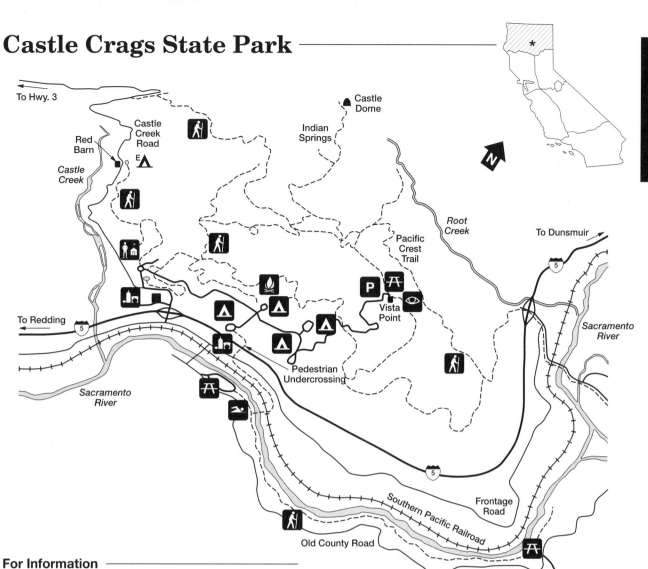

For Information

Castle Crags State Park
P.O. Box 80
Castella, CA 96017-0080
916/235-2684 or 225-2065

Location

Castle Crags State Park is located 6 miles south of Dunsmuir on I-5 in the forest-covered mountains just north of the Sacramento Valley. Elevations at this 4,350-acre park range from 2,000 feet along the river to more than 6,000 feet at the top of the Crags.

Special Notes

The park features soaring spires of ancient granite and includes about 2 miles of the cool, quick-running upper Sacramento River. Seven miles of the Pacific Crest Trail run through the park; hiking trails range from easy to strenuous. The park is surrounded by primitive backcountry and offers a superb view of Mt. Shasta to the north. The park may close seasonally because of snow.

Facilities* & Activities

76 developed campsites
showers
21-foot trailers; 27-foot campers
6 enroute campsites
6 environmental campsites
picnicking
fishing
swimming in Sacramento River
nature & hiking trails
horseback riding trails
visitor center

———
*On state park reservation system.

Del Norte Coast Redwoods State Park

For Information

Del Norte Coast Redwoods State Park
4241 Kings Valley Road
Crescent City, CA 95531
707/464-9533

Location

In the heart of California's rain forest, Del Norte Coast Redwoods State Park is located 7 miles south of Crescent City on US 101. Dense redwood forests grow almost to the ocean's edge at this 6,375-acre park; its elevation is 670 feet and it has 8 miles of coastline.

Special Notes

Del Norte has an average annual rainfall of 110 inches and a temperate, foggy climate fosters tree and plant growth year-round. Although much of the park is virgin forest, the forest at the campground is second-growth redwood, mixed with red alder. In the fall, the leaves of the alders and maples make a colorful display. The campground is 2½ miles off of US 101. The park is closed each winter from November through March or April.

Facilities* & Activities

145 developed campsites
showers
27-foot trailers; 31-foot campers
trailer sanitation station
1 hike/bike campsite
picnicking
fishing
nature trails
15 miles of hiking trails
bike trails
exhibits
extensive summer interpretive programs

*On state park reservation system.

This bicyclist is properly clad with a helmet.

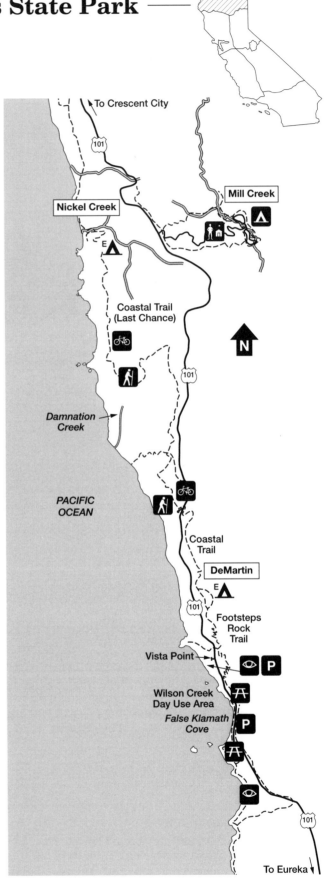

Grizzly Creek Redwoods State Park

For Information

Grizzly Creek Redwoods State Park
16949 Highway 36
Carlotta, CA 95528
707/777-3683

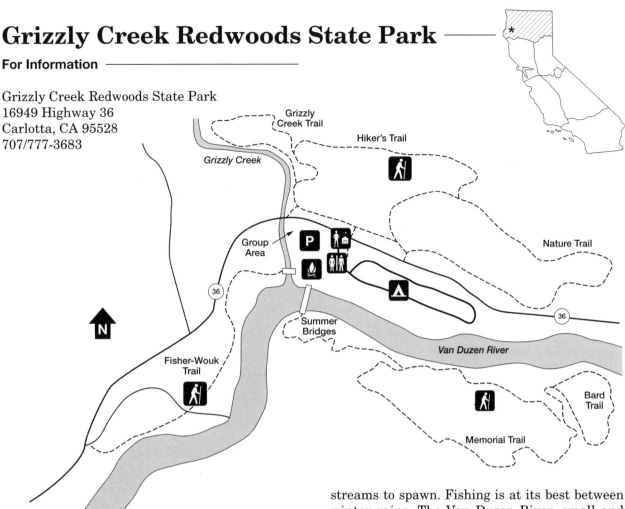

streams to spawn. Fishing is at its best between winter rains. The Van Duzen River, small and peaceful during dry periods, flows mightily during the heavy North Coast rains. Canoeists seek excitement then, and kayakers run the rapids just downstream from the park.

Facilities* & Activities

30 developed campsites
wheelchair accessible campsites
showers
24-foot trailers; 30-foot campers
campsites for hikers & bikers
6 environmental campsites
group camping area*† (40)
picnicking
group picnic area† (40)
fishing
swimming
nature & hiking trails
exhibits/visitor center
summer interpretive programs
state historic landmark

*On state park reservation system
†Phone park for reservations.

Location

Located in the Van Duzen River Valley, Grizzly Creek Redwoods State Park is 17 miles east of US 101 on Highway 36. This 393-acre park, with an elevation of 375 feet, is 30 miles from the Pacific Ocean.

Special Notes

The creek and park were named for the now extinct California grizzly bear; black bears still live here, but are rarely seen. In late fall, anglers seek salmon and steelhead making their way up

Humboldt Lagoons State Park

For Information

Humboldt Lagoons State Park
15336 Highway 101
Trinidad, CA 95570
707/488-2041

Location

Humboldt Lagoons State Park is located 31 miles north of Eureka on US 101. This 1,500-acre park is at sea level and has 3 miles of beach. Lagoons are among the most striking features of the Northern California coastline. Stone Lagoon is a 521-acre estuary fed by many small drainages. Dry Lagoon is a 280-acre freshwater marsh.

To reach the environmental campsites at Stone Lagoon, turn off US 101 at milepost 115.4 to the parking area and the launching area. It's an easy ¾-mile row/paddle across the lagoon to the campsites, which are all within 300 yards of the landing area.

To reach the environmental campsites at Dry Lagoon, turn into the day use area at milepost 114.5. When you register, you will be given the combination to open the gate to the campsite parking area. You must walk 200–400 yards from the parking lot to your campsite.

Registration

If you're northbound on US 101, stop at Patricks Point State Park to register for sites at Humboldt Lagoons. If you're southbound, check the bulletin board next to Stone Lagoon boat launching area at milepost 115.4 for current registration information. Call the park for information or to reserve the sites.

Facilities & Activities

6 environmental campsites at Stone Lagoon
   no drinking water
6 environmental campsites at Dry Lagoon
pit toilets
no pets in environmental camps
day use area/picnicking
fishing
hiking trails
launch ramp/boating/canoeing
exhibits/visitor center (open daily in summer)

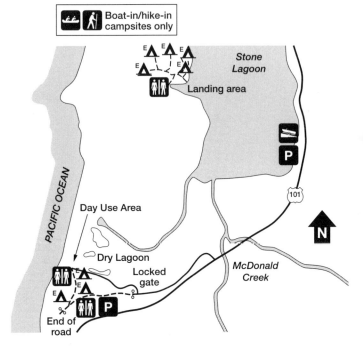

The environmental campsites at Stone Lagoon are an easy ¾-mile row/paddle across the lagoon from the launching area, but this fellow should still be wearing a life jacket.

Humboldt Redwoods State Park

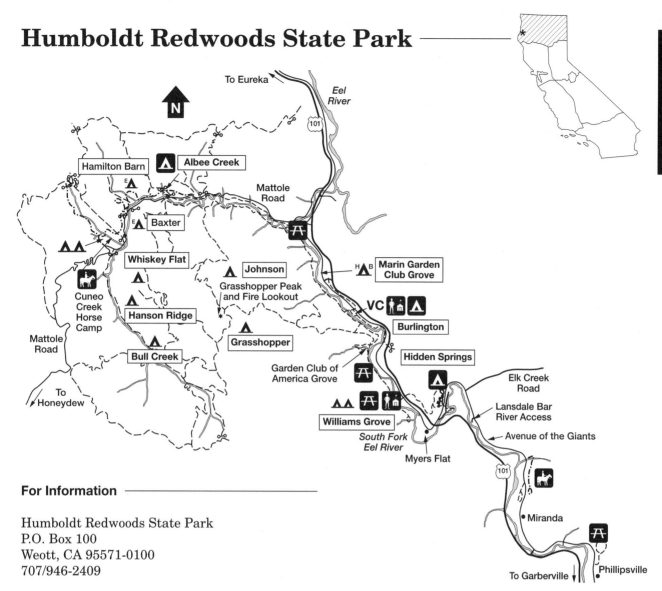

For Information

Humboldt Redwoods State Park
P.O. Box 100
Weott, CA 95571-0100
707/946-2409

Location

Home of the spectacular 33-mile Avenue of the Giants Parkway, Humboldt Redwoods State Park is located 45 miles south of Eureka via US 101 and Highway 254. The 51,143-acre park ranges in elevation from 150 feet at Park Headquarters to 3,379 feet at Grasshopper Peak and Fire Lookout. The park has 3 campgrounds: Burlington is 2 miles south of Weott on Highway 254; Hidden Springs is 1 mile south of Myers Flat on Highway 254; and Albee Creek is 2 miles north of Weott on US 101, then 5 miles west on Mattole Road.

Special Notes

The spectacular 33-mile avenue of the Giants Parkway has many turnouts and parking areas from which short loop trails reach into the forest. Every visitor should stroll through one of the magnificent redwood groves. The park's largest trees—the Dyerville Giant and the Founders Tree—are located in the Founders Grove. The awe-inspiring Tall Tree, Giant Tree, and Flatiron Tree are located in the Rockfeller Forest. A park auto tour is available.

The park features more than 100 miles of hiking and riding trails, and enough river frontage to offer countless opportunities for swimming and fishing. In the rainy season, look for annual runs of silver and king salmon and steelhead.

Facilities & Activities

Burlington Campground
    56 developed campsites/showers
    24-foot trailers; 33-foot campers
    open all year
Hidden Springs Campground

154 developed campsites/showers
   24-foot trailers; 33-foot campers
   closed mid-October through mid-May
Albee Creek Campground
   39 developed campsites/showers
   24-foot trailers; 33-foot campers
   closed October 1 through mid-May
trailer sanitation station at Williams Grove
9 hike/bike campsites at Marin Garden Club Grove
5 environmental campsites
5 trail camps
2 group camping areas at Williams Grove (125)
equestrian camping[†] (50)

picnicking
group picnic area[†] (160)
fishing
swimming
boating
nature & hiking trails
bike & horse trails
summer interpretive programs
exhibits/visitor center
state historic landmark

---

*On state park reservation system.
[†]Phone park for reservations.

Jedediah Smith Redwoods State Park

For Information

Jedediah Smith Redwoods State Park
1375 Elk Valley Road
Crescent City, CA 95531
707/458-3310 or 464-9533

Location

Jedediah Smith Redwoods State Park is located 9 miles east of Crescent City on US 199. The 9,560-acre park is northernmost of the redwood parks that dot the California coast from Monterey County to the Oregon border. Its elevation is 150 feet.

Special Notes

The park lies at the confluence of the Smith River and Mill Creek. Much of the park is very rugged and is best seen from the foot trails that lace the area. There are 18 memorial groves in the park. Stout Memorial Grove contains the park's largest known tree, which is 20 feet in diameter and 340 feet high.

Facilities* & Activities

108 developed campsites
showers
27-foot trailers; 31-foot campers
trailer sanitation station
5 hike/bike campsites

group camping area (50)
picnicking
fishing
swimming
canoeing/kayaking
nature & hiking trails
bike trails
natural history bookstore
summer interpretive programs
exhibits/visitor center

---

*On state park reservation system.

Klamath National Forest

For Information

Supervisor's Office
Klamath National Forest
1312 Fairlane Road
Yreka, CA 96097
916/842-6131

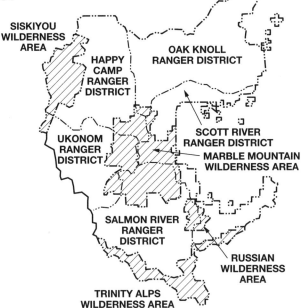

SISKIYOU WILDERNESS AREA

HAPPY CAMP RANGER DISTRICT

OAK KNOLL RANGER DISTRICT

GOOSENEST RANGER DISTRICT

UKONOM RANGER DISTRICT

SCOTT RIVER RANGER DISTRICT

MARBLE MOUNTAIN WILDERNESS AREA

SALMON RIVER RANGER DISTRICT

RUSSIAN WILDERNESS AREA

TRINITY ALPS WILDERNESS AREA

Location

The Klamath National Forest contains 1,695,000 acres in northern California and extends into Oregon. Parts or all of the Klamath, Salmon, Siskiyou, Marble, and Scott mountains are located within the forest. A spur of the volcanic Cascades extends into the forest on the east side.

Special Notes

The rivers of the forest are the Salmon, Scott, and Klamath. All are turbulent streams flowing through mountain valleys and rugged canyons. Most of the campgrounds and picnic sites are located along these rivers. The Klamath River is suitable for kayaking and rafting. Some of the best salmon and steelhead fishing in California is enjoyed here. Elevations range from 600 to 8,300 feet. Weather is usually excellent from June to October. Occasional summer thunderstorms occur, but are usually of short duration.

Wilderness Areas

Klamath National Forest has four wilderness areas. Two of them—Marble Mountain and Rus-

sian—lie wholly within the forest; two of them—Siskiyou and Trinity Alps—are on adjoining forests, as well. Only a small parcel of the **Trinity Alps Wilderness** is along the southern border of the Klamath in the Salmon River and the Scott River ranger districts. Big Flat Campground is an access point to the wilderness.

The 12,000-acre **Russian Wilderness** has steep, rugged slopes and ridges with broad U-shaped glaciated valleys. Meadows, rock pinnacles, bluffs, and alpine lakes in cirque basins are also common.

The **Marble Mountain Wilderness** was one of the earliest designated wilderness areas in California. On April 19, 1931 the area was established as the Marble Mountain Primitive Area. Wilderness designation came in 1953. The 214,500-acre forested area with many meadows is easily traveled; there are 89 lakes stocked with trout.

East side entry into the **Siskiyou Wilderness** is made from the Klamath National Forest; north side entry from Siskiyou National Forest; and west side entry from Six Rivers National Forest. The 153,000-acre wilderness has very steep terrain, narrow ridge lines, some open valleys and sheer rock faces.

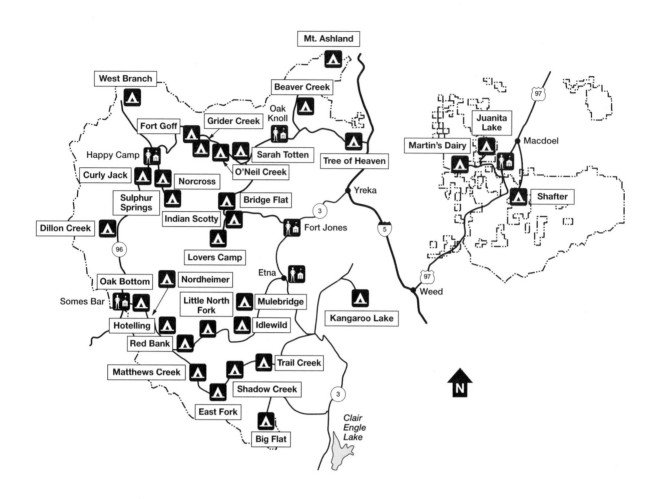

Ukonom Ranger District

For Information

Ukonom Ranger District
P.O. Drawer 410
Orleans, CA 95556
916/627-3291

Campgrounds	Elevation (feet)	# of Units	Drinking Water	Vault Toilets	Trailer Space	Camping Fee
Dillon Creek	800	21	•	•	•	•
Nordheimer	1,000	8	•		•	
Oak Bottom	700	26	•	•	•	•

Notes:
Nordheimer has 4 large group sites.
Campgrounds are open year-round; full services are not offered during winter.

Goosenest Ranger District

For Information

Goosenest Ranger District
37805 Highway 97
Macdoel, CA 96058
916/398-4391

Campgrounds	Elevation (feet)	# of Units	Drinking Water	Vault Toilets	Trailer Space	Camping Fee
Juanita Lake	5,100	23	•	•	•	•
Martin's Dairy	6,000	7	•	•	•	•
Shafter	4,300	10	•	•	•	•

Notes:
Juanita Lake has a 50-person group site; reservations are required.
Camping season is mid-May until mid-October at Juanita Lake.
Martin's Dairy and Shaftner are open year-round with services provided only from May to October.

Klamath National Forest *(continued)*

Happy Camp Ranger District

For Information

Happy Camp Ranger District
P.O. Box 377
Happy Camp, CA 96039
916/493-2243

Campgrounds	Elevation (feet)	# of Units	Drinking Water	Vault Toilets	Trailer Space	Camping Fee
Curly Jack	1,075	18	•	•		•
Norcross Trailhead & Campground	2,400			•		
Sulphur Spring	3,100	7		•		•
West Branch	2,200	15	•	•	•	•

Notes:
Sulphur Springs is open year-round with services provided only from May to October.
West Branch is open from May to October.
Curly Jack has two 30-person group sites.
Norcross Trailhead & Campground has stock corrals; water for stock is available.

Oak Knoll Ranger District

For Information

Oak Knoll Ranger District
22541 Highway 96
Klamath River, CA 96050
916/465-2241

Campgrounds	Elevation (feet)	# of Units	Drinking Water	Vault Toilets	Trailer Space	Camping Fee
Beaver Creek	2,400	8	•	•	•	
Fort Goff	1,300	18	Str.	•		
Grider Creek	1,700	10	Str.	•	•	
Mt. Ashland	6,600	9		•		
O'Neil Creek	1,500	18	Str.	•	•	
Sarah Totten	1,400	17	•	•	•	•
Tree of Heaven	2,100	21	•	•	•	•

Notes:
Sarah Totten has 1 group site; reservations are required.
Beaver Creek, Sarah Totten, & Tree of Heaven are open year-round; services are limited in off-season.
O'Neil Creek is open June 1st thru Nov. 15th.
Tree of Heaven has a boat ramp with parking on the banks on the Klamath River.

Salmon River Ranger District

For Information

Salmon River Ranger District
P.O. Box 280
Etna, CA 96027
916/467-5757

Campgrounds	Elevation (feet)	# of Units	Drinking Water	Vault Toilets	Trailer Space	Camping Fee
Big Flat	5,760	9	Str.	•		
East Fork	2,600	9	•	•	•	
Hotelling	1,760	5		•		
Idlewild	2,600	23	•	•	•	•
Little North Fork	2,000	4	Str.	•		
Matthews Creek	1,760	14	•	•	•	•
Mulebridge	2,800	2	Str.	•		
Red Bank	1,760	4		•	•	
Shadow Creek	2,800	10	•	•	•	•

Notes:
Campgrounds are open year-round but services are provided June through October.
Big Flat is not always accessible in winter due to snow.

Scott River Ranger District

For Information

Scott River Ranger District
11263 North Highway 3
Fort Jones, CA 96032
916/468-5351

Campgrounds	Elevation (feet)	# of Units	Drinking Water	Vault Toilets	Trailer Space	Camping Fee
Bridge Flat	2,000	8	•	•	•	•
Indian Scotty	2,400	36	•	•	•	
Kangaroo Lake	6,500	18	•	•		•
Lover's Camp	4,300	8	•	•		
Trail Creek	4,700	8	•	•	•	•

Notes:
Indian Scotty Group Area is suitable for group picnics & barbecues; reservations are required.
Campgrounds are open year-round, but are managed from June–Oct.
Carter Meadows & Hidden Horse Campground, located near Trail Creek, are horse camps with corrals; ask for details at the District Ranger Office.

Lake Earl State Park

For Information

Lake Earl State Park
1375 Elk Valley Road
Crescent City, CA 95531
707/464-6101 ext. 5151

Location

Lake Earl State Park is located along the northern coast of California, just south of the Oregon border; 5,000 acres of wetlands, wooded hillsides, grassy meadows, sand dunes, and beaches are found within the park boundaries. The lakes and their immediate surroundings comprise the Lake Earl State Wildlife Area, which is administered by the California Department of Fish and Game.

Facilities & Activities

6 walk-in primitive campsites*
 picnic tables, fire ring, nearby toilet, no water
ride-in group horse camp*
 corrals, picnic tables, fire rings, toilets, non-potable water
 available for backpackers when not used by equestrians
picnicking
fishing
boat ramp
20 miles of hiking/horseback riding trails
bike trails
ranger-led nature hikes

---

* Fees are collected at Jedediah Smith or Del Norte campgrounds; you will be given a lock combination for access to the parking areas beyond a locked gate.

The park has a ride-in group horse camp and 20 miles of hiking/horseback riding trails.

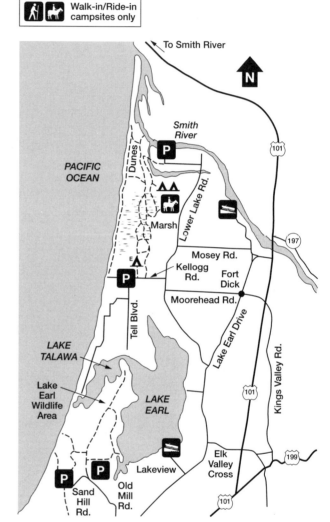

Special Notes

This unique area hosts a wide variety of ecological communities, each with a varied assortment of plants and animals. Hundreds of species of birds can be seen in the forests and wetlands. Sea lions and harbor seals can be seen along the coast, and gray whales may be sighted when migrating from the Arctic to Baja California.

Lassen National Forest

For Information

Supervisor's Office
Lassen National Forest
55 South Sacramento Street
Susanville, CA 96130

Location

Located in northeastern California, the Lassen National Forest covers 1.2 million acres. Elevations range from 1,500 to 8,600 feet. Oak covered foothills that form the eastern boundary of the Sacramento Valley extend to the pine and fir ridges and high peaks of the Southern Cascade and the Northern Sierra Nevada mountain ranges, and then level off to the Modoc Plateau.

Special Notes

The Lassen National Forest is rich in volcanic geology and encircles Lassen Volcanic National Park. Lake Almanor is one of the largest man-made lakes in California at 75 square miles. Eagle Lake, the second largest natural lake in California, supports the Eagle Lake trout, a fish native only to this lake. More than 130 miles of the Pacific Crest National Recreation Trail cross the Lassen where elevations along the trail range from 2,700 to 7,600 feet.

Wilderness Areas

Thousand Lakes Wilderness contains 16,300 acres of primitive type mountain terrain. There are entrances to the area from all four directions. Elevations range from 5,000 to 9,000 feet with the most dominant topographic features being Magee Peak at 8,550 feet and Crater Peak at 8,677 feet. The main attraction is Thousand Lakes Valley. The best travel time is mid-June through September; most years, snow is on the ground until June. Mosquitoes are a problem the first part of the summer.

The 20,500-acre **Caribou Wilderness** is not an area of lofty mountains and majestic views. Most of the trails are located on gentle slopes with very few steep pitches. The average elevation is between 6,800 and 7,000 feet. The land itself is rough and broken; reminders of its volcanic and glacial origin can be seen in the numerous depressions that have become beautiful, timber-edged lakes. The best travel time is mid-June through September; most

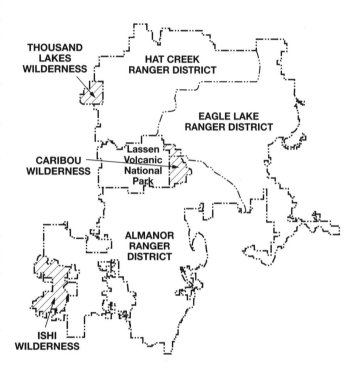

years, the lakes are frozen and snow is on the ground in June. Summer thunderstorms are common and mosquitoes are a problem the first part of the summer.

The **Ishi Wilderness** is best described as a pine-oak woodland with interspersed grassland and chaparral. Areas near streams at higher elevation are forested with ponderosa pine and Douglas fir. The highest elevation in this 42,900-acre wilderness is 4,488 feet at Barkley Mountain, and the lowest point is 900 feet on Deer Creek. The mild climate is conducive to nearly year-round use. There are many unique and interesting rock formations through the area, making it popular with hikers. Access to the wilderness is from the east or north.

Lassen National Forest *(continued)*

Almanor Ranger District

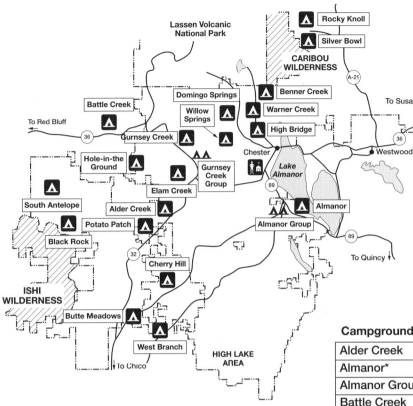

For Information

Almanor Ranger District
P.O. Box 767
Chester, CA 96020

Eagle Lake, the second-largest natural lake in California, supports the Eagle Lake Trout, a fish native only to this lake.

Campgrounds	Elevation (feet)	# of Units	Drinking Water	Toilets Vault/Flush	Trailer Space	Camping Fee
Alder Creek	3,900	6	Str.	V	•	•
Almanor*	4,550	101	•	V	•	•
Almanor Group*	4,450	1	•	V	•	•
Battle Creek	4,800	50	•	V/F	•	•
Benner Creek	5,562	5	Str.	V		•
Black Rock	2,100	5	Str.	V		•
Butte Meadows	4,600	13	•	V	•	•
Cherry Hill	4,700	26	•	V	•	•
Domingo Springs	5,060	18	•	V	•	•
Elam Creek	4,400	15	•	V	•	•
Gurnsey Creek	4,700	52	•	V	•	•
Gurnsey Creek Group*	4,700	1	•	V	•	•
High Bridge	5,200	12	•	V		•
Hole-in-the-Ground	4,300	13	•	V		•
Potato Patch	3,400	32	•	V	•	•
Rocky Knoll	6,000	18	•	V	•	•
Silver Bowl	6,000	18	•	V	•	•
South Antelope	2,700	4	Str.	V		
Warner Creek	5,040	13	Str.	V	•	•
West Branch	5,000	15	•	V		•
Willow Springs	5,100	14	Str.	V		•

Notes:
*On reservation system. Phone: 1-800-280-CAMP.
Almanor Group Camp has a max. of 100; Guernsey Creek
  Group Camp has 20 sites for a max. of 100.
Most campgrounds are open May 1–Nov. 1, weather
  permitting.
Black Rock & South Antelope are open year-round.
Warner Creek, West Branch, & Willow Springs are open
  May 30–Nov. 1.

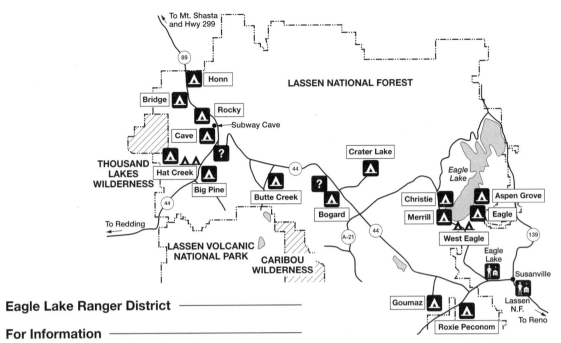

Eagle Lake Ranger District

For Information

Eagle Lake Ranger District
477-050 Eagle Lake Road
Susanville, CA 96130
916/257-4150

Campgrounds	Elevation (feet)	# of Units	Drinking Water	Toilets Vault/Flush	Trailer Space	Camping Fee
Aspen Grove (tents only)	5,100	26	•	F		•
Bogard	5,600	22	•	V	•	•
Butte Creek	5,600	20		V	•	
Christie	5,100	69	•	F	•	•
Crater Lake	6,800	17	•	V		•
Eagle*	5,100	50	•	F	•	•
Goumaz	5,200	5		V		•
Merrill*	5,100	181	•	F	•	•
Roxie Peconom (walk-in)	4,800	10	•	V		
West Eagle Group #1*	5,100	1	•	F	•	•
West Eagle Group #2*	5,100	1	•	F	•	•

Notes:

*Reservations available: Phone: 1-800-280-CAMP.

All campgrounds are open May through Oct., except Aspen Grove & Crater Lake.

Aspen Grove is open May through Sept. and Crater Lake is open June through Oct.

Also, part of Merrill Campground at Eagle Lake is open until end of fishing season, weather permitting.

West Eagle group camps use parking lots: maximum of 100 at Group #1 & 75 at Group #2; reservations only.

Hat Creek Ranger District

For Information

Hat Creek Ranger District
P.O. Box 220
Fall River Mills, CA 96028
916/336-5758

Campgrounds	Elevation (feet)	# of Units	Drinking Water	Toilets Vault/Flush	Trailer Space	Camping Fee
Big Pine	4,500	19	•	V		•
Bridge	4,000	25	•	V	•	•
Cave	4,300	46	•	V/F	•	•
Hat Creek*	4,300	75	•	V/F	•	•
Hat Creek Group*	4,300	3	•	V/F		•
Honn	3,400	6		V		•
Rocky	4,000	8		V		•

Notes:

*On reservation system. Phone: 1-800-280-CAMP.

All campgrounds are open late April through October.

Lassen Volcanic National Park

For Information

Lassen Volcanic National Park
P.O. Box 100
Mineral, CA 96063-0100
916/595-4444

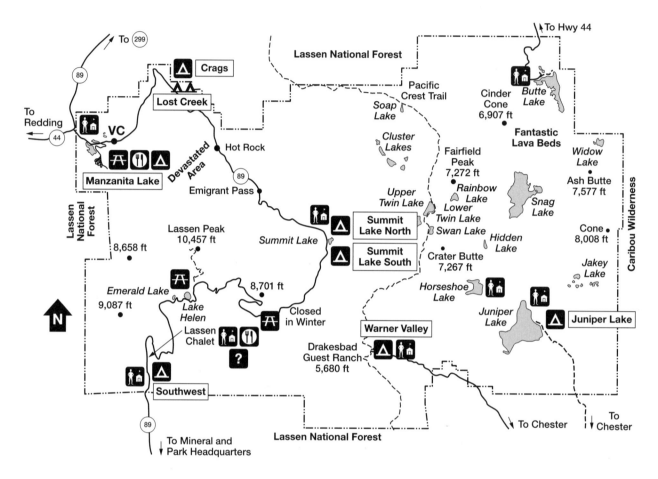

Location

This national park is located between Redding and Susanville. From the north and south, the park is reached via Highway 89; off of Highway 44 to the north and Highway 36 to the south. Lassen Peak, one of the world's largest plug dome volcanoes, is the park's highest elevation at 10,457 feet. Before the 1980 eruption of Mount St. Helens in Oregon, Lassen Peak was the most recent volcanic outburst in the contiguous 48 states. In May 1914, Lassen Peak began a 7-year cycle of sporadic volcanic outbursts. The peak is near the southernmost point in the Cascade Range. The 106,372-acre park has 78,982 acres designated as wilderness.

Points of Interest

▲ The western part of the park features great lava pinnacles, huge mountains created by lava flows, jagged craters, and steaming sulfur vents; it is cut by spectacular glaciated canyons and dotted by lakes.
▲ Studded with small lakes and forested, the eastern part of the park is a vast lava plateau more than 1 mile above sea level featuring small cinder cones—Fairfield Peak, Hat Mountain, and Crater Butte.
▲ The forested, steep Warner Valley with its gorgeous meadows marks the southern edge of the Lassen plateau and features hot springs areas—

Lassen Volcanic National Park *(continued)*

Boiling Springs Lake, Devils Kitchen, and Terminal Geyser.

▲ Markers on the scenic 35-mile Lassen park road denote various natural and historic features between the Raker Memorial and the Manzanita Lake entrance; an auto tour guide book explaining these features is for sale at any information center. The park road closes in late October due to snow, and usually reopens in late May or early June.

▲ Winter sports are centered in an area near the southwest entrance; marked trails for the ski tourer or snowshoer are in the vicinity of Manzanita Lake and Lassen Chalet.

General Information

▲ An entry fee is charged and is valid for 7 consecutive days. Three of the park entrances have a self-registration stand; the permit should be displayed on the dashboard.

▲ Two opportunities to get acquainted with the park include the visitor center at the northwest entrance and the information station near the southwest entrance.

▲ All campgrounds are above 5,650 feet; persons with problems aggravated by high elevation should consult their physician.

▲ Campground fees are charged at all campgrounds. Campgrounds are open from about Memorial Day weekend through most of September; exact dates depend on road and weather conditions. All sites are available on a first-come, first-served basis and are self-registering.

▲ Limit of stay is 14 days per year at all but 3 campgrounds; the limit at Summit Lake (North and South) and the Lost Creek group campground is 7 days per year.

▲ Warner Valley and Juniper Lake campgrounds are not recommended for trailers because of the poor roads.

▲ Campsites are available for organized groups of 10 to 25 people; reservations are required. Contact the park headquarters.

▲ Camping is prohibited along roadsides or in picnic areas; RV camping is permitted at the Chalet parking lot for a small fee.

▲ Southwest Campground is available for snow camping with restroom facilities nearby.

▲ Backcountry camping is permitted; a free wilderness permit is required and may be requested 2 weeks before the trip by mail or telephone. Camping is limited to 14 days per year. Groups are limited to 10 people per camp, although groups up to 20 may hike together.

▲ Camping is not allowed in the backcountry within one mile of developed areas or park roads or within ¼ mile in all directions of closed areas near a named feature. Ask about these closed areas when applying for a permit.

▲ When hiking, stay on marked trails on Lassen Peak and the Cinder Cone, and on boardwalks in thermal areas where the ground may be dangerously thin.

▲ Bicycles are permitted on park roads and in campgrounds, but are prohibited on all park trails.

▲ The park's 150 miles of trails includes a 17-mile section of the Pacific Crest Trail. A trail booklet is available that describes popular hikes.

▲ Backcountry users may leave vehicles at trailhead parking lots for the length of the trip.

▲ Use of horses and other stock is permitted under certain restrictions and regulations. Pack and saddle stock may stay overnight only in the corrals provided at Summit Lake and Juniper Lake. Reservations are required. Contact park headquarters to receive specific information and to reserve corral space.

▲ Fishing requires a valid California fishing license and knowledge of park regulations and catch and possession limits.

Lassen Peak, the park's highest point at 10,457 feet, is one of the world's largest plug dome volcanoes! (Photo: National Park Service)

Lassen Volcanic National Park *(continued)*

▲ Motorized boats, including electric motors, are prohibited on all park lakes and waterways. Rowboats, canoes, and other non-power boats are permitted on all park lakes except Emerald, Helen, Reflection, and Boiling Springs. There are no boat rentals in the park.

▲ Technical climbers should talk with a ranger before climbing here. Volcanic rock is generally unstable and poorly suited to rock climbing.

▲ Several designated routes for the ski tourer or snowshoer are marked with triangular red or orange or round yellow markers. These routes provide a variety of terrain and scenery and have been selected to help avoid the most hazardous areas; they start in the vicinity of Manzanita Lake and the Lassen Chalet.

▲ Visitor services inside Lassen Volcanic National Park include:

Lassen Summer Chalet is located at the southwest entrance: cafe serves breakfast and lunch, outside deck dining, gift shop, dinners on Fridays and Saturdays; call for schedule; 916/595-3376.

Manzanita Lake Camper Store is located at Manzanita Lake: camping supplies, gasoline, propane, groceries, espresso snack bar, gift shop, showers, laundromat, fishing tackle; 916/335-7557.

Drakesbad Guest Ranch is located 18 miles from Chester in Warner Valley area: full American Plan, lodging, meals, swimming pool, horseback riding (phone for availability), reservations advisable. Ask the operator in Susanville for Drakesbad Toll Station #2.

Facilities & Activities

375 RV and tent campsites
9 group campsites
backcountry camping
picnicking
fishing
boating (non-power)
self-guiding nature trails
150 miles of hiking/backpacking trails
17-mile section of Pacific Crest Trail
horseback riding
downhill/cross-country skiing
snowshoeing
camper store at Manzanita Lake
Lassen Chalet near southwest entrance
guest ranch in Warner Valley area
35-mile self-guiding auto tour
ranger-led walks and talks
evening programs at Summit Lake & Manzanita
    Lake amphitheaters
visitor center/exhibits

Campgrounds	Elevation (feet)	Total Sites	RVs	Tents	Fee	Drinking Water	Toilets: Flush/ Pit/Chemical
Crags	5,700	45	•	•	•	•	C
Juniper Lake	6,792	18		•			P
Manzanita Lake*	5,890	179	•	•	•	•	F
Southwest (walk-in)	6,700	21		•	•	•	F
Summit Lake-North	6,695	46	•	•	•	•	F
Summit Lake-South	6,695	48	•	•	•	•	C
Warner Valley	5,650	18		•	•	•	P
Group Campgrounds							
Juniper Lake	6,792	2		•			P
Lost Creek	5,700	7		•	•	•	F

*Has showers and sanitary dump.

The western portion of the park features cinder cones, steaming sulfur vents, jagged craters, and great lava pinnacles. (Photo: National Park Service)

Latour State Forest

For Information

Latour State Forest
1000 Cypress Avenue
Redding, CA 96001
916/225-2508

Location

Part of the Cascade Range, Latour State Forest is located in a remote area on the western edge of Lassen National Forest near the Thousand Lakes Wilderness. The 9,013-acre state forest is about 50 miles east of Redding and north of Highway 44, and can be reached via Whitmore Road and Bateman Road. Elevations range from 3,800 to 6,740 feet. Rock exposures in the area are of volcanic origin; two old cinder cones are located nearby. The forest was established in 1946.

Special Notes

Those who travel by horseback are required to supply sufficient feed for their riding stock; the stock is not to be turned loose to graze. Pets, such as dogs and cats, must be confined to a vehicle or on a leash no longer than 6 feet, or be in restrictive control always. The use of vehicles, such as dune buggies, motor bikes, scooters, carts, etc. is restricted to the forest roads; all such vehicles used within the forest must be street legal.

Hunting is permitted under applicable state game laws and regulations; don't discharge firearms in or around campgrounds. There is a 320-acre area closed to hunting around the forest station. Build campfires in a cleared area well away from tree roots. Fishing is permitted under applicable state laws and regulations. Many roads are suitable for nature hikes.

Facilities & Activities

3 designated campgrounds
   Butcher Gulch
   Old Cow Creek
   South Cow Creek
2–3 campsites at each campground
tables, stoves, toilets
acquire water from the creek
fishing
nature walks/hiking
horseback riding
hunting
normally accessible from late June until early
   November

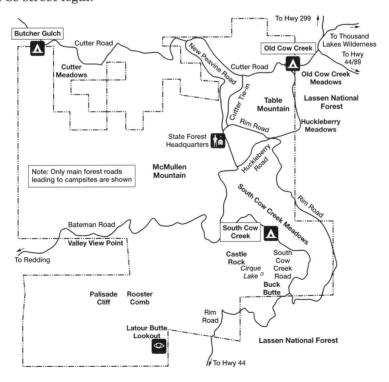

Lava Beds National Monument

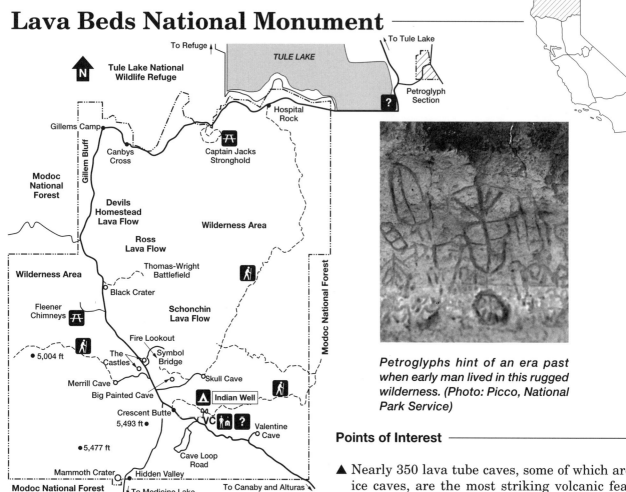

Petroglyphs hint of an era past when early man lived in this rugged wilderness. (Photo: Picco, National Park Service)

Points of Interest

▲ Nearly 350 lava tube caves, some of which are ice caves, are the most striking volcanic features in Lava Beds.

▲ Mushpot Cave, an extension of the visitor center, has lights, a paved trail, and exhibits that explain how the tubes formed; see other caves off of Cave Loop Road and throughout the monument.

▲ Lava flows, spatter cones, cinder cones, and craters are other unique volcanic features.

▲ Captain Jack's Stronghold, Thomas-Wright Battlefield, Canby's Cross, and Gillem's Camp are historic reminders of the Modoc War between U.S. Army troops and native Modoc Indians in 1872–73.

▲ The annual *Return to the Stronghold Gathering* commemorates the Modoc People.

General Information

▲ An entry fee is charged; camping fees are charged year-round.

▲ Visitor center is open year-round except Thanksgiving and Christmas Day; it is open 5 days a week during the winter. Exhibits interpret the cultural and natural history of the area. Maps and sales publications are available; lights can be checked out free.

For Information

Lava Beds National Monument
P.O. Box 867
Tulelake, CA 96134-0867
916/667-2282

Location

This national monument is located near the California-Oregon border and is a landscape of lava flows and lava tubes dotted with cinder cones. Because it is sheltered from the moisture-laden winds of the Pacific Ocean, it is a dry and rugged region covered with sagebrush, western juniper, and mountain mahogany trees. The 46,600-acre monument, which includes 28,460 acres of designated wilderness, ranges in elevation from 4,000 to 5,700 feet. The road through the monument is off of Highway 139, 5 miles south of Tulelake and 26 miles north of Canby.

Lava Beds National Monument
(continued)

▲ Ranger-guided morning walks, cave trips, and evening campfire programs are offered daily in the summer. During the winter season, rangers conduct tours by advance reservation.

▲ Indian Well campground is open all year on a first-come, first-served basis. In the winter the water in the campground is turned off; a pit toilet is nearby. Water and flush toilets are always available at the visitor center. Limit of stay is 14 days but can be extended in winter.

▲ Backcountry camping is permitted; check in at the visitor center. There is no potable water available in the backcountry.

▲ Take proper precautions when exploring the lava caves: wear adequate clothing because the caves are cool; wear protective headgear; wear hard-soled shoes because the lava can be sharp; and carry more than one light source.

▲ Snow has been recorded in nearly all months. In the winter daily high temperatures average around 40°F; lows are 20°F. Fog is frequent throughout the winter.

▲ Summers are moderate, with daytime highs averaging from 75 to 80°F and lows about 50 °F.

▲ The campground, visitor center, and picnic areas are accessible for the mobility impaired; the trails and caves have different degrees of accessibility.

▲ Food, lodging, gasoline, auto repairs, etc. are not available in the monument.

Facilities & Activities

44 campsites for tents, pickup campers and small trailers
drinking water/flush toilets
backcountry camping
2 picnicking sites; no water
self-guiding trails
hiking trails
21 caves accessible for exploration
visitor center/exhibits
ranger-led walks & cave trips
evening campfire programs

Man's activities in this rugged volcanic landscape have been nearly as violent as the natural forces that created it. This is a pathway in the lava-land stronghold of Captain Jack, the Modoc leader who fought the Army in 1872 to keep from being sent to a reservation. (Photo: National Park Service)

McArthur-Burney Falls Memorial State Park

For Information

McArthur-Burney Falls Memorial State Park
24898 Highway 89
Burney, CA 96013
916/335-2777

Location

McArthur-Burney Falls Memorial State Park is located 11 miles northeast of Burney on Highway 89 in the beautiful evergreen forests of the Pit River country. The 850-acre park is halfway between Mount Shasta and Lassen Peak on the edge of the Modoc Plateau at 3,000-foot elevation. The surrounding area includes some of the finest trout fishing streams in the nation.

Facilities & Activities

2 campgrounds: 128 developed sites
wheelchair accessible campsites
showers
32-foot trailers; 45-foot campers
trailer sanitation station
5 enroute campsites
2 hike/bike campsites
6 environmental campsites
picnicking
fishing
swimming
boating/rentals
launch ramp
water skiing
nature & hiking trails
horseback riding trails
food service/supplies
exhibits/visitor center

*On state park reservation system.

Special Notes

The most spectacular scenic feature within the park itself is the 129-foot waterfall, Burney Falls. The park has nearly 2 miles of frontage along Burney Creek and a bit of shoreline on Lake Britton, a 9-mile long man-made lake where all water sports are popular.

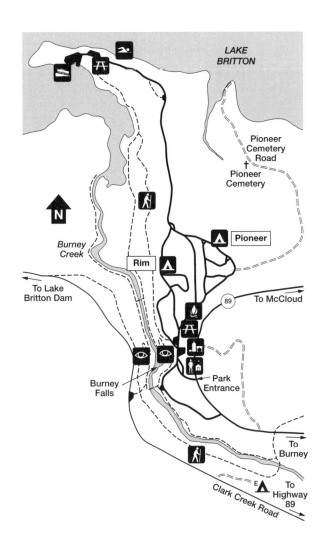

The park has 2 hike/bike campsites.

Modoc National Forest

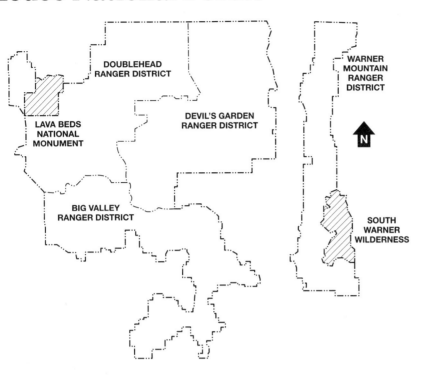

DOUBLEHEAD RANGER DISTRICT

WARNER MOUNTAIN RANGER DISTRICT

LAVA BEDS NATIONAL MONUMENT

DEVIL'S GARDEN RANGER DISTRICT

N

BIG VALLEY RANGER DISTRICT

SOUTH WARNER WILDERNESS

For Information

Supervisor's Office
Modoc National Forest
800 West 12th Street
Alturas, CA 96101-3132
916/233-5811

Location

The Modoc National Forest is located in the northeastern corner of California. It is bordered on the west by an isolated spur of the Cascade Range known as the Warner Mountain Range, to the west by a plateau region of forest meadows, timber, and open range land, and to the north by the state of Oregon. The forest boundary encompasses some 1,980,000 acres.

Special Notes

There are unique vistas of rugged obsidian mountains, lava caves, and craters in the Medicine Lake Highlands, located along the west boundary of the forest, directly southeast of the Lava Beds National Monument. To the east, the Warner Mountains offer a variety of fishing opportunities. There are crystal clear lakes, beautiful streams, and the Pit River to provide an abundance of fishing waters for all types of anglers.

Wilderness Areas

The 70,400-acre **South Warner Wilderness** is located in the southern portion of the Warner Mountains. The western face of the Warner Mountains has moderate to steep slopes while the eastern face is very steep. Elevations range from 5,000 to 9,900 feet. The wilderness encompasses areas of pleasant beauty, some spectacular scenery, and the highest peaks in northeastern California; seven high mountain peaks dominate the scene. Eagle Peak towers at 9,892 feet in the south central section.

Modoc National Forest provides an abundance of fishing waters for all types of anglers.

Modoc National Forest *(continued)*

Big Valley Ranger District

For Information

Big Valley Ranger District
P.O. Box 159
Adin, CA 96006
916/299-3215

Map #/ Campgrounds	Elevation (feet)	# of Units	Drinking Water	Vault Toilets	Trailer Space	Camping Fee
1—Ash Creek	4,800	7	•	•	•	
2—Lava Camp	4,400	12		•	•	
3—Lower Rush Creek	4,400	10	•	•	•	•
4–Upper Rush Creek	5,200	13	•	•	•	•
5—Willow Creek Camp	5,200	8	•	•	•	•

Notes:
Campgrounds close about mid-October; these reopen about June 1.

Devil's Garden Ranger District

For Information

Devil's Garden Ranger District
800 West 12th Street
Alturas, CA 96006
916/233-5811

Map #/ Campgrounds	Elevation (feet)	# of Units	Drinking Water	Vault Toilets	Trailer Space	Camping Fee
6—Cottonwood Flat	4,700	10	•	•	•	
7—Howards Gulch	4,700	11		•	•	

Notes:
Campgrounds close about mid-October; these reopen in late May.

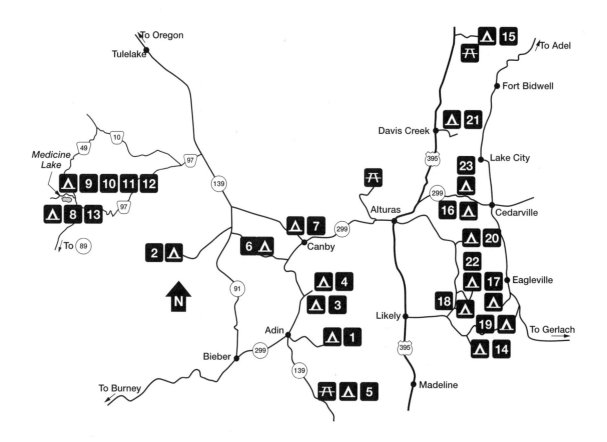

Modoc National Forest *(continued)*

Doublehead Ranger District

For Information

Doublehead Ranger District
P.O. Box 369
Tulelake, CA 96134
916/667-2246

Map #/ Campgrounds	Elevation (feet)	# of Units	Drinking Water	Vault Toilets	Trailer Space	Camping Fee
8—Bullseye Lake	8,500	10			•	
9—Headquarters	6,700	9	•	•	•	•
10—Hemlock	6,700	19	•	•	•	•
11—Hogue	6,700	24	•	•	•	•
12—Medicine Camp	6,700	22	•	•	•	•
13—Paynes Spring	6,500	6			•	

Notes:
Campgrounds close about mid-October; these reopen in late May.

Warner Mountain Ranger District

For Information

Warner Mountain Ranger District
P.O. Box 220
Cedarville, CA 96104
916/279-6118

Map #/ Campgrounds	Elevation (feet)	# of Units	Drinking Water	Vault Toilets	Trailer Space	Camping Fee
14—Blue Lake	6,000	48	•	•	•	•
15—Cave Lake	6,600	6	•	•	•	
16—Cedar Pass	5,900	17		•	•	
17—Emerson	6,000	4		•		
18—Mill Creek Falls	5,700	19	•	•	•	•
19—Patterson	7,200	5		•	•	
20—Pepperdine	6,680	5	•	•	•	
21—Plum Valley	5,600	7		•	•	
22—Soup Springs	6,800	8		•	•	
23—Stough Reservoir	6,200	14		•		

Notes:
Campgrounds close about mid-October; Plum Valley reopens about May 1, Cedar Pass, Mill Creek Falls, & Stough Reservoir reopen in late May or early June, and the others reopen about July 1.

Trailer space is available at most campgrounds in the Modoc National Forest; camping fees are charged at fewer than half.

Patrick's Point State Park

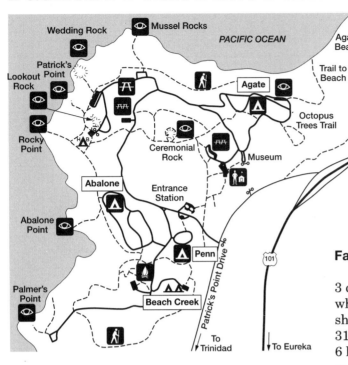

For Information

Patrick's Point State Park
4150 Patrick's Point Drive
Trinidad, CA 95570
707/677-3570

Location

Patrick's Point State Park is a 632-acre tree-and-meadow-covered headland with a broad sandy beach, located 25 miles north of Eureka on US 101. The shoreline ranges from broad sandy beach to 100-foot-high precipitous cliffs. The elevation of the park is 200 feet; there is beach access.

Special Notes

Whale-watching from high bluffs, wandering miles of beach and exploring tide pools, and searching for agates are typical activities at Patrick's Point. Although the park is in the heart of California's coast redwood country, the principal trees are spruce, hemlock, pine, fir, and red alder. Like all the north coast, the park has night and morning fog almost year-round. However, beautiful, crystal-clear days can often be enjoyed in spring and fall.

Facilities* & Activities

3 campgrounds: 124 developed sites
wheelchair accessible campsites
showers
31-foot trailers; 31-foot campers
6 hike/bike campsites
group camping area (150)
picnicking
group picnic area[†] (200)
fishing
nature & hiking trails
bike trails
exhibits/visitor center
state historic landmark

*On state park reservation system.
[†]Phone park for reservations.

Exploring tide pools and searching for agates are typical activities at Patrick's Point. (Photo: Lillian Morava)

Prairie Creek Redwoods State Park

For Information

Prairie Creek Redwoods State Park
127001 Newton B. Drury Scenic Parkway
Orick, CA 95555
707/488-2171 or 464-9533

Location

Located 50 miles north of Eureka on US 101, this 12,544-acre park features magnificent groves of coast redwoods, among the tallest trees in the world. Many are 300 feet or more in height. The park has an elevation of 150 feet. The park has 2 campgrounds: Elk Prairie is 5 miles north of Orick on US 101; and Gold Bluffs Beach is 3 miles north of Orick via US 101 and Davison Road (Fern Canyon turnoff).

Special Notes

Popular attractions include Fern Canyon Trail, where lush ferns cover 50-foot rock walls; Revelation Trail, with 17 informative stopping points; and Cathedral Trees Trail, where stately Roosevelt elk, California's largest land animal, have been known to browse. Bears frequent campgrounds; food should be secured.

Facilities* & Activities

Elk Prairie Campground
   75 developed campsites/showers
   wheelchair accessible campsites
   24-foot trailers; 27-foot campers
Gold Bluffs Beach Campground
   25 developed campsites/showers
   campers 24-foot by 8-foot wide
trailer sanitation station
9 hike/bike campsites at Elk Prairie
6 environmental campsites near Gold Bluff
2 trail camps
picnicking
fishing
nature & bike trails
75 miles of hiking trails
summer interpretive programs
exhibits/visitor center
state historic landmark

---

*On state park reservation system.

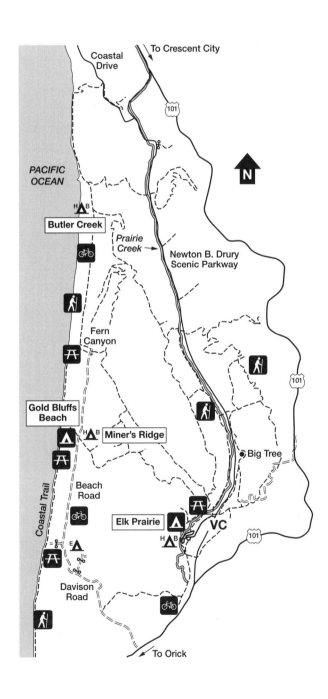

Redwood National and State Parks

For Information

Redwood National and State Parks
1111 Second Street
Crescent City, CA 95531-4123
707/464-6101

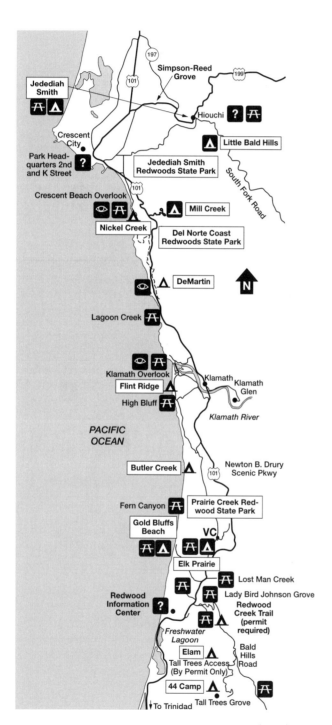

Location

Redwood National and State Parks stretch for 33 miles along California's North Coast from Orick to Crescent City. US 101 runs north and south through the park, providing a scenic drive along the coast. The 106,000-acre park includes more than 28,000 acres and is cooperatively managed by the National Park Service and the California Department of Parks and Recreation. It includes 4 parks: Del Norte Coast Redwoods State Park, Jedediah Smith Redwoods State Park, Prairie Creek Redwoods State Park, and Redwood National Park.

Points of Interest

▲ Redwood's coastline is rugged, with stretches of steep, rocky cliffs broken by rolling slopes; its tidal zone is generally rocky, other than a 7-mile stretch of dunes and sandy beach at Gold Bluffs Beach.
▲ Taller than all other trees in the world, coast redwoods grow in a narrow strip along the Pacific Coast of California and southwestern Oregon.
▲ The park's tallest known tree (367.8 feet), located along the alluvial terraces of Redwood Creek, is accessible via a 3-mile round-trip hike on Tall Trees Trail.
▲ Roosevelt elk, the park's largest mammal, can best be seen along the beach and trails at Prairie Creek Campground and Gold Bluffs Beach.
▲ Located along the Pacific Flyway, the park boasts sightings of some 370 bird species.
▲ More than half of the park's birds are marine species, some of which nest in sea cliffs: murrelets, cormorants, puffins, auklets, gulls, and pigeon guillemots.

General Information

▲ Camping and overnight parking are allowed only in designated areas. Fees are charged at the 4 campgrounds that are operated by the California Department of Parks and Recreation; fees are not charged for the primitive campsites operated by the National Park Service.

Redwood National and State Parks
(continued)

▲ There are 4 visitor centers—

Park Headquarters: 2nd and K Street in Crescent City, open year-round

Hiouchi Information Center: on US 199, 8 miles northeast of Crescent City, open June–September

Prairie Creek Information Center: located just west of US 101 near Elk Prairie Campground

Redwood Information Center: 1 mile south of Orick off US 101 near Freshwater Lagoon, open year-round

▲ Visitor centers provide exhibits and interpretive publications. In summer, a variety of interpretive programs is offered. Printed information on handicapped accessible facilities and trails is available.

▲ The 4 state-run campgrounds inside the park have a 15-day limit of stay from June to September; the rest of the year it is 30 days. Mill Creek Campground is open April to October; others are open all year.

▲ All of the state campgrounds, except Gold Bluffs Beach, are on the DESTINET reservation system from mid-May through Labor Day; the rest of the year they are first-come, first-served. RVs longer than 20 feet and trailers are not permitted at Gold Bluffs Beach because the access road is unpaved, narrow, and winding; wet weather sometimes makes it inaccessible.

▲ In state campgrounds, campers with dogs must have proof of rabies vaccination; additional fees are charged for dogs.

▲ The Park Service operates 4 backcountry campsites: DeMartin, Flint Ridge, Nickel Creek, and Little Bald Hills. They are open all year on a first-come, first-served basis, and have a 14-day limit. Butler Creek, also located along the Coastal Trail, is operated by Prairie Creek Redwoods State Park.

▲ Primitive camping is also allowed along Redwood Creek, but only on gravel bars a stipulated distance from the trailhead and from the Tall Trees Grove. Obtain free permits at Redwood Information Center and check with a ranger for camping options.

▲ Several scenic roads, both paved and unpaved, provide access to trails, beaches, ocean views, elk viewing, picnic areas, etc. Do not take trailers or large campers on roads other than main highways without first asking if the roads can handle them; check at an information center.

▲ Do not swim in the ocean. Swift currents, cold water, and undertow make swimming dangerous even on calm summer days. Smith River and Redwood Creek are better suited for swimming.

▲ Smith River, the only major undammed river in California, flows through the park's north section.

▲ Smith River and Klamath River are famous for salmon and steelhead. The Klamath River merely crosses the park from east to west, but the park protects its mouth. Redwood Creek flows through the park's southern section.

Coastal redwood forests with virgin groves of ancient trees, including the world's tallest (367.8 feet) thrive in the foggy climate prevalent almost daily in summer.

Redwood National and State Parks
(continued)

▲ Although seldom seen, black bears number several hundred in the park. Help prevent wild bears from becoming problem bears by using sound food storage practices in the backcountry and in the campgrounds.

▲ The inland part of the park is warmer in summer than the coast. July temperatures average 70–90°F inland and 50–60°F on the coast. The annual rainy season is from November through mid-April. One winter, 174 inches of rain was recorded, with 46 inches for one month.

Facilities & Activities

350 developed campsites at the 3 state parks
4 primitive campsites along the Coastal Trail
backcountry camping along Redwood Creek
picnicking
swimming
river fishing/surf fishing
shoreline walks and beachcombing
self-guiding interpretive trails/exhibits
hiking/bicycle trails
horseback riding
scenic drives
4 visitor centers
ranger-guided talks/walks, evening programs

Campgrounds	Total Sites	State/National Park	Fee	Drinking Water	Showers	Toilets Flush/Pit	Sanitary Dump
Jedediah Smith	106	S	•	•	•	F	•
Mill Creek	145	S	•	•	•	F	•
Elk Prairie*	75	S	•	•	•	F	•
Gold Bluffs Beach	24	S	•	•	solar	F	
Little Bald Hill (hike-in)	4	N				P	
Nickel Creek (walk-in)	5	N				P	
DeMartin (walk-in)	10	N		•		P	
Flint Ridge (walk-in)	10	N		•		P	
Butler Creek (hike-in)	3	S	•			P	
Redwood Creek (hike-in)	ltd.	N					

*Has separate campsites for hikers and bicyclists.

More than half of the park's birds are marine species. The Redwood Information Center, one mile south of Orick off US 101 near Freshwater Lagoon, is an excellent spot to sight some of them.

Shasta-Trinity National Forests

For Information

Supervisor's Office
Shasta-Trinity National Forests
2400 Washington Ave.
Redding, CA 96001
916/246-5222

Location

The Shasta-Trinity National Forests are located in the central part of northern California between the interior Coast Range on the west and the Cascade Range to the east. Elevations range from 1,000 feet along the southern and eastern edges of the forests to 14,162 feet at the summit of Mt. Shasta. The two forests, totaling 2.1 million acres, were combined into one administrative unit in 1954.

Special Notes

The forests include low-elevation grass and oak woodlands, as well as heavily forested slopes and granite peaks. The terrain varies from deep, steep-sided canyons to gentler rolling plateaus. There are 114 named natural lakes, 11 man-made reservoirs, 1,377 miles of trails, over 100 miles of rivers that have been designated as components of the National Wild and Scenic Rivers System, over 150 miles of the Pacific Crest Trail, and the volcano, Mt. Shasta.

The Whiskeytown-Shasta-Trinity National Recreation Area was established in November 1965. Three separate units make up the 203,587-acre area. The Whiskeytown unit is administered by the National Park Service. The Shasta & Trinity Units

of the National Recreation Area are within the Shasta-Trinity National Forests and are administered by the U.S. Forest Service. See pages 63 and 66 for maps and campground information for these two units; it is not repeated in this section.

Wilderness Areas

The 11,000-acre **Castle Crags Wilderness** has spectacular sheer granite cliffs and spires along the high east-west ridge, five small lakes and numerous streams—some spring fed. Elevations range from 2,300 to 7,200 feet. The Pacific Crest Trail bisects the area in the east-west direction. The area adjoins Castle Crags State Park.

The 8,200-acre **Chanchelulla Wilderness** has steep (up to 70%) slopes; mostly brush fields on southern slopes and mixed conifer on north slopes. Chanchelulla Peak is the highest point in the wilderness at 6,400 feet. North side entry is from Hayfork Ranger District and south side entry is from Yolla Bolla Ranger District.

The **Mount Shasta Wilderness** contains many unique geologic and scenic features: a hot sulfur spring, glaciers, lava flows, waterfall, buttes, and canyons. Much of this 37,700-acre area is above the timberline; elevations range from 4,300 to 14,000 feet. Mt. Shasta is a landmark that dominates the

Shasta-Trinity National Forests
(*continued*)

aerial view for several hundred miles in all directions. There are no established trails up the mountain and it is snow-covered most of the year. Hikers normally need crampons and an ice axe.

The **Trinity Alps Wilderness** is the second largest wilderness in California. The largest portion of this 513,100-acre wilderness is in Shasta-Trinity National Forests, while smaller portions are in Klamath and Six Rivers. The rugged, isolated area consists of mountain ridges and deep canyons between the Trinity River and Salmon River with more than 55 lakes and streams, scattered timber stands, large meadows, barren rock cliffs, and peaks. Elevations range from 2,000 to 8,000 feet. The area is accessible from mid-June to mid-October; wilderness permits are required. South side entry is from the Weaverville Ranger District.

The **Yolla Bolly-Middle Eel Wilderness** is located between the North and South Yolla Bolly Mountains in rugged country of the headwaters of the Middle Fork of the Eel River. It is open for use longer than most wilderness areas in California due to its relatively low elevations. Elevations range from 2,700 to 8,000 feet, although the average elevation is 4,000 to 6,000 feet. Heavy snows do not fall until December and most of the area is open by late May. Water is scarce after July 1. This 154,000-acre wilderness area is shared with Six Rivers and Mendocino National Forests. North side entry is from the Yolla Bolla Ranger District.

Big Bar Ranger District

For Information

Big Bar Ranger District
HC 1, Box 10
Big Bar, CA 96010
916/623-6123

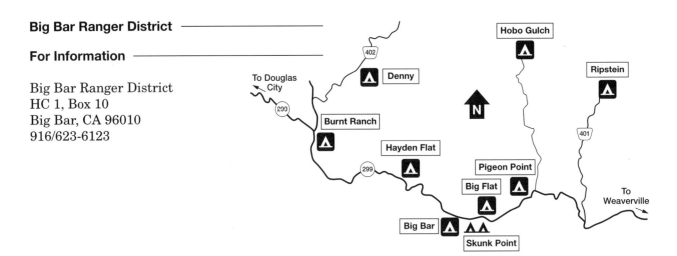

Campgrounds	Elevation (feet)	# of Units	Drinking Water	Vault Toilets	Trailer Space	Camping Fee
Big Bar	1,200	3	•	•		
Big Flat	1,300	10	•	•	•	•
Burnt Ranch	1,000	16	•	•	•	•
Denny	1,400	16	•	•	•	
Hayden Flat	1,200	35	•	•	•	•
Hobo Gulch	3,000	10		•		
Pigeon Point	1,100	10		•	•	
Ripstein	2,600	10		•		
Skunk Point Group*	1,200	2		•		•

Notes:
*Reservations required. Phone: 1-800-280-CAMP.
Skunk Point Group Campground capacity: 2 units, 30 each.
Hayden Flat, Pigeon Point, & Skunk Point Group have a beach.
Hobo Gulch has a corral.

Many of the lakes in the Trinity Alps Wilderness are surrounded by sheer granite rock formations. (Photo: California Office of Tourism)

Shasta-Trinity National Forests
(*continued*)

Campgrounds	Elevation (feet)	# of Units	Drinking Water	Toilets Vault/Flush	Trailer Space	Camping Fee
Ah-Di-Na	2,300	16	•	F		•
Algoma	3,800	8		V		
Cattle Camp	3,800	30		V		
Fowlers Camp	3,600	39	•	V	•	•
Harris Springs	4,800	15	•	V	•	
Trout Creek	5,100	10		V		

Notes:
Access to Ah-Di-Na includes a 4-mile unpaved road.
Access to Trout Creek includes a 1-mile unpaved road.

Mt. Shasta Ranger District

For Information

Mt. Shasta Ranger District
204 West Alma
Mt. Shasta, CA 96067
916/926-4511

Campgrounds	Elevation (feet)	# of Units	Drinking Water	Toilets V=Vault; F=Flush	Trailer Space	Camping Fee
Castle Lake	5,280	6		V	•	
Gumboot	6,080	4		V	•	
Mc Bride Springs	4,880	9	•	V	•	•
Panther Meadows	7,450	10		V		
Sims Flat	1,600	20	•	F/V	•	•
Toad Lake	6,940	6		V		

Notes:
Panther Meadows is a walk-in campground.
Toad Lake Campground involves a ¼-mile hike from road.

McCloud Ranger District

For Information

McCloud Ranger District
P.O. Box 1620
McCloud, CA 96057
916/964-2184

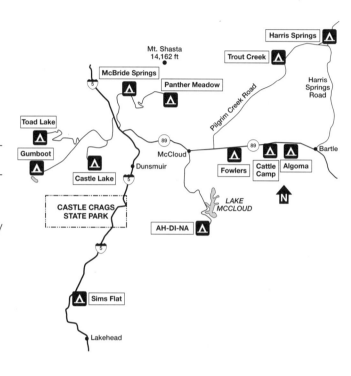

Many of the lakes in the Trinity Alps Wilderness are surrounded by sheer granite rock formations. (Photo: California Office of Tourism)

Shasta-Trinity National Forests
(*continued*)

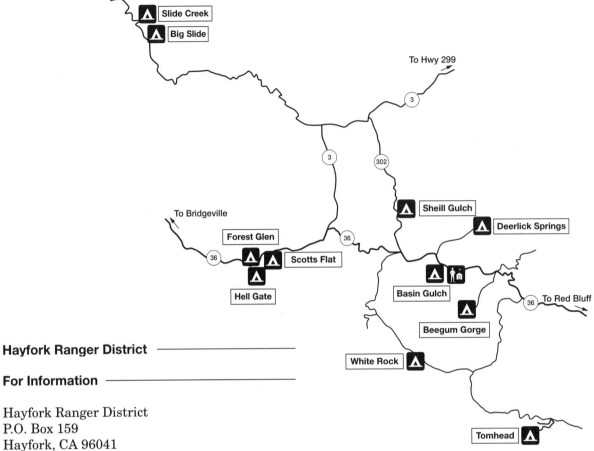

Hayfork Ranger District

For Information

Hayfork Ranger District
P.O. Box 159
Hayfork, CA 96041
916/628-5227

Campgrounds	Elevation (feet)	# of Units	Drinking Water	Vault Toilets	Trailer Space	Camping Fee
Big Slide	1,250	8		•		
Forest Glen	2,300	15	•	•	•	
Hell Gate	2,300	17	•	•	•	
Scotts Flat	2,300	10		•	•	
Slide Creek	1,250	5		•		
Sheill Gulch	2,600	5		•		

Notes:
Scotts Flat & Sheill Gulch have unpaved access.
Hell Gate & Scotts Flat have a beach.

Yolla Bolla Ranger District

For Information

Yolla Bolla Ranger District
HC 1, Box 400
Plantina, CA 96076
916/352-4211

Campgrounds	Elevation (feet)	# of Units	Drinking Water	Vault Toilets	Trailer Space	Camping Fee
Basin Gulch	2,700	13		•	•	
Beegum Gorge	2,200	2		•		
Deerlick Springs	3,100	13		•		
Tomhead Saddle	5,600	5		•		
White Rock	4,800	3		•		

Notes:
Camp trailers are not recommended for Beegum Gorge.
Tomhead Saddle has a horse corral.

Shasta-Trinity National Forests (*continued*)

Shasta Lake and Weaverville Ranger Districts

For Information

Shasta Lake Ranger District
14225 Holiday Rd.
Redding, CA 96003
916/275-1587

Weaverville Ranger District
P.O. Box 1190
Weaverville, CA 96093
916/623-2121

Campgrounds	Elevation (feet)	# of Units	Drinking Water	Vault Toilets	Trailer Space	Camping Fee
Shasta Lake						
Deadlun	2,750	30		•	•	
Madrone	1,500	13		•	•	
Trinity Lake						
Bridge Camp*	2,700	10	•	•	•	•
Clear Creek	3,400	8		•	•	
Eagle Creek*	2,800	17	•	•	•	•
East Weaver*	2,700	15	•	•	•	•
Goldfield	3,000	6		•		
Horse Flat	3,200	16		•		
Preacher Meadow*	2,900	45	•	•	•	•
Scott Mountain	5,400	7		•		
Trinity River*	2,500	7	•	•	•	•

Notes:
*Reservations available. Phone 1-800-280-CAMP.
Eagle Creek, East Weaver, and Trinity River are open year-round.
Clear Creek has an unpaved access road.

Note

Numerous campgrounds are located around Shasta Lake and Trinity Lake; they are administered by the Shasta Lake Ranger District and the Weaverville Ranger District, respectively. Most of these campgrounds are located within the Whiskeytown-Shasta-Trinity National Recreation Area; information about them appears on pages 61–67, so it is not duplicated in this section.

The campgrounds displayed below are within the Shasta-Trinity National Forests but not within the National Recreation Area. The general location of each campground is shown; a more detailed map should be consulted to determine the exact location and best travel route.

Weaverville Ranger District

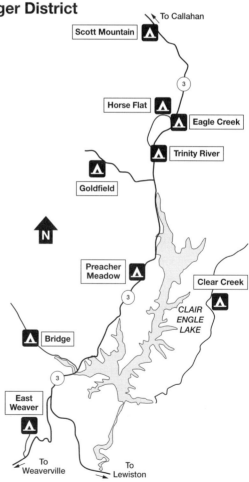

Shasta Lake Ranger District

Six Rivers National Forest

For Information

Supervisor's Office
Six Rivers National Forest
1330 Bayshore Way
Eureka, CA 95501
707/442-1721

Location

The Six Rivers National Forest lies in northwestern California and stretches southward from the Oregon border for about 140 miles. US 101, the famed "Redwood Highway," parallels the inland forest in a north-south direction on the coast side. The forest is just east of the Redwood National Park.

Special Notes

This 1,118,247-acre forest is named Six Rivers because of the six major streams that drain or pass through it—the Smith, Klamath, Trinity, Mad, Van Duzen, and Eel rivers. Six Rivers offers an unparalleled range of river experiences for water enthusiasts. Whether you like white-water rafting or kayaking, fishing for trout or salmon, or just swimming in deep, rock-lined pools, you'll find it somewhere along the many waterways of the forest. Six Rivers contains 366 miles of wild, scenic, or recreational rivers—35% of California's Wild and Scenic Rivers. Four of its rivers—the Eel, Smith, Trinity and Klamath—have been designated as Wild and Scenic Rivers. Always contact the local ranger district office or call the Flow Phone (707/443-9305) before taking a trip to determine water conditions.

Fishing on the major streams is considered the finest in California for the popular salmon and steelhead. Tremendous runs of these large fish come in from the ocean from September through February, and an estimated 70,000 fishermen come from all over to enjoy this sport annually. Elevations range from 300 to 6,400 feet, and the climate is moderate.

Highways 199 and 299, which traverse the Six Rivers National Forest, are both designated as national scenic byways. Highway 299, the 150-mile Trinity Scenic Byway, winds along the Trinity River gorge, skirts the spectacular Trinity Alps and descends into the moist coastal redwood forests from the Sacramento Valley. Highway 199, the 33-mile, Smith River Scenic Byway, is a paved, two-lane road that winds inland from the Northern

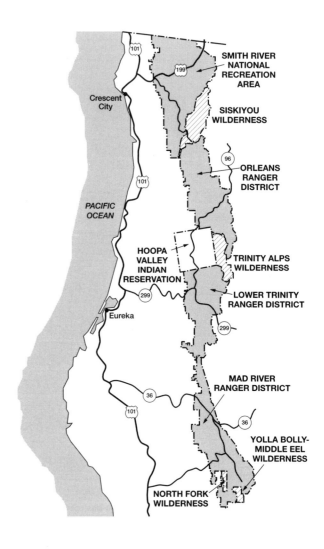

California coast to the Oregon border through towering redwood trees. It passes through Smith River National Recreation Area, a 305,000-acre recreation area managed by the Six Rivers National Forest. In 1990, it became the 16th national recreation area on national forest lands. Information is presented in greater detail on pages 59–60 for this northernmost area of the forest.

Six Rivers National Forest
(*continued*)

Wilderness Areas

The **North Fork Wilderness** occupies 8,100 acres; it highlights the Wild and Scenic North Fork of the Eel River. The terrain of this area is steep and rugged and access to the wilderness is rather limited. South-facing slopes are covered with grass, manzanita, and scrub oak, while north-facing slopes have Douglas-fir, ponderosa pine, and incense cedar.

The 153,000-acre **Siskiyou Wilderness** is in three national forests—Siskiyou, Klamath, and Six Rivers. It offers a wide diversity of flora and fauna, steep forested ridges and peaks, fragile mountain meadows, and shallow mountain lakes. The Upper South Fork Smith River, a designated Wild and Scenic River, and the South Kelsey National Recreation Trail are both in the northern part of the area. Cross country travel is almost impossible due to dense vegetation. West side entry is from Six Rivers National Forest.

The 513,100-acre **Trinity Alps Wilderness** is in four national forests—Shasta, Trinity, Klamath, and Six Rivers. The second-largest wilderness in California, this rugged, isolated area consists of mountain ridges and deep canyons between the Trinity River and Salmon River. Elevations range from 2,000 to 8,000 feet. Salmon Summit, Horse Trail Ridge, and Devil's Backbone national recreation trails are all within this area and offer spectacular views of the Marble Mountain Wilderness and the Trinity Alps. Visitor permits are required.

The **Yolla Bolly-Middle Eel Wilderness** encompasses 154,000 acres and is in three national forests—Mendocino, Trinity, and Six Rivers. The area is located between the North and South Yolla Bolla Mountains in rugged country of the headwaters of the Middle Fork of the Eel River. Elevations range from 2,700 to 8,000 feet. An extensive trail system exists. Hiking season extends May to October; water is scarce after July 1.

Lower Trinity and Mad River Ranger Districts

For Information

Lower Trinity Ranger District
P.O. Box 68
Willow Creek, CA 95573
916/629-2118

Mad River Ranger District
HC Box 300
Bridgeville, CA 95526
707/574-6233

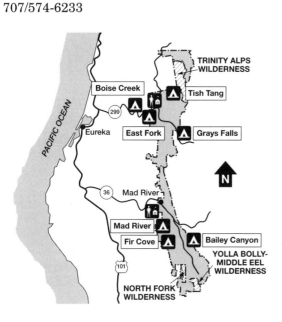

Campgrounds	Elevation (feet)	# of Units	Drinking Water	Toilets	Trailer Space	Camping Fee
Lower Trinity Ranger District						
Boise Creek	1,000	17	•	V	•	•
East Fork	1,000	9		V	•	•
Grays Falls	1,000	33	•	F	•	•
Tish Tang	400	40	•	V	•	•
Mad River Ranger District						
Bailey Canyon	2,600	25	•	P	•	•
Fir Cove*	2,600	19	•	P	•	•
Fir Cove Group*	2,600	3	•	P	•	•
Mad River	2,500	40	•	P	•	•

Notes:

*Fir Cove single sites are available for individual family camping from Friday at 2 p.m. to Monday at 2 p.m.

*Group camping at Fir Cove is available from Monday at 2 p.m. to Friday at 2 p.m. Reservations are required. Phone 707/574-6223.

East Fork is open year-round; other campgrounds open the last week of May and close the first week in Sept., except Tish Tang & it remains open until the end of Sept.

Six Rivers National Forest
(*continued*)

Orleans Ranger District and Smith River National Recreation Area

For Information

Orleans Ranger District
Drawer B
Orleans, CA 95556
916/627-3291

Smith River National Recreation Area
P.O. Box 228
Gasquet, CA 95543
707/457-3131

Campgrounds	Elevation (feet)	# of Units	Drinking Water	Toilets Vault/Flush	Trailer Space	Camping Fee
Orleans Ranger District						
Aikens Creek	340	29	•	F	•	•
E-Ne-Nuck	360	11	•	V	•	•
Fish Lake	1,750	24	•	V	•	•
Pearch Creek	400	10	•	V	•	•
Smith River National Recreation Area						
Big Flat	660	28		V	•	•
Grassy Flat*	500	19	•	V	•	•
Panther Flat*	500	39	•	F	•	•
Patrick Creek*	800	13	•	F	•	•

Notes:
*Reservations available. Phone 1-800-280-CAMP.
Panther Flat has showers.
Panther Flat is open year-round ; other campgrounds in the
Smith River NRA open the last week of May and close the
first week of Sept.
Aikens Creek West closes Dec. 31; other campgrounds in
Orleans RD close the first week in November; Fish Creek
opens the first week in April, Pearch Creek opens the last
week in May, and the other 3 open the last week in July.

Highways 199 and 299, both designated as national scenic byways, traverse the forest amid towering redwood trees.

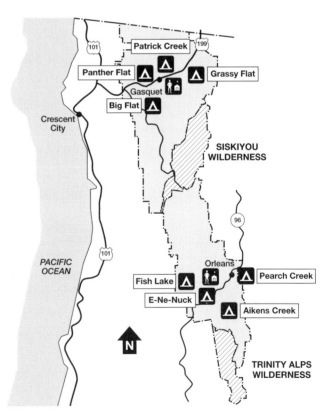

Because six major streams drain or pass through the forest, an unparalleled range of experiences for water enthusiasts exists.

Smith River National Recreation Area

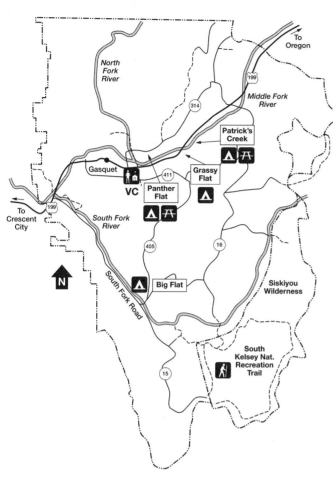

For Information

Smith River National Recreation Area
Box 228, Hwy. 199 N.
Gasquet, CA 95543-0228
707/457-3131

Location

On November 16, 1990, Smith River became the 16th national recreation area on national forest lands; it is located within the Six Rivers National Forest. The Forest Service has been designated as the steward of the 305,337-acre Smith River National Recreation Area to provide recreational opportunities and to manage this area of special scenic value. Located in the extreme northwestern corner of California, the recreation area is the heart of one of the largest wild and scenic river systems (315 miles) in the United States. A national scenic byway, which begins northeast of Crescent City at the junction of US 101 and 199 and ends at Collier Tunnel near the California-Oregon border, passes through the heart of the recreation area.

Points of Interest

▲ Twenty-seven miles of the 33-mile Smith River Scenic Byway weave through the National Recreation Area; frequent turnouts allow views of the striking scenery along the Middle Fork of the Smith River.
▲ Recreational opportunities abound along the free-flowing river and include exciting rafting, kayaking, and steelhead fishing.
▲ 59,000 acres of the Siskiyou Wilderness lie within the borders of the Smith River National Recreation Area; its steep forested ridges and craggy, steep peaks are accessible to hikers and backpackers.
▲ Over 65 miles of designated trails are provided for hiking, horseback riding and mountain biking; trail lengths vary from 9/10 of a mile to 16 miles.

General Information

▲ Headquarters for this national recreation area are located at the Smith River Visitor Center along the Smith River Scenic Byway. It is open Monday through Friday, year-round; during the summer months it is also open on weekends.
▲ All 4 developed campgrounds have RV and tent sites; all charge a fee. Panther Flat Campground is open year-round while the rest are open in the summer. Panther Flat Campground has showers.
▲ Campgrounds have running water, toilets, a parking spur, picnic table, and fire ring or stove at each site. Garbage disposal is available at all campgrounds except Big Flat.
▲ Dispersed camping, that is, camping along roadways or along streams outside designated campgrounds, is allowed. Unless specifically prohibited, most land in the forest is open to camping free of

Smith River National Recreation Area (*continued*)

charge; visits are limited to 30 days. Campfire permits are required and are free of charge.

▲ Patrick's Creek and Panther Flat Campgrounds have barrier-free campsites and restrooms.

▲ River access points are clearly marked along the roads that parallel the Middle Fork (US 199) and the South Fork (Highway 427) of the Smith River; they provide access to sandy beaches and river pools. A *Boating Recreation Map & Guide* is available for each river at the visitor center.

▲ Information and guidelines for experiencing the Siskiyou Wilderness are available at the visitor center.

▲ Scenery is outstanding from the paved two-lane Scenic Byway, but even more can be seen by traveling the 124 miles of county and 142 miles of national forest roads.

▲ Winter temperatures drop into the 40s and 50s, with an occasional snow storm. Summer highs are a pleasant 75–85°F. The relatively dry months of May through September provide weather ideal for camping, hiking, and swimming.

▲ The rainy season normally runs from October through April with an average annual rainfall of 94 inches in Gasquet. Winter rains raise the undammed waters of the Smith River, making it ideal for white-water rafting, canoeing, kayaking, and fishing for salmon, trout, and steelhead.

Facilities & Activities

100 RV and tent campsites
dispersed camping
picnicking
swimming
white-water rafting
canoeing/kayaking
fishing
hunting
65 miles of designated trails
hiking
backpacking
4-wheel drive/ATV/mountain bike areas
horseback riding
touring the scenic roads
visitor center

Developed Campgrounds	Elevation (ft)	Camp Units	Toilets Vault/Flush	Picnic Sites	River Access
Big Flat	660	30	V		•
Grassy Flats	500	19	V	10	
Panther Flat*	500	39	F	2	•
Patrick Creek	800	12	F		•

Notes:
* Panther Flat has showers.
Fees are charged at all campgrounds; RV size limit is 25 feet.

Smith River is the heart of one of the largest wild and scenic river systems in the United States.

Whiskeytown-Shasta-Trinity National Recreation Area

Location

Whiskeytown-Shasta-Trinity National Recreation Area consists of three separate units—Shasta, Trinity, and Whiskeytown. Each unit comprises its lake and surrounding lands. The Trinity and Shasta Units are administered by two different ranger districts within the Shasta-Trinity National Forest of the U.S. Forest Service; the Whiskeytown Unit is administered by the National Park Service. The 203,587-acre recreation area, authorized by an Act of Congress in 1965, features four lakes including Shasta Lake, the largest reservoir in California. Each lake offers its own special attractions. A dominant landscape feature, the dormant Mt. Shasta Volcano, is a scenic regional backdrop to Shasta Lake. The rugged, granite peaks of the 517,500-acre Trinity Alps Wilderness provide a picturesque backdrop to Trinity Lake.

Facilities & Activities

Whiskeytown Unit
   60 RV campsites
   105 tent campsites
   2 group campgrounds
Shasta Unit
   368 RV and tent campsites
   3 group campgrounds
Trinity Unit
   444 RV and tent campsites
   3 group campgrounds
backcountry campsites in all units
picnicking
group picnic areas
fishing
swimming
snorkeling/scuba diving
sailing/canoeing
boat ramps
boating/boat rentals/marinas
water skiing/jet skiing
house boating
hunting
hiking
horseback riding
snowmobiling/cross-country skiing/snowshoeing
   on the Shasta and Trinity Units
resorts/restaurants/groceries
ranger-guided programs/activities
visitor centers/exhibits

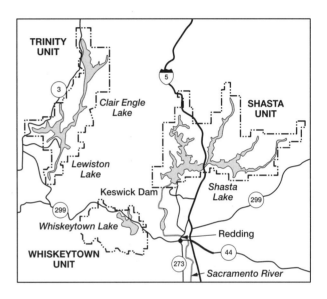

Points of Interest

▲ Opportunities are unlimited for recreation on, in, and around water.
▲ Houseboats, patio boats, jet skis, ski boats, sailboards, and fishing boats with gear and tackle are available for rental from marinas located throughout the area.
▲ Interesting historical sites can be found throughout the area; free brochures are available at each lake's information centers.
▲ With a campfire permit, you can camp just about anywhere accessible by boat, car, or foot on the Shasta and Trinity Units.
▲ Lewiston and Whiskeytown are both constant level lakes; Trinity and Shasta Lakes may fluctuate as much as 1–2 feet each day.

Whiskeytown Unit

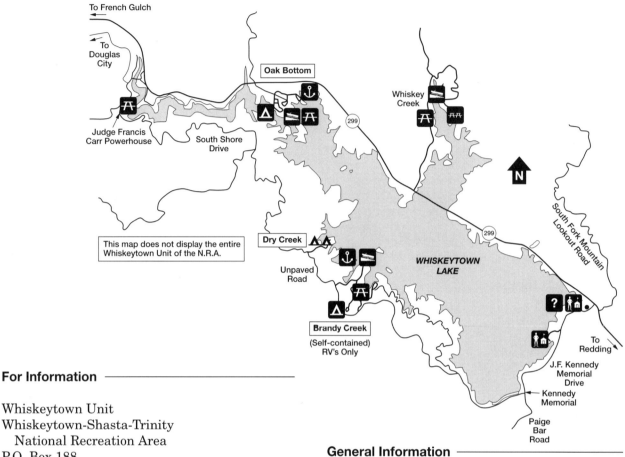

For Information

Whiskeytown Unit
Whiskeytown-Shasta-Trinity
  National Recreation Area
P.O. Box 188
Whiskeytown, CA 96095
916/241-6584

Location

The Whiskeytown Unit of the recreation area lies on Highway 299 off I-5 near Redding. Whiskeytown Lake, the smallest of the recreation area's 4 impounded lakes, has approximately 36 miles of shoreline. Its constant level in the summer makes it ideal for recreational use. Whiskeytown Dam and Lake store and regulate waters being diverted from the Trinity River via the 11-mile Clear Creek Tunnel from Lewiston Dam. The water next goes by tunnel to Keswick Reservoir, to be mixed with water from Shasta Dam and released through the Keswick power plant into the Sacramento River. The Whiskeytown Unit encompasses 42,500 acres; the highest point is Shasta Bally Mountain at 6,209 feet and the lowest point is Clear Creek Canyon at 830 feet.

General Information

▲ The visitor information center is located at the intersection of Highway 299 and Kennedy Memorial Drive. It offers an orientation map, exhibits about the area, an information desk, and publications for sale. The center is open year-round, but days and hours of operation vary with the season.

▲ Interpretive activities are provided from mid-June through Labor Day. Evening programs are held at the Oak Bottom Amphitheater. Other activities include ranger-guided walks and gold panning demonstrations.

▲ Camping is permitted in designated campgrounds and in the backcountry. A 14-day limit applies from May 15 through September 15; there is a 30-day limit otherwise. Brandy Creek and Oak Bottom campgrounds are open all year; the group campground is open seasonally.

▲ Brandy Creek offers a 37-unit RV campground for self-contained units only; camping is on a

first-come, first-served basis. There are no restrooms; no fees are charged. A sanitary dump station and drinking water are provided.
▲ Oak Bottom offers a 22-unit RV campground with dump station. Water and modern restrooms are nearby. A walk-in tent campground has 105 sites with fireplaces, picnic tables, and modern restrooms. Fees are charged and reservations are available through DESTINET.
▲ Two group campgrounds are available at Dry Creek for RVs and tents; maximum number of persons per site is 80. Reservations are required; contact the Whiskeytown Unit of the recreation area. Water is available; limit-of-stay is 7 days.
▲ All overnight backcountry use requires a back-country use permit issued free at headquarters.

With permit, you may camp anywhere in the backcountry except within 1 mile of the lake shore. Many backcountry roads are only suitable for 4-wheel-drive vehicles. Check for other restrictions when you obtain your permit.
▲ Concessionaire-operated marinas are located at Oak Bottom and Brandy Creek; they offer launch ramp, snack bar, camper store, and boat rentals. Whiskey Creek also has a launch ramp.
▲ Gold panning may be done for recreational purposes only, not to make money. It must be done in the historical manner, using a metal or plastic gold pan with the aid of small hand tools only; a permit is required.
▲ The extensive backcountry provides ample hiking, mountain biking, and horseback riding opportunities. Ask a ranger for advice on the best trails.

Shasta Unit

For Information

Shasta Lake Ranger District
Shasta-Trinity National Forest
14225 Holiday Road
Redding, CA 96003
916/275-1589

Location

Shasta Lake is the largest man-made reservoir in California. When full, it has a 370-mile shoreline and a surface area of 30,000 acres. Shasta is the second largest and tallest concrete dam in the United States. The construction of Shasta Dam impounded three major rivers (Pit, McCloud, and Sacramento), and Squaw Creek. Referred to as arms, each one retains its own character, environment, history, and recreation opportunities. The Sacramento Arm is the busiest and most developed arm of Shasta Lake. The O'Brien Area, on the McCloud Arm, is at the hub of the lake and provides central access to all arms. The Squaw Creek Arm is rugged, remote and one of the lake's most popular houseboating areas. The Pit Arm is the longest one on the lake. The largest inland marina on the West Coast is at Bridge Bay; high above is the Pit River Bridge, the highest double-decker bridge in the United States.
Spectacular views of Mt. Shasta and Mt. Lassen backdrop the steep shores and islands in a wide basin formed by the confluence of the Sacramento and Pit Rivers directly behind Shasta Dam. Interstate-5, north from Redding, is the main access

road to the area, but much of the Shasta Unit of the national recreation area is accessible only by boat. Every year Shasta Lake has a substantial drawdown that occasionally exceeds 100 feet. The result is a new lake and an explorer's paradise because areas of geological and historical interest are no longer submerged.

General Information

▲ Visitor information centers at the following locations provide maps, brochures, exhibits, campfire permits, and general information: Shasta Lake Information Center is at the Mountain Gate/Wonderland Boulevard exit from I-5, phone, 916/275-1589; and, the Shasta Dam Information Center is at the dam, exit from I-5 on Shasta Dam Boulevard, phone 916/275-4463.
▲ The Shasta Unit offers 20 Forest Service campgrounds near the lake. All charge fees except the boat access campgrounds. Some have flush toilets, but most have pit or vault type facilities. All sites are first-come, first-served. The limit of stay is either 7 or 14 days, as posted at the campground entrance.
▲ Most campgrounds are open from May through September; several remain open all year. During the winter months, many water systems are shut down, but restroom facilities are available. Check at the information centers for seasonal closures or temporary closures due to low water level.
▲ Four campgrounds are accessible only by boat: Arbuckle Flat, Gooseneck Cove, Greens Creek,

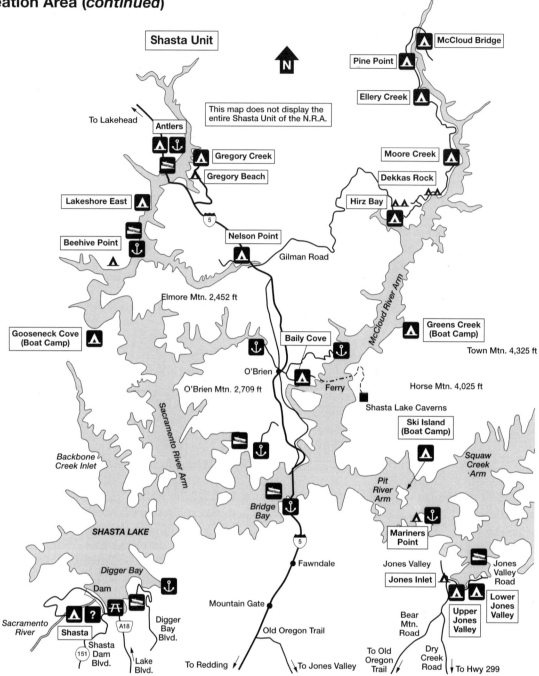

Shasta Unit

This map does not display the entire Shasta Unit of the N.R.A.

and Ski Island. These camps have tables, stoves, and toilets. Three road-accessible campgrounds have primitive campsites: Beehive Point, Gregory Beach, and Jones Inlet. Fees are charged; drinking water is not available.

▲ Three group campgrounds will accommodate up to 120 people each. Reservations are required and may be made by calling 1-800-280-CAMP, starting the first business day after January 1st.

▲ Camping is permitted in undeveloped areas except where posted otherwise. Beach area use is limited to 30 days per year. Garbage should be packed out to the nearest container; do not bury it or dispose of it at floating restrooms.

▲ The upper section of the McCloud Arm is known to be bear country. Keep food in secure containers inside vehicles and make every effort to avoid attracting bears to the campsite.

Whiskeytown-Shasta-Trinity Recreation Area (*continued*)

▲ A campfire permit is required for building fires or using gas or charcoal stoves along the shoreline during fire season (usually May through October). This permit is free and may be obtained from either information center. Fire permits are not required for campfires in developed campgrounds. Gathering dead wood for campfires is allowed; no permit is necessary.

▲ Shasta Lake has several short trails for the casual hiker. A brochure is available that describes 12 trails ranging in length from one-half mile to 8 miles. Hiking trails are generally open all year.

▲ Shasta Lake has no developed swimming areas. During the summer, the water is comfortably warm. Many people swim from the shore near their campgrounds or from boats. Swimming is prohibited in the main channels and within 200 feet of any launch ramp.

▲ Water skiing is popular everywhere on the lake, but the Sacramento Arm and Jones Valley areas are particularly favored. Skiing can be hazardous in the Pit Arm where snags and floating debris have not been removed. Waterskiing is prohibited in some of the smaller coves and bays; these areas are posted by buoys.

▲ There are over a dozen public and commercial boat ramps at Shasta Lake. The public ramps charge a fee and are open all year. Commercial ramps, associated with marinas or resorts, usually charge a fee, and some close during the winter. Contact an information center for a map and list of boat ramp locations and the chart that shows which public boat ramps are in service at lower lake levels.

▲ Most boats must be registered and numbered; out-of-state registration is valid for 90 days. Houseboats require a Forest Service permit to be on the lake in excess of 30 days per calendar year; this restriction applies primarily to boats equipped for overnight use.

▲ The Jones Valley area provides the best access to the Pit and Squaw Arms, considered by many to provide the best overall fishing. Other popular spots are located where the major rivers and streams empty into the lake.

▲ The commercially-operated Shasta Lake Caverns are open to the public with guided tours hourly between 9 and 4 from April 1 through October 31; there are three tours daily the rest of the year. From I-5 at O'Brien, turn at Shasta Cav-

erns Road and travel east; the Caverns' headquarters chalet is less than 2 miles.

▲ Commercial campgrounds with full hookups, resorts, marinas, restaurants and other services are within the Shasta Unit; ask for a complete listing of these at an information station.

▲ Facilities have been constructed or modified to assist the physically disabled. Several campgrounds, picnic areas, and boat ramps are handicap accessible. Contact the Shasta Lake Information Center for assistance in finding suitable areas or more information.

Campgrounds	Total Sites	Fee	Drinking Water	Toilets Vault/Flush	Trailer Max. Length (feet)
Antlers*	59	•	•	F/V	30
Arbuckle Flat Boat Camp	11			V	
Bailey Cove	7	•	•	F	30
Beehive Point (P)			•	V	30
Ellery Creek	19	•	•	V	30
Gooseneck Cove Boat Camp	11			V	
Greens Creek Boat Camp	8			V	
Gregory Beach (P)		•		V	30
Gregory Creek	18	•	•	F	16
Hirz Bay*	48	•	•	F	30
Jones Valley Inlet (P)		•	•	V	30
Lakeshore East	26	•	•	F	30
Lower Jones Valley	14	•	•	V	16
Mariners Point (P)		•	•	V	16
McCloud Bridge	20	•	•	F/V	16
Moore Creek	12	•	•	V	16
Nelson Point	9	•		V	16
Pine Point	14	•	•	V	24
Shasta	23	•	•	V	30
Ski Island Boat Camp	23			V	
Upper Jones Valley	13	•	•	V	16
Group Campgrounds*					
Dekkas Rock Group Camp	2	•	•	V	16
Hirz Bay Group Camp #1	1	•	•	V	30
Hirz Bay Group Camp #2	1	•	•	V	30

Notes:
*On reservation system: 1-800-280-CAMP.
P = Primitive campsites.

Trinity Unit

For Information

Weaverville Ranger District
Shasta-Trinity National Forest
P.O. Box 1190
Weaverville, CA 96093-1190
916/623-2121

Location

The Clair Engle-Lewiston Lakes Unit is commonly called the Trinity Unit. Clair Engle Lake is referred to locally as Trinity Lake; when full, it is approximately 20 miles long and has a 145-mile shoreline with a surface area of 17,000 acres. Highway 3 (Trinity Heritage National Scenic Byway) off of Highway 299 at Weaverville provides the main access to the Trinity Unit. The Stuart Fork Arm is the "hub" of most of the activity on and around the lake; it extends to the west and is fed by the Stuart Fork River. This arm is popular with houseboaters and is one of the choicest waterskiing areas on the lake. Swimming at Trinity Lake is extremely popular because the surface water temperature

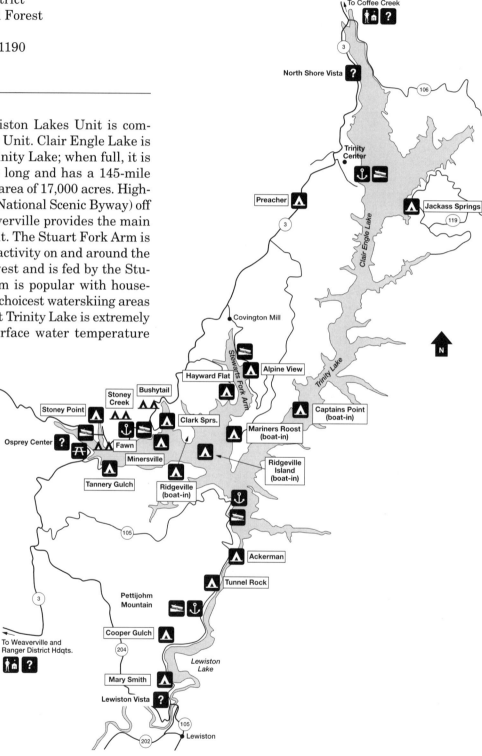

during the summer can get into the 80s. The water level can fluctuate as much as two or three feet per day during times of heavy rains or release.

Lewiston Lake, just downstream from Trinity Lake, is 5 miles long with 15 miles of shoreline and a surface area of 960 acres. Lewiston Lake caters primarily to the camper and fisherman. Because of the narrow width of Lewiston Lake, boat speed is limited to 10 mph. Always kept at full capacity, the water here is considerably colder than Trinity Lake; it seldom climbs above the 50°F mark, so is exceptionally good for trout. The 2-mile fly-fishing-only stretch of the Trinity River just below Lewiston Dam attracts fishermen who try their skills on browns and rainbows.

For Information

▲ Visitor information in the form of maps, brochures, exhibits, campfire permits, and general information may be obtained from the ranger stations in Weaverville and Coffee Creek. Coffee Creek Station is open summers only. Self-service information stations are located at Osprey and Mule Creek Station, and 3 vista points: Lewiston, North Shore, and Trinity.

▲ The Trinity Unit offers 15 Forest Service campgrounds. Seven of them are developed; they have drinking water and flush toilets. Fees are charged except in the off season when water is not provided. Limit of stay at improved campgrounds is generally limited to 14 days per year.

▲ Most campgrounds are open from Memorial Day through Labor Day; more than half remain open year-round. Most water systems are shut down during the winter months, but restroom facilities are available. Check at the ranger stations for seasonal closures or temporary closures due to low water level.

▲ Four campgrounds are boat access only: Captain's Point, Mariner's Roost, Ridgeville, and Ridgeville Islands. They are open year-round; they do not have drinking water, nor are fees charged.

▲ Three group campgrounds are available from the first of May through the end of September. Advance registrations are required through the Weaverville Ranger District office.

▲ Camping outside of a developed campground, either out in the forest or along a lakeshore, is permitted on the Trinity Unit. Camping is permitted along the shoreline at Trinity Lake, except were specifically prohibited; however, at Lewiston Lake, camping is not permitted on the

Campgrounds	Total Sites	Fee	Drinking Water	Toilets Vault/Flush	Trailer Max. Length (feet)
Ackerman (S)	66	•	•	F	27
Alpine View	66	•	•	F	32
Captain's Point (BI)	3			V	
Clark Springs	21	•	•	F	
Cooper Gulch	9	•		V	16
Hayward Flat (R)	97	•	•	V	40
Jackass Spring	21			V	32
Mariner's Roost (BI)	7			V	
Mary Smith (T)	18	•	•	F/V	
Minersville	21	•	•	F	18
Ridgeville (BI)	21			V	
Ridgeville Islands (BI)	3			V	
Stoney Point	22	•	•	F	
Tannery Gulch (R)	84	•	•	F/V	40
Tunnel Rock	6	•		V	
Group Campgrounds*	Max. Persons				
Bushytail Group	200	•	•	F	
Fawn Group	300	•	•	F	37
Stoney Creek	50	•	•	F	

Notes:
*Reservations required; contact Ranger District office.
BI = Boat-In camping.
R= On National Reservation System: 1-800-280-CAMP.
S = Sanitary dump.
T = Tent camping only; no trailers allowed.

shoreline except in developed campsites. Limit of stay is 30 days at any one location.

▲ Commercial campgrounds with full hookups, resorts, marinas, restaurants, and other services are within the Trinity Unit; pick up a complete listing of these at an information station.

▲ Grills and fire rings are provided at campgrounds and picnic areas. Campfire permits are not required at developed sites; however, they are required elsewhere, including shoreline camping.

▲ Any boat designed or converted for overnight occupancy requires a houseboat permit from the Forest Service. Temporary permits are good for 30 days per year.

▲ Boat ramps at Trinity Lake are operational from full lake to a specific number of feet down. Prior to bringing a boat that requires a launch ramp, check with the Forest Service regarding which ramps are open; many are closed during periods of low water level.

Region 2

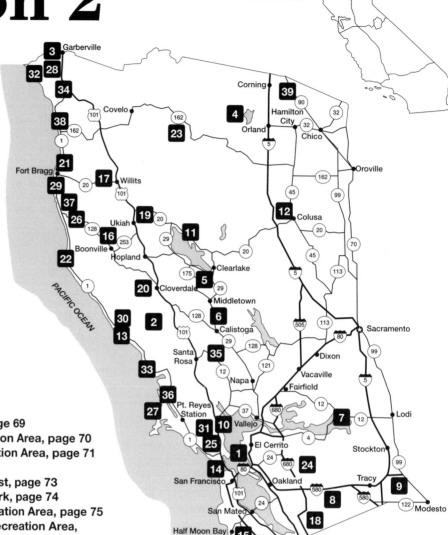

1—Angel Island State Park, page 69
2—Austin Creek State Recreation Area, page 70
3—Benbow Lake State Recreation Area, page 71
4—Black Butte Lake, page 72
5—Boggs Mountain State Forest, page 73
6—Bothe-Napa Valley State Park, page 74
7—Brannan Island State Recreation Area, page 75
8—Carnegie State Vehicular Recreation Area, page 76
9—Caswell Memorial State Park, page 77
10—China Camp State Park, page 78
11—Clear Lake State Park, page 79
12—Colusa-Sacramento River State Recreation Area, page 80
13—Fort Ross State Historic Park, page 81
14—Golden Gate National Recreation Area, page 82
15—Half Moon Bay State Beach, page 84
16—Hendy Woods State Park, page 85
17—Jackson State Forest, page 86
18—Lake Del Valle State Recreation Area, page 88
19—Lake Mendocino, page 89
20—Lake Sonoma, page 90
21—MacKerricher State Park, page 91
22—Manchester State Park, page 92
23—Mendocino National Forest, page 101
24—Mount Diablo State Park, page 105
25—Mount Tamalpais State Park, page 107
26—Navarro River Redwoods State Park, page 108
27—Point Reyes National Seashore, page 109
28—Richardson Grove State Park, page 111

29—Russian Gulch State Park, page 112
30—Salt Point State Park, page 113
31—Samuel P. Taylor State Park, page 114
32—Sinkyone Wilderness State Park, page 115
33—Sonoma Coast State Beach, page 117
34—Standish-Hickey State Recreation Area, page 119
35—Sugarloaf Ridge State Park, page 120
36—Tomales Bay State Park, page 121
37—Van Damme State Park, page 122
38—Westport-Union Landing State Beach, page 123
39—Woodson Bridge State Recreation Area, page 124

Angel Island State Park

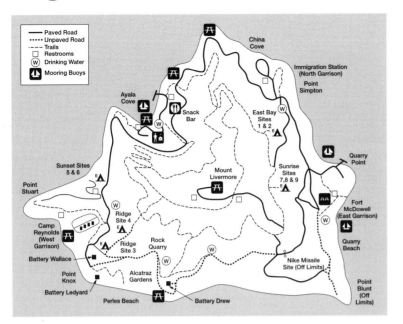

Walk-in Campsites Only

For Information

Angel Island State Park
P.O. Box 318
Tiburon, CA 94920
415/435-1915

Location

Angel Island State Park is located in San Francisco Bay on a 740-acre mountainous, forest-covered island. The elevation of the island ranges from sea level to 781 feet at the summit of Mount Livermore. The park is reached by ferry from Tiburon (415/435-2131), from Pier 43½, San Francisco (415/546-2628), or from Vallejo 415/705-5444; ferry prices include the park entry fee. Spectacular views of San Francisco and the Golden Gate await the Angel Island State Park visitor.

Special Notes

A special feature at the park is the "Cove to Crest Nature Trail," a 2-mile loop that explores the natural terrain of the island. Bicycles can be brought to Angel Island on the ferry and used to circle the island on the main road. However, most of the other roads on the island are either too rough or too steep for safe cycling. Angel Island's past includes use as an immigrant quarantine station, a Nike missile base, and a military overseas staging area. In the summer, there are elephant train tours.

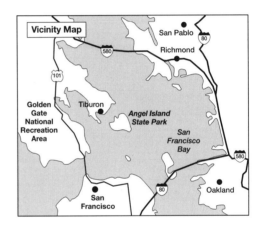

Facilities* & Activities

9 environmental campsites
    water, pit toilet, open year-round
    sites #7, 8, & 9 available as a group camp for 24
picnicking
group picnic area† (150)
fishing
nature trail
13 miles hiking trails
bicycling/rentals
boat mooring/day-use dock facility
snack bar (open summers & spring weekends)
guided tours (415/435-3522)
visitor center
state historic landmark

---

*On state park reservation system.
†Phone park for reservations.

Austin Creek State Recreation Area

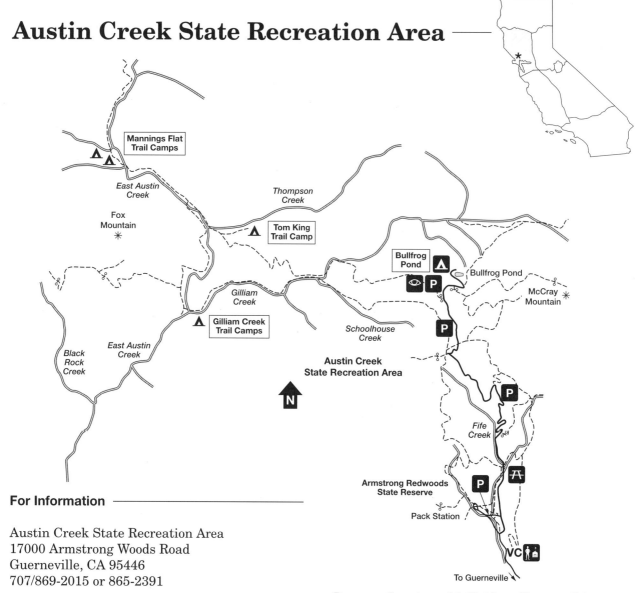

For Information

Austin Creek State Recreation Area
17000 Armstrong Woods Road
Guerneville, CA 95446
707/869-2015 or 865-2391

Location

Located 3 miles north of Guerneville on Armstrong Woods Road, Austin Creek State Recreation Area covers 4,236 acres. Elevation ranges from 150 feet to 1,940 feet at the top of McCray Mountain.

The park is accessible via a steep, one-lane road that begins at Armstrong Redwoods picnic area; the road is considered unsafe for motor homes or trailers.

Special Notes

Austin Creek rewards the explorer with panoramic wilderness views; with 20 miles of trails, it is a paradise for the hiker and equestrian. Although the park is close to urban areas, its rugged topography gives a real sense of isolation.

Its open forests and hillsides offer a striking contrast to the dark forest of the adjacent Armstrong Redwoods State Reserve. Horse trailers should be parked at the Armstrong Redwoods entrance or picnic area. Campsites are open all year except in the summer during periods of high fire danger.

Facilities & Activities

24 campsites
    flush toilets, potable water
    no washing facilities
no trailers or vehicles over 20 feet
4 primitive trail camps
equestrian camping* (30)
picnicking
hiking trails
horseback riding trails

*Phone park for reservations.

Benbow Lake State Recreation Area

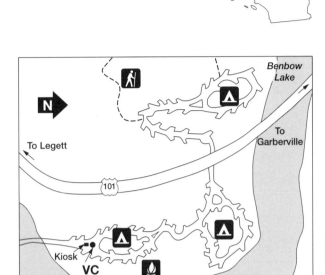

For Information

Benbow Lake State Recreation Area
1600 Highway 101 #8
Garberville, CA 95542
707/247-3318

Location

Benbow Lake State Recreation Area is located 2 miles south of Garberville on US 101 and 5 miles north of Richardson Grove State Park. The 786-acre recreation area, adjacent to the banks of the South Fork of the Eel River, has an elevation of 400 feet.

Special Notes

Benbow Lake is a seasonal lake; every May through September, Benbow Dam is used to create a 26-acre summer lake. The recreation area has 6 miles of lake and river frontage. During high water in the winter, the park is closed.

Facilities* & Activities

76 developed campsites
cold outdoor showers
24-foot trailers; 30-foot campers
trailer sanitation station
enroute campsites
1 hike/bike campsite
group camping area[†] (350)
picnicking
fishing
swimming
windsurfing
canoeing/boating (no power boats)
launch ramp/boat rentals
hiking trails
interpretive center
summer nature programs

---
*On state park reservation system.
[†]Phone park for reservations.

REGION 2

Austin Creek is a paradise for the hiker and equestrian. With 20 miles of trails, its rugged topography gives a real sense of isolation. (Photo: Lillian Morava)

Black Butte Lake

For Information

Black Butte Lake
19225 Newville Road
Orland, CA 95963-8901
916/865-4781

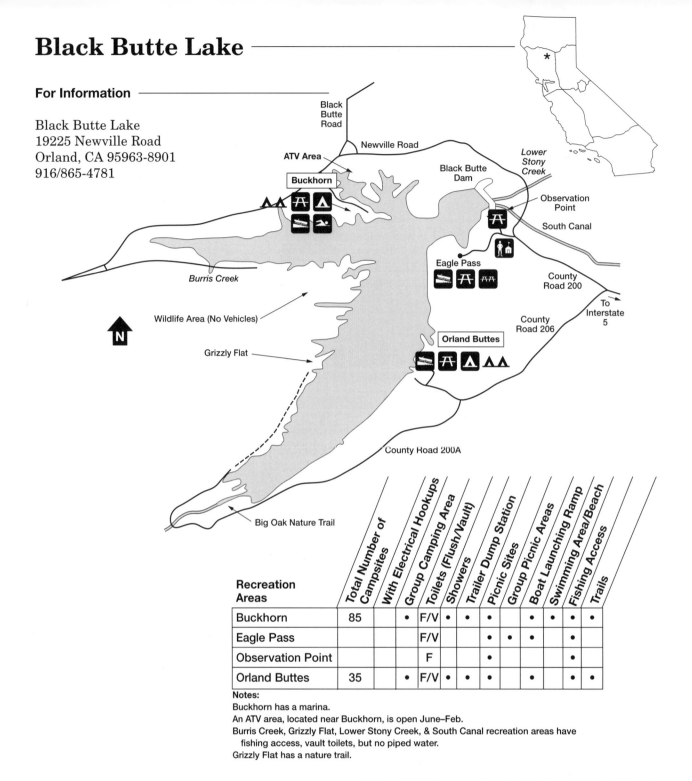

Recreation Areas	Total Number of Campsites	With Electrical Hookups	Group Camping Area	Toilets (Flush/Vault)	Showers	Trailer Dump Station	Picnic Sites	Group Picnic Areas	Boat Launching Ramp	Swimming Area/Beach	Fishing Access	Trails
Buckhorn	85		•	F/V	•	•	•		•	•	•	•
Eagle Pass				F/V			•	•	•		•	
Observation Point				F			•				•	
Orland Buttes	35		•	F/V	•	•	•		•		•	•

Notes:
Buckhorn has a marina.
An ATV area, located near Buckhorn, is open June–Feb.
Burris Creek, Grizzly Flat, Lower Stony Creek, & South Canal recreation areas have fishing access, vault toilets, but no piped water.
Grizzly Flat has a nature trail.

Location

Black Butte Lake is on Stony Creek, a tributary of the Sacramento River. Situated at the northern end of the Central Valley, it is 10 miles west of Orland. The water level of Black Butte Lake changes with the season. In the summer and fall, the lake is down; in the winter and spring, it's up. This quiet lake, surrounded by beautiful, dark volcanic buttes, is well known for outstanding fishing and sailing.

Lake Statistics

2,718-acre surface area
7 miles long
23 miles of shoreline

Boggs Mountain State Forest

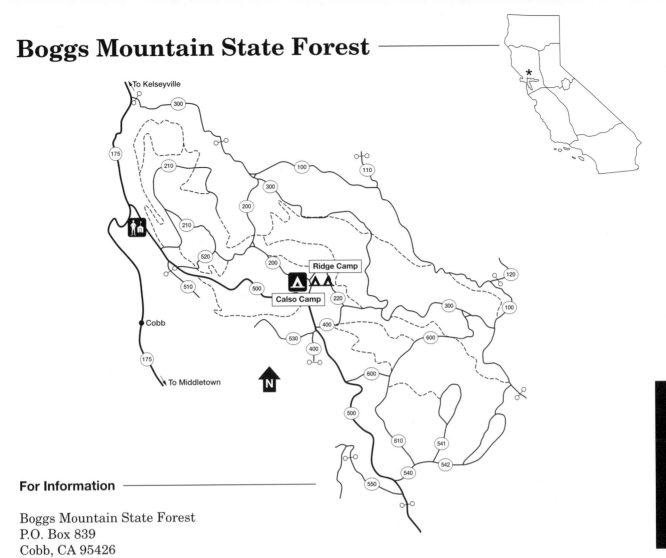

For Information

Boggs Mountain State Forest
P.O. Box 839
Cobb, CA 95426
707/928-4378

Location

Boggs Mountain State Forest is located north from Middletown on Highway 175 through Cobb. The 3,493-acre state forest has an elevation range of 2,400 to 3,750 feet. Established in 1949, the forest is 46% Ponderosa pine, 48% mixed conifer, 3% Douglas fir, and 3% brush and grass.

Facilities & Activities

15 primitive campsites at Calso Camp
2 large group campsites at Ridge Camp
tables, fire rings, toilets
water is not available at campsites; it is normally available at forest entrance
picnicking
hiking trails
mountain bicycling
horseback riding
hunting

Special Notes

A system of trails and secondary roads for hiking, mountain biking, and horseback riding exists on the forest and covers a variety of terrain, including meadows, ridgetops, and dense forests. All motor vehicles are restricted to existing roads and are prohibited from trails and cross-country travel; all must be licensed. Keep pets leashed and controlled in camp areas and keep horses out of camp areas. Garbage and trash should be taken with you when you leave because there is no garbage pickup service. The campground is open year-round.

Obtain a "Campfire and Special Use Permit" from the forestry office before camping, igniting a campfire, or using an open gas stove. Campfires should be built only in fire rings or stoves at camping areas and attended at all times. Hunting is permitted under applicable state game laws and regulations; no hunting or shooting is permitted within 150 yards of any camp area. None of the intermittent streams contain fish.

Bothe-Napa Valley State Park

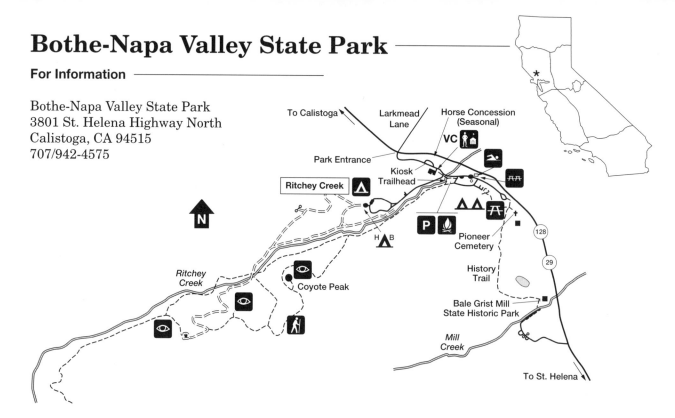

For Information

Bothe-Napa Valley State Park
3801 St. Helena Highway North
Calistoga, CA 94515
707/942-4575

Location

Bothe-Napa Valley State Park is 4 miles north of St. Helena on Highway 29/128. Located in the heart of the beautiful Napa Valley wine country, this 1,983-acre park has an elevation ranging from 320 feet to 2,100 feet.

Most of the park is rugged, and only foot and horse travel go beyond the parking area and campground.

Special Notes

Most of the park is rugged, and only foot and horse travel go beyond the parking area and campground. The hiking and horse trails go through some of the most easterly stands of coast redwoods as well as forests of Douglas fir, tan oak, and madrone. The swimming pool is open mid-June through Labor Day.

Facilities* & Activities

50 developed campsites
wheelchair accessible campsites
pay showers
24-foot trailers; 31-foot campers
trailer sanitation station
1 hike/bike campsite
group camping area (30)
picnicking
group picnic area† (60)
swimming pool
hiking & horseback riding trails
bicycle trails
exhibits/visitor center
state historic landmark

---

*On state park reservation system.
†Phone park for reservations.

Brannan Island State Recreation Area

For Information

Brannan Island State Recreation Area
17645 Highway 160
Rio Vista, CA 94571
916/777-6671 or 777-7701

Location

Brannan Island State Recreation Area is located 3 miles south of Rio Vista on Highway 160. The 336-acre park is located on the east bank of the Sacramento River 13 miles northeast of Antioch and 4 miles downstream from Rio Vista. Its elevation is 25 feet.

Special Notes

The 1,000 miles of rivers, sloughs, levees, marshes, and old river channels has made the Sacramento-San Joaquin River Delta one of the outstanding water recreation areas of the world. For the bicycle rider there are miles of quiet scenic levee roads, free ferry rides, and historic towns.

Facilities* & Activities

102 developed campsites
pay showers/water hookups
31-foot trailers; 31-foot campers
trailer sanitation station
2 hike/bike campsites
6 group camping areas (180)
boat-in primitive camping
   32 boat berths in Delta Vista Boat Campsite
picnicking
group picnic area (100)
fishing
swimming
boating/launch ramp
mooring/boat berth sites
pump out facility
water skiing/windsurfing
canoe/boat tours[†]
exhibits
visitor center (open only on weekends)

---

*On state park reservation system.
[†]Phone park for reservations.

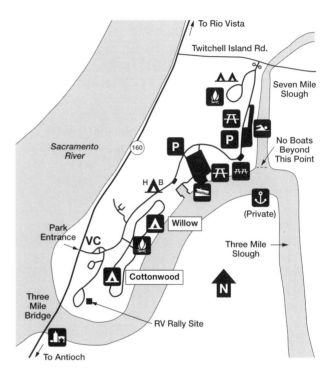

The sloughs at Brannan Island are ideal for exploring by canoe.

Carnegie State Vehicular Recreation Area

For Information

Carnegie State Vehicular Recreation Area
17999 Tesla Road
Livermore, CA 94550
510/447-9027 or 447-0426

Special Notes

Only motorcycles and ATVs are allowed. The terrain offers enough variety—from rolling hills to steep slopes, canyons, and gulches—to challenge the off-road skills of the beginner to expert. Each motorcycle must have a U.S. Forest Service-approved spark arrester in place at all times. Ground fires are not allowed because of extremely high fire hazard. The park is open 7 days a week.

Facilities & Activities

50 primitive campsites
large RVs o.k.
flush toilets/no showers
picnicking
100 miles of motorcycle trails
food service
concession store

Location

This vehicular recreation area is located 10 miles west of Tracy (6 miles west of I-580) on Tesla/Corral Hollow Road. Its 1,540 acres offer a wide variety of terrain from 600 feet to 3,000 feet elevation.

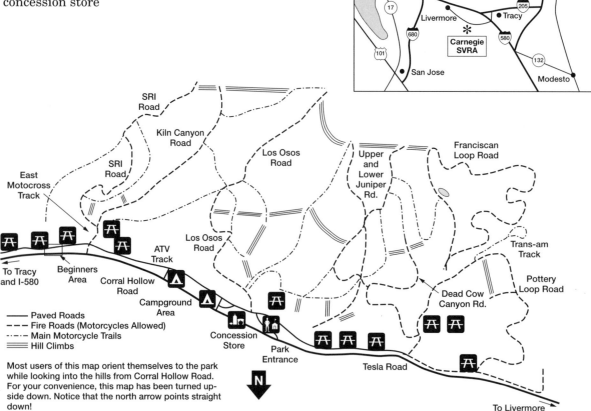

Caswell Memorial State Park

For Information

Caswell Memorial State Park
28000 South Austin Road
Ripon, CA 95366-9527
209/599-3810

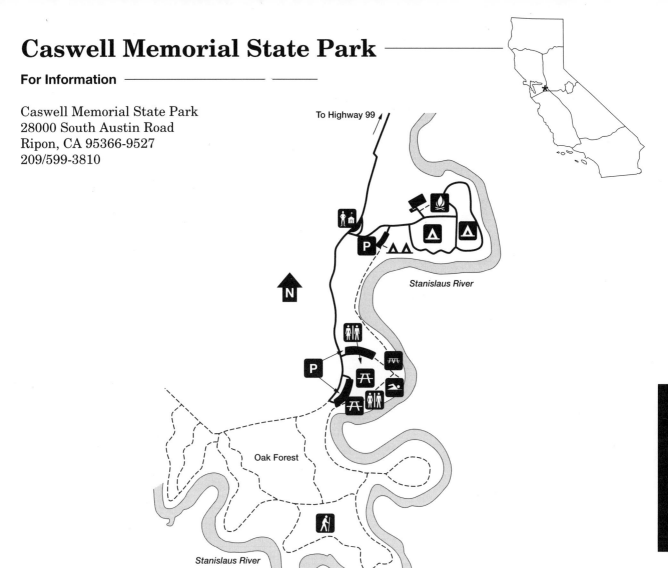

Location

Caswell Memorial State Park is located in the San Joaquin Valley, 6 miles west of Ripon off of Highway 99 on Austin Road. The 258-acre park is 40 feet above sea level. The Stanislaus River may be closed seasonally; contact the park for information.

Special Notes

The Stanislaus River winds through the park; a beach and swimming area are close to the day-use facilities and campground. The river provides salmon fishing in the fall and fishing for striped bass, sturgeon, and black bass all year. The park's stand of valley oak is native only to California. Some of the stands protected in the park contain trees more than 60 feet high and girths of over 17 feet.

Facilities* & Activities

65 developed campsites
showers
21-foot trailers; 24-foot campers
group camping area (50)
picnicking
group picnic area† (40)
fishing
swimming
hiking trails
exhibits

*On state park reservation system.
†Phone park for reservations.

China Camp State Park

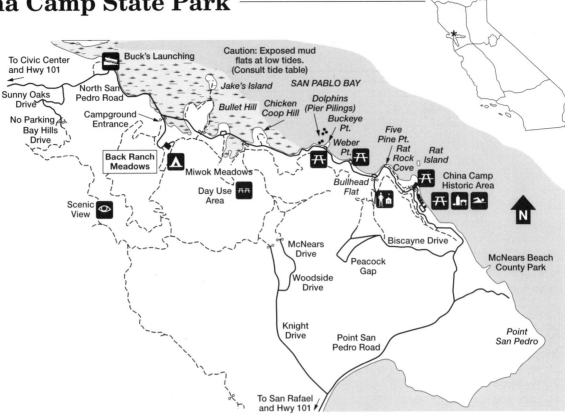

For Information

China Camp State Park
Route 1, Box 244
San Rafael CA 94901
415/456-0766 or 456-1286

Location

China Camp State Park is located on the southwest shore of San Pablo Bay; from US 101 in San Rafael, take San Pedro Road north for 2½ miles to the park entrance. This 1,512-acre park is just a 30-minute drive from San Francisco by way of the Golden Gate Bridge. The elevation ranges from sea level to 1,000 feet.

Special Notes

The park has a variety of natural scenery and some fine trails along San Pablo ridge that feature magnificent panoramic (360°) views of the North Bay Area. The human history of this area adds still another dimension to the park. Visitors usually stop first at the site of the old village. It preserves San Francisco Bay's last Chinese shrimp-fishing village that thrived here in the 1880s. The campground is a walk-in, tent-only campground; campers must carry their equipment from the parking lot to the campsites, some 30 to 100 yards.

Facilities* & Activities

30 walk-in developed sites (tents only)
wheelchair accessible campsites
pay showers
enroute campsites
campsites for hikers & bikers
picnicking
group picnic area at Miwok Meadows**
wading/swimming
fishing
windsurfing
boating (small boats only)
launch ramp
hiking & horseback riding trails
bike trails
food service
group tours†
exhibits/visitor center
state historic landmark

*On state park reservation system.
**Phone 415/456-1286 for reservations.
†Phone park for reservations.

Clear Lake State Park

For Information

Clear Lake State Park
5300 Soda Bay Road
Kelseyville, CA 95451
707/279-4293 or 279-2267

Facilities* & Activities

4 campgrounds (147 developed sites)
   21 tents only at Lower Bayview
   35 camper sites at Upper Bayview (21-foot)
   26 camper sites at Cole Creek (24-foot)
   65 trailer/camper sites at Kelsey Creek (35-foot)
     wheelchair accessible campsites
showers
trailer sanitation station
2 hike/bike campsites
picnicking
group picnic area[†] (150)
fishing
swimming
boating/launch ramp
boat mooring
water skiing
nature & hiking trails
exhibits/visitor center

---

*On state park reservation system.
[†]Phone park for reservations.

Location

Clear Lake State Park is located 3½ miles northeast of Kelseyville on Soda Bay Road. The 565-acre park has hilly terrain, with elevations of 1,320 to 1,600 feet.

Special Notes

Clear Lake is 19 miles long and 8 miles wide at its widest point; it has about 100 miles of shoreline. The lake was created thousands of years ago when a landslide blocked the broad valley's drainage into the Russian River. The main attractions are water sports; life guards are on duty only during the summer at the buoyed swimming area just below Lower Bayview Campground.

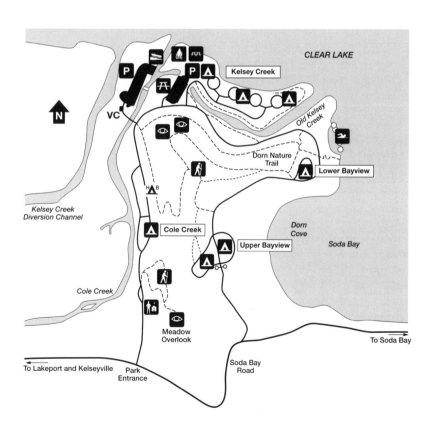

Colusa-Sacramento River State Recreation Area

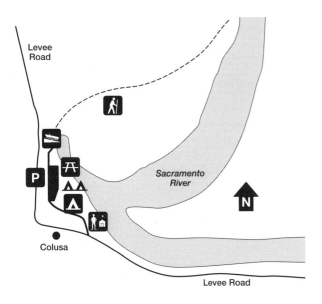

For Information

Colusa-Sacramento River State Recreation Area
P.O. Box 207
Colusa, CA 95932-0207
916/458-4927

Location

This 67-acre recreation area is in Colusa along the west bank of the Sacramento River; be aware that the area may close due to flooding. The river-bank cottonwoods and willows shelter one of the finest fishing stretches in California; the river yields king salmon, steelhead, rainbow trout, and striped bass. Colusa is 9 miles east of I-5 via Highway 20; it has an elevation of 60 feet. The river is also on a major migratory route for birds of the Pacific flyway, and provides homes for an amazing number of species.

Facilities* & Activities

14 developed campsites
wheelchair accessible campsites
showers
24-foot trailers; 27-foot campers
trailer sanitation station
10 enroute campsites
group camping area[†] (40)
picnicking
fishing
boating/boat launch for small boats

---

*On state park reservation system.
[†]Phone park for reservations.

The Sacramento River is one of the finest fishing stretches in California; the recreation area may close due to seasonal flooding.

Fort Ross State Historic Park

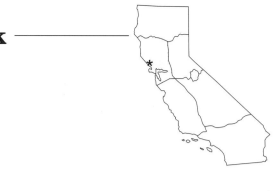

For Information

Fort Ross State Historic Park
19005 Coast Highway 1
Jenner, CA 95450
707/847-3286

Location

This 3,315-acre park is 12 miles northwest of Jenner on Highway 1. Fort Ross is located on a narrow, flat, coastal terrace between the ocean to the west and the high, forest-covered hills to the east; the elevation is 90 feet. The San Andreas Fault runs along the base of the hills. The southern portion of the park is characterized by steep bluffs that drop several hundred feet into the ocean.

Special Notes

Fort Ross, a reconstructed 19th century Russian settlement, marks Russia's southernmost permanent California outpost. It was established in 1812 by 25 Russians and 80 Aleuts to protect their claim against the Spanish. Extensive restoration and reconstruction work has been done, so that today you can again see Fort Ross somewhat as it looked when the Russians were here.

Ocean access points are located at Windermere Point, 1 mile north of the unit entrance, and on the marine terrace, which can be reached by way of the campground entrance. The campground is not suitable for large RVs because of very limited turning space. Camping is not permitted during the winter, but is available from March 15 through November.

Facilities & Activities

20 primitive campsites
   tables, grills, food lockers
   drinking water & toilets nearby
picnicking
designated underwater area
surf fishing
hiking
exhibits
visitor center
state historic landmark

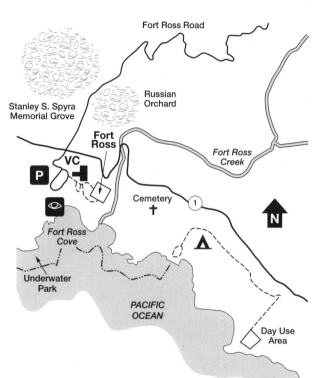

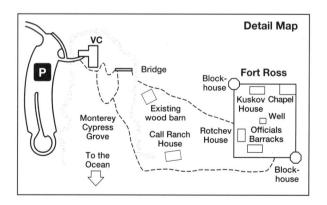

Golden Gate National Recreation Area

For Information

Golden Gate National Recreation Area
Fort Mason
San Francisco, CA 94123
415/556-0560

Location

In San Francisco, Golden Gate National Recreation Area (GGNRA) follows the city's northern and western shoreline. With approximately 74,000 acres within its authorized boundaries, the recreation area encompasses shoreline areas of San Francisco, Marin, and San Mateo counties. GGNRA is the largest national park in an urban setting in the world, and is the most heavily visited of the U.S. national parks. Its North Pacific Coast landscape includes beaches, headlands, grasslands, forests, lakes, streams, estuaries, and marshes. Fort Point National Historic Site, Muir Woods National Monument, a cultural center at Fort Mason, and Alcatraz Island, site of the famous penitentiary, are among the park's historic wealth.

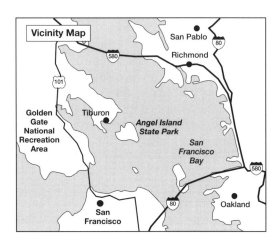

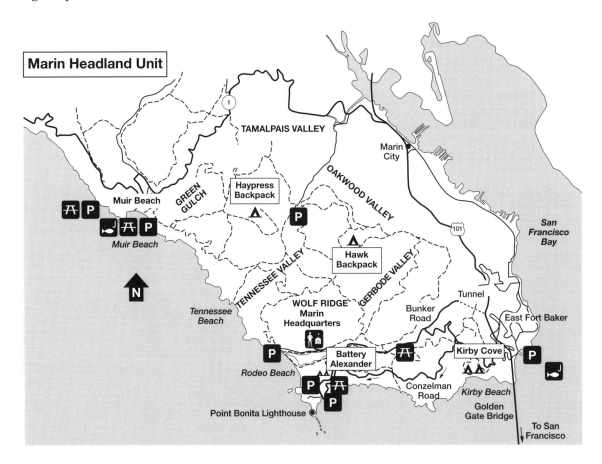

Golden Gate National Recreation Area
(continued)

Special Notes

Because opportunities for camping exist only in the Marin Headlands, only this unit of the Golden Gate National Recreation Area (GGNRA) is included. Opportunities for recreation and sight-seeing activities in the San Francisco portion of the GGNRA are numerous but do not include camping. Obtain a GGNRA brochure from park headquarters at Fort Mason or one of the other visitor centers. The Marin Headlands unit is located north of San Francisco across the Golden Gate Bridge; Highway 101 provides access.

Points of Interest

▲ San Francisco, San Francisco Bay, and the 4,200-foot-long Golden Gate Bridge are clearly visible in the distance from many camping areas in the Marin Headlands.
▲ A feeling of wilderness prevails in the Marin Headlands amid the coastal woods, sandy beaches, and windswept hills and valleys.
▲ To the north and south of the Golden Gate, GGNRA follows the Pacific shoreline creating a vast coastal preserve; the redwood forests, beaches, grassy hillsides, marshes, and rocky shoreline provide a natural retreat from the city.
▲ No unit of the GGNRA is more than an hour's drive from San Francisco; a day's trip will provide enough time to visit any area of the park.

General Information

▲ No fees are charged to enter or camp in Marin Headlands.
▲ The Marin Headlands Visitor Center, located at Fort Barry, is open daily. For information and campground reservations phone: 415/331-1540.
▲ There is no car camping at GGNRA, only tent camping; group and individual campsites are available; reservations are required and accepted

Opportunities for camping exist only in the Marin Headlands unit of the Golden Gate National Recreation Area. It is located north of San Francisco across the Golden Gate Bridge; US 101 provides access.

no more than 90 days in advance; the limit of stay is 3 days, but the number of days of stay may be extended to 5 during periods of low demand.
▲ Backcountry camping is allowed all year. Bicentennial has 3 walk-in campsites; Haypress is a gentle ¾-mile walk from the parking lot and has 7 campsites; and Hawk is a 3-mile backpack trek up the Bobcat Trail and has 3 campsites. There is no drinking water.
▲ Kirby Cove and Battery Alexander group sites have fire rings and Kirby Cove also has barbecue pits; bring your own firewood and kindling. Fires are not allowed at the 3 backcountry sites.
▲ Battery Alexander group campground is open all year. Kirby Cove, with 4 group sites, is open from April 1 to October 31; exact dates depend on weather and road conditions.
▲ The number and type of vehicles permitted in the group campgrounds are restricted; groups can drive close to the sites.
▲ Wheelchair-accessible toilets are available at both Kirby Cove and Battery Alexander group campgrounds.
▲ Cliffs are prone to landslides and often covered with poison oak; avoid climbing them.
▲ Weather at the park is variable. Wind and fog are common from June to September, especially near the Golden Gate. Fall is the season of sun and warmth; most rainfall occurs from November to April.

Facilities & Activities

3 hike-in backcountry camping areas (13 sites)
2 group campgrounds for tents only
picnicking
group picnic areas
hiking
swimming
ranger station/visitor center

Half Moon Bay State Beach

For Information

Half Moon Bay State Beach
95 Kelly Avenue
Half Moon Bay, CA 94019
415/726-8819

Location

Half Moon Bay State Beach has 4 miles of ocean frontage. This 170-acre state beach is located ½ mile west of Highway 1 on Kelly Avenue at Half Moon Bay. There are 3 parking and beach access points within the state beach: Francis Beach at the end of Kelly Ave. in the city of Half Moon Bay, Venice Beach at the end of Venice Blvd. off Highway 1, and Dunes Beach at the end of Young Ave. off Highway 1.

Special Notes

Developed campsites are at Francis Beach; enroute campsites are at Venice Beach during high use periods when Francis Campground is full; and the group camping area is at Sweetwood. The Coastside Trail, located on the marine terrace above the beach, is now open the entire length of

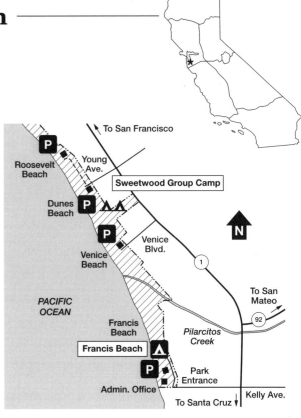

Half Moon Bay from Kelly Ave. at the south end to Mirada Ave. at the north end. Swimming is not recommended because of the 50°F water temperature, hazardous surf, and recurring rip currents. The major weather pattern is fog in the summer, crisp and clear days in the fall and spring, and wet, windy winters.

Facilities & Activities

55 developed campsites at Francis Beach
wheelchair accessible campsites
cold outdoor showers
36-foot trailers; 36-foot campers
trailer sanitation station
44 enroute campsites at Venice Beach
4 hike/bike campsites
group camping area at Sweetwood* (50)
picnicking
fishing
walk/jog/bicycle on Coastside Trail
horseback riding trail between Dunes & Francis
    beaches
horse rentals nearby
summer interpretive programs

Swimming is not recommended at many north coast beaches because of the cold water temperature, boulder-strewn water, hazardous surf, and recurring rip currents.

*On state park reservation system; 12 vehicle max., tents only—no tent trailers or RVs.

Hendy Woods State Park

For Information

Hendy Woods State Park
P.O. Box 440
Mendocino, CA 95460
707/895-3141 or 937-5804

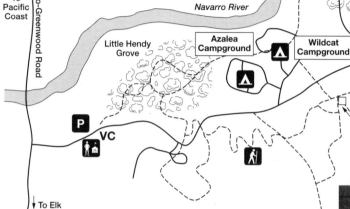

Location

Hendy Woods State Park is located on the south side of Highway 128, 8 miles west of Boonville, then ½ mile south on Greenwood Road. The 693-acre park is bordered by the Navarro River and has an elevation of 200 feet.

Special Notes

This unique park features 2 virgin redwood groves: 80-acre Big Hendy and 20-acre Little Hendy. Big Hendy has a ½-mile self-guided discovery trail and a ¼-mile trail accessible to visitors in wheelchairs. The Navarro River is enjoyed by fishermen, canoeists, and kayakers during the late winter and spring months.

Facilities* & Activities

92 developed campsites
wheelchair accessible campsites
showers
24-foot trailers; 30-foot campers
trailer sanitation station
12 hike/bike campsites

One of the nature trails through the virgin redwood groves at Hendy Woods is accessible to visitors in wheelchairs. (Photo: Lillian Morava)

picnicking
canoeing/kayaking
nature & hiking trails
bike trails
horseback riding trail
exhibits

---

*On state park reservation system.

Jackson State Forest

For Information

Jackson State Forest
802 N. Main Street
Fort Bragg, CA 95437
707/964-5674

Location

Jackson State Forest is located along Highway 20 that runs east from Highway 1, just south of Fort Bragg, to Willits on US 101. The 50,200-acre state forest ranges in elevation from 200 to 1,948 feet; it is the largest of 8 state forests in California. Coast redwoods are seen along all of the trails and roads.

Special Notes

There are 2 main overnight camping areas: Camp One and Camp 20. Camp One is located in the west end of the forest just north of Highway 20 with access via Forest Road 350. Day-use areas and campsites are at 17 different locations along the South Fork of the Noyo River and the North Fork of the South Fork Noyo River. Camp 20 is located in the east end of the forest along Highway 20 and Forest Road 810, which runs parallel to Highway 20. Two day-use areas and campsites are at 7 different locations.

Campsites are primitive, furnished with picnic tables, fire rings, and pit toilets. There is no developed water supply at any of the campgrounds; most sites are adjacent to rivers. Camping is limited to designated sites for 14 consecutive days for a maximum stay of 30 days per year. Groups can reserve the day-use areas, equestrian camps, and designated group camps by contacting the forest headquarters in Fort Bragg. Campsites and day-use areas are available at no charge. Permits are

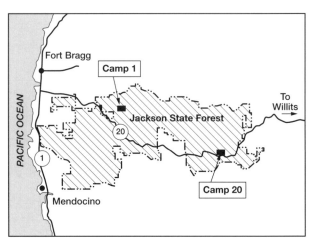

required for overnight camping; they may be obtained from the resident camp host.

Facilities & Activities

65 primitive campsites
4 group camping areas
3 backcountry campsites for hikers/bikers/equestrians
picnicking
swimming
fishing/hunting
8 developed trails
hiking/biking
horseback riding

Jackson State Forest has 3 backcountry campsites for equestrians and numerous roads and trails designated for riding. (Photo: Marsha Elmore)

Jackson State Forest (continued)

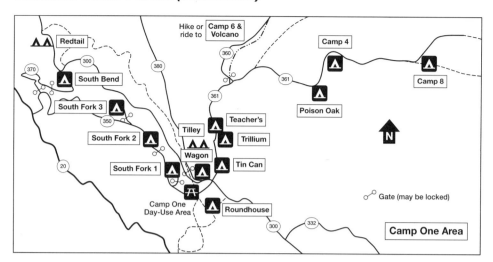

Camp One Area

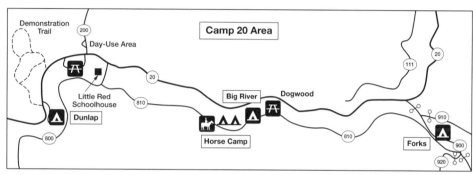

Camp 20 Area

Campsites	# Sites	Comments
Camp One Area		
Day Use Area		Camp Host, trail
South Fork 1	1	Seasonal
South Fork 2	1	Seasonal
South Fork 3	1	Seasonal
Roundhouse	3	Trail, handicap restroom
Wagon	5	Weekends only
Tilley Group Camp	1	Large groups, weekends
Tin Can	1	
Triullium	2	
Teacher's	1	
Poison Oak	1	Seasonal
Camp 4	1	Seasonal
Camp 6	1	Hike-in, equestrian
Camp 8	1	Seasonal, near 2 trails
Redtail	10	Equestrians, groups
South Bend	1	Seasonal, groups
Volcano	1	Hike-in, equestrian
Camp 20 Area		
Day Use Area		Trails
Dunlap	16	Camp Host
Indian Springs	1	Hike-in, equestrians
Big River	6	Seasonal
Dogwood		Day-Use Only
Horse Camp	6	Equestrians, groups
Forks Camp	1	Seasonal

A state forest is an ideal place for viewing wildlife; don't forget your binoculars.

Lake Del Valle State Recreation Area

For Information

Lake Del Valle State Recreation Area
2950 Peralta Oaks Court
P.O. Box 5381
Oakland, CA 94605-0381
510/373-0332

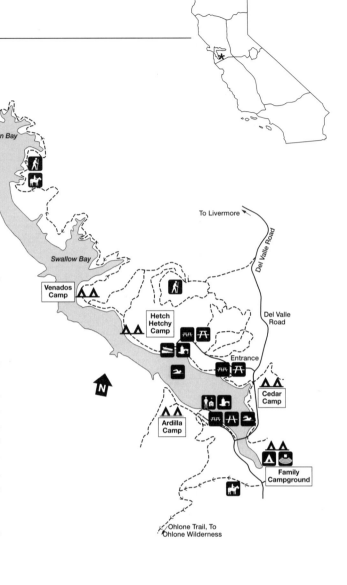

Location

Lake Del Valle State Recreation Area is about 9 miles south of Livermore. To reach the park from west of Livermore, take I-580 west to the N. Livermore exit. Go south on N. Livermore through the city of Livermore; going south, N. Livermore Ave. becomes Tesla Road. From Tesla Road, turn right onto Mines Road; follow Mines Road to Del Valley Road and turn right onto Del Valle Road, and continue on to the park entrance. To reach the park from east of Livermore, take I-580 west to the Vasco Road south exit. Follow Vasco to Tesla Road; turn right. At Mines Road turn left and follow the directions above.

Facilities & Activities

150 developed campsites*
   21 sites with water & sewage hookups
   showers/flush toilets
backpack campsites[†]
4 hike-in group camps[†]
2 group camps with vehicle access[†]
picnicking
13 group picnic sites[†]
2 swimming beaches
fishing
boat launch/food, bait, tackle
boating/windsurfing
rental boats/tour boat
hiking & equestrian trails
bicycle trails
food concession
amphitheater
visitor center

*Reservations available: 510/373-0332 for information.
[†]Reservations required: 510/636-1684.

Special Notes

This park is designated as a state recreation area but is operated by East Bay Regional Park District (510/635-0135); it is also known as Del Valle Regional Park. The water level at Lake Del Valle fluctuates seasonally from a high of 703 feet in the summer to a low of 678 feet in the winter. The speed limit on the entire lake water is 10 mph; any size boat is accepted. All watercraft must be off the lake at the boat ramp one half hour before sundown.

The campground is open year-round and has provisions for both tent camping and motor homes. Backpack camping sites are available for the Ohlone Wilderness Trail. Organized group camping is available at 4 group camps that are hike-in only, and 2 group camps that are located in the family campground.

Lake Mendocino

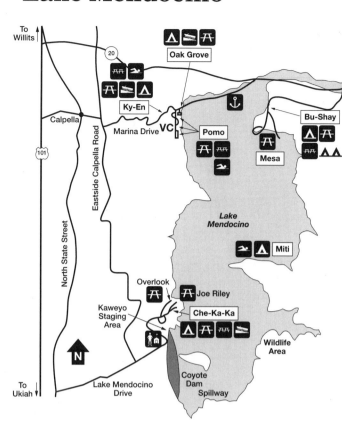

For Information

Lake Mendocino
1160 Lake Mendocino Drive
Ukiah, CA 95482-9404
707/462-7581

Location

Created by Coyote Valley Dam on the East Fork of the Russian River, Lake Mendocino is in the Northern Coast Range. From Ukiah on US 101, travel 3 miles north, then east on Lake Mendocino Drive. Although small in comparison with some other lakes in California, the quality of its facilities is exceptional. Fishing, hiking, and boating are all available.

Lake Statistics

1,740-acre surface area
3 miles long
15 miles of shoreline

Recreation Areas	Total Number of Campsites	With Electrical Hookups	Group Camping Area	Toilets (Flush/Vault)	Showers	Trailer Dump Station	Picnic Sites	Group Picnic Areas	Boat Launching Ramp	Swimming Area/Beach	Fishing Access	Trails
Bu-Shay	164	1	•	F/V	•	•	•	•			•	•
Che-Ka-Ka	23			F/V			•	•	•		•	•
Ky-En	103	4		F/V	•	•	•	•	•	•	•	•
Marina	20			•		•			•		•	•
Mesa				•			•				•	•
Miti (boat-in)	18			V					•	•	•	•
Oak Grove				•			•		•		•	
Pomo				V	•		•	•		•	•	•

Notes:
Joe Riley & Overlook have picnic facilities, rest rooms, & fishing access.
Che-Ka-Ka & Pomo have bicycle trails; Che-Ka-Ka has equestrian trails.
Kaweyo is an equestrian staging area; camping is by permit only.

Lake Sonoma

A detailed brochure on the trail system is available at the visitors center.

Lake Statistics

2,700-acre surface area
9 miles long (Dry Creek arm)
4½ miles long (Warm Spring arm)
60 miles of shoreline

For Information

Lake Sonoma
3333 Skaggs Springs Road
Geyserville, CA 95441-9644
707/433-9483

Location

Lake Sonoma is in the Russian River Basin, just below the confluence of Dry Creek and Warm Springs Creek. This 17,615-acre recreation area is located off of US 101, about 13 miles northwest of Healdsburg on Dry Creek Road, and 9 miles south of Cloverdale. The lake is nestled in the oak-covered hills and wine-growing region of Sonoma County. Camping facilities at this picturesque lake include one developed campground and 15 primitive campgrounds, accessible either by boat or by the hiking and equestrian trails. Backcountry camp permits are required and are obtained at the visitor center without cost. The trail system is closed to bicycle and horse traffic each winter while crews work on erosion and other weather-related problems; check at the visitor center about seasonal closure dates. The Warm Springs arm of the lake is subject to closure due to fluctuating water levels.

Facilities & Activities

100 developed campsites at Liberty Glen
  wheelchair accessible campsites*
  showers/flush toilets
  trailer sanitation station
  2 group camping areas* (100)
15 primitive campgrounds (113 sites)
  accessible only by boat, horse, or foot
  portable restrooms/no water
2 group camps: Island View & Loggers Camp
  accessible only by boat, horse, or foot
  portable restrooms/no water
4 day-use picnic areas
group picnic areas at Warm Springs Dam & Yorty
  Creek
swimming beach at Yorty Creek
fishing
boating/sailing/water skiing
2 boat launch ramps
car-top-only launch area at Yorty Creek
marina/fuel, rentals, boat slips, store
nature trails at visitor center, Warm Springs Dam,
  & Overlook
40 miles of hiking & equestrian trails
trailhead parking at 4 locations
4-mile trail loop for mountain bikes
ranger-led programs
fish hatchery (tours available)
visitor center

*Reservations required; one group area has hitching facilities
 for equestrian campers.

MacKerricher State Park

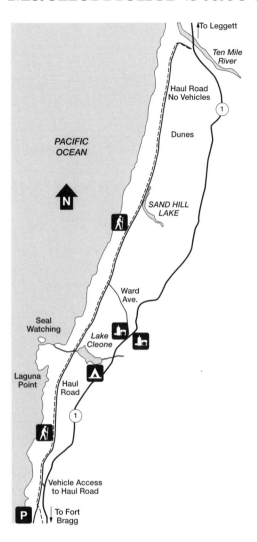

For Information

MacKerricher State Park
P.O. Box 440
Mendocino, CA 95460
707/964-9112 or 937-5804

Location

MacKerricher State Park is located 3 miles north of Fort Bragg on Highway 1. The 1,598-acre park has an elevation of 50 feet. The park offers a wide variety of habitats: beach, bluff, headland, dune, forest, and wetland. There are 2 campgrounds: Pinewood and Cleone.

Special Notes

Pudding Creek Beach, at the southern end of the park is a popular beach play area. There are horse trails through the park and beach area. Hikers have many opportunities: the trail around Cleone Lake, the 6 miles of beach and dune in the northern portion of the park, or the trail down the headlands toward Fort Bragg. Bicycling is also popular.

Facilities* & Activities

2 campgrounds
143 developed campsites
wheelchair accessible campsites
pay showers
35-foot trailers; 35-foot campers
trailer sanitation station
10 hike/bike campsites
picnicking
fishing
boating (non-motorized)
launch ramp
designated underwater area
hiking & horseback riding trails
bike trails
summer programs

*On state park reservation system.

Detail Map

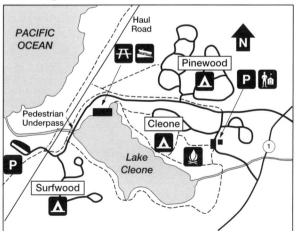

REGION 2

Manchester State Park

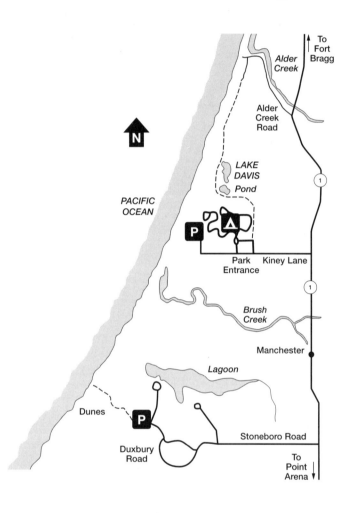

For Information

Manchester State Park
P.O. Box 440
Mendocino, CA 95460
707/882-2437 or 937-5804

Location

Manchester State Park is located 7 miles north of Point Arena on Highway 1; the elevation of this 1,419-acre park is cited as 0 feet.

Special Notes

The beach at this park has nearly 18,000 feet of seashore. The beach line curves gently to form a "catch basin" for sea debris, which accounts for the tremendous amount of driftwood found here. The beach is unsafe for swimming, but is known as one of the best surf fishing beaches in Mendocino County. There are 2 streams in the park that offer good steelhead and salmon fishing in the winter.

Facilities & Activities

48 primitive campsites
22-foot trailers; 30-foot campers
trailer sanitation station
1 hike/bike campsite
10 environmental campsites in dune area
group camping area* (40)
picnicking
fishing
designated underwater area
hiking

———
*On state park reservation system.

The beach at Manchester curves gently to form a "catch basin" for sea debris, which accounts for the tremendous amount of driftwood found here. (Credit: Lillian Morava)

Taller than all other trees in the world, coast redwoods grow in a narrow strip along the Pacific Coast of California and southwestern Oregon. Giant sequoias, their cousins, grow larger in diameter and bulk, but not in height.

Mickey Little

Mickey Little

A word of caution to those beach strollers who delight in finding stairs to access the beach—remember to pause long enough to determine whether the tide is coming in or going out.

Mickey Little

Words alone cannot describe the scenic boulder-strewn beaches of the north coast. They are extraordinary!

Mickey Little

Yosemite National Park has over 800 miles of hiking and backpacking trails. Free wilderness permits are required and there are quotas for overnight use. ▲

The view is impressive, even if you don't descend the 300 steps to the Point Reyes Lighthouse.

Eight miles of beach at MacKerricher State Park offer refuge for harbor seals; a seal-watching station provides a close-up view. ▼

Take time to read the exhibits along self-guided nature trails because you can learn much about the fauna, geology, and history of the area that will greatly enhance your visit. ▲

Vernal Fall is one of five prominent waterfalls around Yosemite Valley's perimeter; it is beyond the Happy Isles Nature Center and is reached via a hiking trail.

In the early morning fog that is typical of a summer day in the Redwood National Park area, ethereal beauty abounds in the Lady Bird Johnson Grove. ▼

95

The lakes along Highway 120 from Lee Vining to Yosemite's Tioga Pass entrance are typical mountain lakes—clear, cold, and beautiful (above and top).

Cross-country skiing provides the perfect opportunity to see nature at its best.

Roosevelt elk, Redwood National Park's largest mammal, can best be seen along the beach and trails at Prairie Creek Campground and Gold Bluffs Beach.▲

The Smith River National Recreation Area is the heart of one of the largest wild and scenic river systems in the United States; it is located within the Six Rivers National Forest.

Lassen Peak, the highest peak at Lassen Volcanic National Park, is one of the world's largest plug dome volcanoes.▼

North coast tent campers are either lulled to sleep at night by the sound of the pounding waves, or they are awake all night wondering if their tents will withstand the wind.

The sounds and sights at a beach can be very therapeutic, and everyone can do their own "thing."▲

Much of California's north coast is a wild and rugged place where waves pound against the rocks and groves of 300-foot-tall redwoods grow.

Tidepools along northern California's coast form in rocky beach outcroppings to shelter life forms found only in these environments. These areas are protected, so remember to take nothing but pictures!▼

D. L. Bliss State Park and Emerald Bay State Park offer magnificent panoramas of Lake Tahoe, which to the Indians meant "lake in the sky."▲

Whiskeytown Lake's constant level in the summer makes it ideal for recreational use; it is the smallest of the four impounded lakes at Whiskeytown-Shasta-Trinity National Recreation Area.

Legendary Half Dome looms over Yosemite Valley and hints of the park's magnificent scenery. This backpacker has taken the shortest, but not fastest, route to Glacier Point.▼

Big Tree is an awesome specimen of the coast redwoods that tower over all other trees in the world.

Merely to walk within a redwood grove is inspiring; it's like hearing a sermon without words!

Sunset on the California coast is a photographer's dream . . . and a dreamer's paradise!

Mickey Little

100

Mendocino National Forest

For Information

Supervisor's Office
825 North Humboldt Avenue
Willows, CA 95988
916/934-3316

Location

The Mendocino National Forest is located in northwestern California and is about 65 miles long, north to south, and about 35 miles wide. It extends from the Yolla Bolly Mountains in the north to Clear Lake in the south. Elevations range from less than 1,000 feet along the forest boundary, to more than 8,000 feet at the crest of the mountains.

Special Notes

The Mendocino National Forest offers an array of recreation opportunities to the visitor including fishing in lakes and streams, camping, picnicking, boating, hiking, horseback riding, viewing wildlife, hunting, hang-gliding, winter snow play, wilderness experiences, mountain biking, and a large off-road vehicle trail system.

The forest has many species of wildlife; wildlife biologists estimate that the forest is home for 20,000 blacktailed deer, and 350 black bears. Steelhead and salmon fishing on the branches of the Eel River is also popular.

Except within the two wilderness areas, the forest is open to travel by 2-wheel, 4-wheel, and all-terrain vehicles. Driving conditions are a bit different from other national forests; there are no roads in the forest that are entirely paved. Maintained primary roads, or "M" routes, are surfaced with gravel or dirt and occasionally with pavement. They offer continuous routes through the forest.

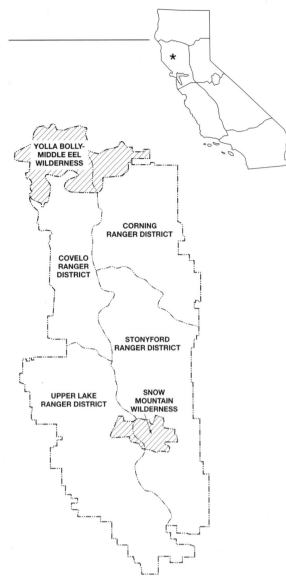

What do we have here? Could this be the answer to getting a good night's sleep at the trailhead before the trek into the wilderness begins?

Mendocino National Forest *(continued)*

Wilderness Areas

The central feature of the 37,000-acre **Snow Mountain Wilderness** is the large, broad-topped Snow Mountain, which drains water toward the Sacramento River on the east and Eel River Basin on the west. The area is ecologically unique because it lies at the transition from the Coast Range to the Lower Valley foothills. The wilderness ranges in elevation from 1,800 feet in the gorge of the Middle Fork of Stony Creek to 7,056 feet on the summit of East Peak.

The **Yolla Bolly-Middle Eel Wilderness** straddles the crest of the California Coast Range and runs from the North Yolla Bollys to the South Yolla Bollys. The 168,824-acre area contains 8,100-foot Mt. Linn, the highest point in the Coastal Range and is on three national forests—Six Rivers, Trinity, and Mendocino. The area is traversed by trails open to hikers and horseback riders, usually from mid-June through October. Solitude and panoramic views are key attractions of the area.

These backpackers were surprised by an early snowfall, but it appears that they were prepared.

Upper Lake Ranger District

For Information

Upper Lake Ranger District
10025 Elk Mountain Road
Upper Lake, CA 95485
707/275-2361

Campgrounds	Elevation (feet)	# of Units	Drinking Water	Vault Toilets	Trailer Space	Camping Fee
Bear Creek	2,000	16	Str.	•	•	
Deer Valley	3,700	13	•	•	•	
Lakeview	3,400	9	•	•	•	
Lower Nye	3,300	6	•	•		
Middle Creek	2,000	16	•	•	•	•

Notes:
Middle Creek is open year-round.
Deer Valley is open April 1 to Nov. 1; Lower Nye is open
   May 1 to Sept. 15.
Bear Creek & Lakeview are open May 1 to Oct. 15.

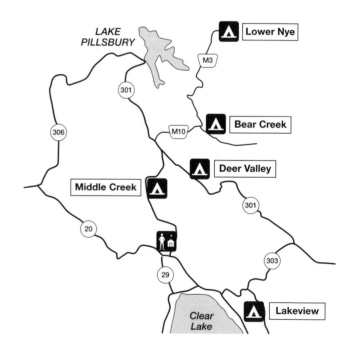

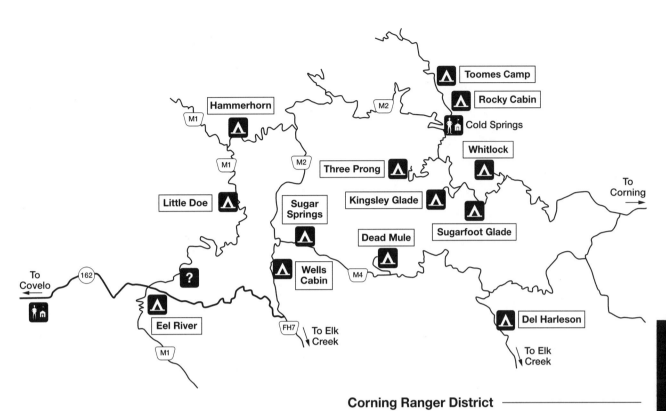

Covelo Ranger District

For Information

Covelo Ranger District
78150 Covelo Road
Covelo, CA 95428
707/983-6118

Campgrounds	Elevation (feet)	# of Units	Drinking Water	Vault Toilets	Trailer Space
Eel River	1,500	16	•	•	•
Hammerhorn Lake	3,500	9	•	•	•
Little Doe	3,600	13		•	

Notes:
None of these campgrounds charges fees.
All campgrounds close October 1; Eel River opens May 1, Hammerhorn Lake opens June 1, and Little Doe opens June 15.

Corning Ranger District

For Information

Corning Ranger District
22000 Corning Road
P.O. Box 1019
Corning, CA 96021
916/824-5196

Campgrounds	Elevation (feet)	# of Units	Drinking Water	Vault Toilets	Trailer Space
Dead Mule	5,100	2		•	•
Del Harleson	4,500	2	•	•	
Kingsley Glade	4,500	6	•	•	•
Rocky Cabin	6,250	3	•	•	•
Sugarfoot Glade	4,200	6		•	•
Sugar Springs	5,400	2	•	•	•
Three Prong	5,800	6	•	•	•
Toomes	6,000	2	•	•	•
Wells Cabin	6,300	25	•	•	
Whitlock	4,300	3	•	•	•

Notes:
None of these campgrounds charges fees.
All but 3 campgrounds are open June 1 to October 31; Del Harleson is open April 15 to Nov. 15, Sugarfoot Glade is open May 15 to Nov. 15, and Wells Cabin is open July 1 to Oct. 31.

REGION 2

Stonyford Ranger District

For Information

Stonyford Ranger District
P.O. Box 160
Stonyford, CA 95979
916/963-3128

The two small lakes at Plaskett Meadows are for trout fishing; no motorized boats are allowed.

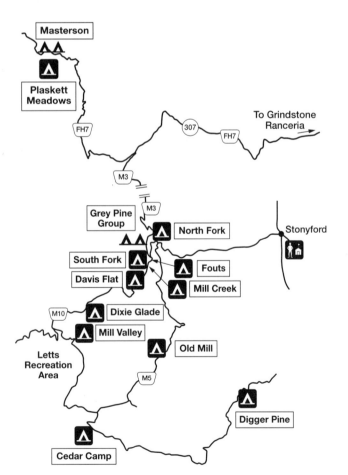

Campgrounds	Elevation (feet)	# of Units	Drinking Water	Vault Toilets	Trailer Space	Camping Fee
Cedar Camp	4,300	5		•		
Davis Flat	1,700	12	•	•	•	
Digger Pine Flat	1,500	7		•	•	
Dixie Glade	3,700	5		•	•	
Fouts	1,700	11	•	•	•	
Letts Lake Complex	4,500	40	•	•	•	•
Mill Creek	1,700	6		•		
Mill Valley	4,200	15	•	•	•	•
North Fork	1,700	6		•		
Old Mill	3,700	10	•	•	•	
Plaskett Meadows	6,000	32	•	•	•	•
South Fork	1,900	5		•	•	
Group Campgrounds*						
Gray Pine Group	1,700	70 max.	•	•	•	
Masterson Group	6,000	90 max.	•	•		•

Notes:
*Reservations are required for both group campgrounds.
Letts Lake Complex has 4 camps (Main Letts, Saddle, Stirrup, & Spillway); the 30-acre lake is for non-motorized boating, trout fishing, & swimming.
The 2 small lakes at Plaskett Meadows are for trout fishing; no motorized boats are allowed.
The campgrounds that are open year-round have high OHV use Oct. 1 to June 1.
The seasons for campgrounds that are not open year-round are:
4/15–11/1 for Letts Lake Complex & Mill Valley.
5/1–11/1 for Old Mill.
6/15–10/15 for Cedar Camp, Plaskett Meadows, & Masterson Group.

Mount Diablo State Park

For Information

Mount Diablo State Park
P.O. Box 250
Diablo, CA 94528
510/837-2525

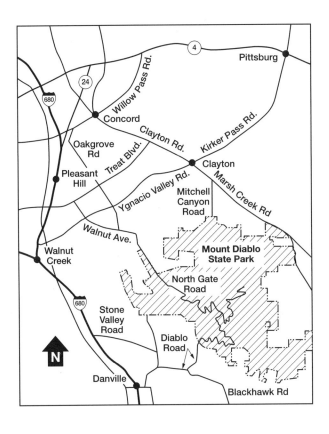

Location

At the eastern fringe of the San Francisco Bay Region, Mount Diablo—elevation 3,849 feet—stands on the edge of California's great Central Valley. The 19,000+-acre park is 5 miles east of I-680 at Danville on Diablo Road. The park can also be reached via North Gate Road off of Ygnacio Valley Road near Walnut Creek. The 2 roads that lead into the park are quite winding; trailers longer than 19 feet are not advised.

Special Notes

The park entrance gates are closed from one hour after sunset to 8 a.m. The view from the summit is unexcelled; when conditions are best, you can see almost 200 miles. The best time to come for the view is in winter and early spring after a storm clears the air. During the summer months campsites are available on a first-come, first-served basis due to possible last-minute park closures during extreme fire danger. The park has 3 campgrounds: Juniper, Junction, and Live Oak.

Facilities* & Activities

3 campgrounds
60 developed campsites
wheelchair accessible campsites
19-foot trailers; 31-foot campers
4 group camping areas (110)
2 equestrian camping areas† (8 & 84)
picnicking
2 group picnic areas† (150)
hiking & horseback riding trails
bike trails
exhibits/visitor center
state historic landmark

---

*On state park reservation system.
†Phone park for reservations.

Because the park entrance gates at Mount Diablo are closed from one hour after sunset to 8 a.m., campers have to forego an evening on the town.

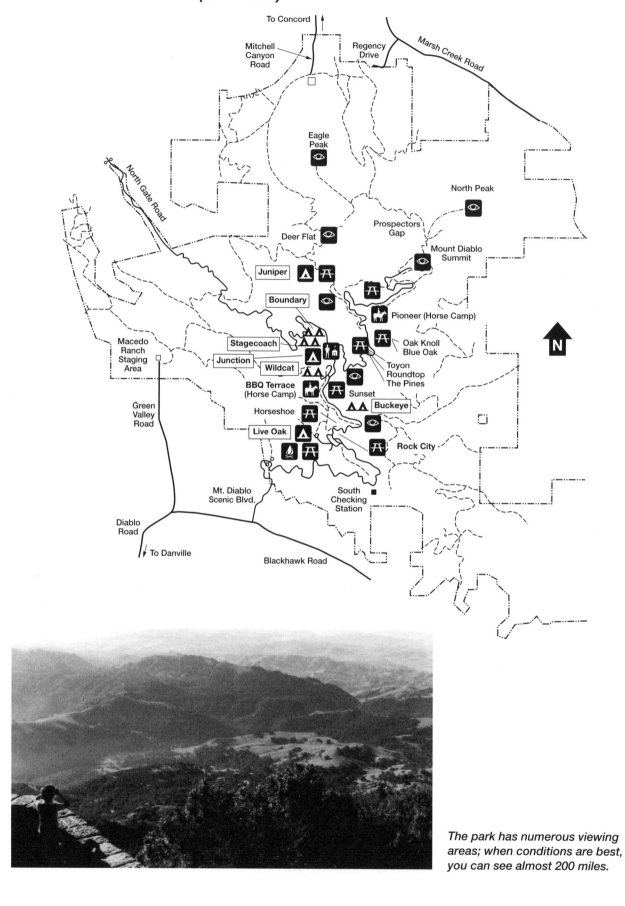

To Concord

Mitchell Canyon Road

Regency Drive

Marsh Creek Road

Eagle Peak

North Peak

North Gate Road

Prospectors Gap

Deer Flat

Mount Diablo Summit

Juniper

Boundary

Pioneer (Horse Camp)

N

Macedo Ranch Staging Area

Stagecoach

Junction

Wildcat

Oak Knoll Blue Oak

Toyon Roundtop The Pines

Green Valley Road

BBQ Terrace (Horse Camp)

Sunset

Buckeye

Horseshoe

Live Oak

Rock City

Mt. Diablo Scenic Blvd.

South Checking Station

Diablo Road

To Danville

Blackhawk Road

The park has numerous viewing areas; when conditions are best, you can see almost 200 miles.

Mount Tamalpais State Park

For Information

Mount Tamalpais State Park
801 Panoramic Highway
Mill Valley, CA 94941
415/388-2070

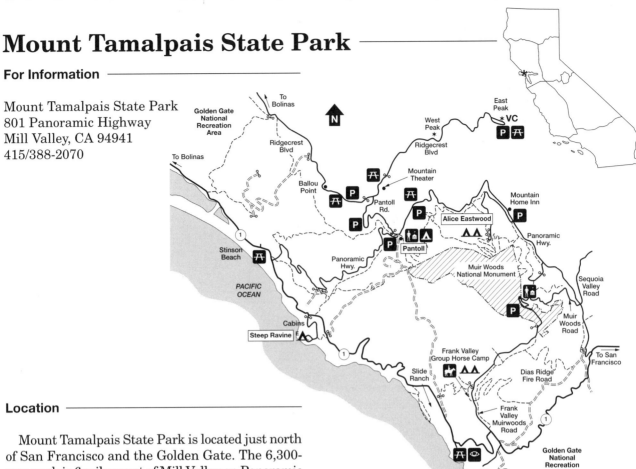

Location

Mount Tamalpais State Park is located just north of San Francisco and the Golden Gate. The 6,300-acre park is 6 miles west of Mill Valley on Panoramic Highway. From US 101, take Highway 1/Stinson Beach Exit and follow the signs up the mountain. The park surrounds Muir Woods National Monument, and is bordered by Marin Municipal Water District land on the north and by the Golden Gate National Recreation Area on the south.

Special Notes

Mount Tamalpais State Park is one of the oldest and most popular units of the California State Park system. The view from the summit is awe-inspiring. San Francisco can be seen to the south, the bay and Mount Diablo to the east, and the blue Pacific to the west. In springtime, the slopes of Mount Tamalpais come alive with wildflowers.

East Peak Summit features a visitor center, refreshment stand, phone, picnic tables, and a wheelchair accessible restroom. "Mountain Theater," a beautiful natural stone amphitheater, has been the site for the traditional Mountain Play each spring since 1913.

The trails of "Mount Tam" are one of its greatest attractions. More than 50 miles of trails lie within the park and connect to some 200 miles of trails on adjacent public land. Bicyclists are allowed on fire trails only. Horses are allowed on all fire trails and on certain clearly posted trails.

Facilities & Activities

16 developed walk-in campsites
wheelchair accessible campsites
enroute campsites at Pantoll (25-foot RVs)
1 hike/bike campsite
6 environmental walk-in campsites at Steep Ravine*
10 rustic cabins at Steep Ravine*
2 group camping areas* (25 & 50)
equestrian camping[†]
picnicking
group picnic area (50)
fishing
nature & hiking trails
horseback riding trails
bike trails
food service
group tours
exhibits/visitor center
state historic landmark

*On state park reservation system.
[†]Phone park for reservations.

Navarro River Redwoods State Park

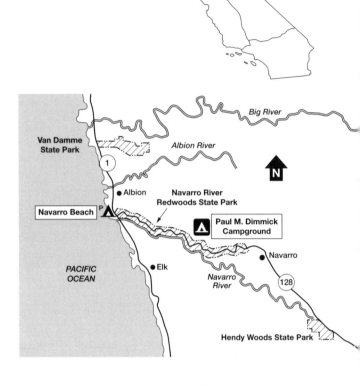

For Information

Navarro River Redwoods State Park
P.O. Box 440
Mendocino, CA 95460
707/895-3141 or 937-5804

Location

This 673-acre park follows Highway 128 along the north side of the Navarro River from the mouth of the river at Highway 1 for about 12 miles. The park's elevation ranges from 0 to 50 feet from the coast through the "redwood tunnel"—the name given by travelers to the second growth redwood groves that stretch the length of the park.

Special Notes

Paul M. Dimmick campground is located on Highway 128, 8 miles east of the junction with Highway 1 at the coast. The campground is very popular with anglers, canoeists, and kayakers in the late winter and spring. However, the river occasionally causes major flooding at the campground during heavy rains in winter. Navarro Beach contains the estuary of the Navarro River—the largest river between the Eel and the Russian rivers; it is available for day use and primitive camping.

Facilities & Activities

27 primitive campsites at Dimmick
  picnic tables/fire rings
  food lockers/pit toilets
  piped water (April to October)
  21-foot trailers; 30-foot campers
primitive camping at Navarro Beach
  picnic tables, fire pits
  pit toilets/no drinking water
  24-foot trailers; 30-foot campers
picnicking
snorkeling/scuba diving
beachcombing/hiking
fishing from Philo-Greenwood Bridge down stream
canoeing/kayaking (seasonal)

These birders are certainly intent on their endeavor; however, the tall trees make identification rather difficult.

Point Reyes National Seashore

Hike-in Campsites Only

For Information

Point Reyes National Seashore
Point Reyes, CA 94956-9799
415/663-1092

Backcountry Campsites	Individual Sites	People Per Site	Available Group Sites	People Per Site	Tents Only
Coast	14	4–8	2	9–25	•
Glen	12	8			•
Sky	12	8	1	9–25	•
Wildcat	7	4		9–25*	•

Note: Reservations and permits required for all sites.
* Or maximum group size of 40 at Wildcat.

Location

This national seashore is located approximately 35 miles north of San Francisco via US 101 and Sir Francis Drake Boulevard, or via Highway 1 near Mill Valley. This 65,303-acre peninsula is noted for its long beaches backed by tall cliffs, lagoons and esteros, and forested ridges. The elevation ranges from sea level to 1,407 feet at Mt. Wittenberg.

Points of Interest

▲ Bear Valley Visitor Center not only has an extensive display of exhibits, specimens, and artifacts, but a ⁷⁄₁₀-mile walk along the San Andreas Fault and Kule Loklo, a replica of a Coast Miwok Indian village.

▲ The impressive view from the Point Reyes Lighthouse overlooks rocky shelves and offshore rocks below, the home for thousands of common murres and basking sea lions.

▲ Gray whales migrating southward to Baja, California and back to the Bering Sea are best seen from the lighthouse observation platform in December to April.

▲ Palomarin and McClures beaches are good places to explore tidepools; Estero de Limantour is a favorite of birdwatchers for its variety and number of birds; and beachcombing is good at Point Reyes Beach North and South.

▲ Mount Vision Overlook affords a panoramic view of the curves of Drakes and Point Reyes beaches that extend to the southern tip of the peninsula.

▲ Pierce Point Road ends at the Tule elk range where a herd of Tule elk have been returned to this wilderness area after an absence of almost a century.

Point Reyes National Seashore
(continued)

General Information

▲ No fees are charged to enter or camp in the park.

▲ The lighthouse and visitor center are open Thursday through Monday, weather permitting.

▲ Always check at a visitor center for information on local weather, safety, and tide conditions. There are 3 visitor centers:

Bear Valley Visitor Center, at the Bear Valley entrance to the park; 415/663-1092

Kenneth C. Patrick Visitor Center on Drakes Bay; 415/669-1250

Point Reyes Lighthouse Visitor Center; 415/669-1534

▲ Camping is by permit only and reservations are required. There is no car camping at Point Reyes, only hike-in tent camping; group and individual campsites are available. Telephone reservations will only be accepted between the hours of 9:00 a.m. and noon, Monday through Friday, at 415/663-1092.

▲ Free camping permits must be obtained at the Bear Valley Visitor Center before starting a trip; permits are checked by park rangers in the backcountry; 4 consecutive nights of camping are permitted.

▲ Camping is restricted to 4 backpack campgrounds and can be reserved up to 2 months in advance:

Coast Camp is on an open grassy bluff about 650 feet above the beach; there are no trees. It is 8.9 miles from the Bear Valley trailhead.

Glen Camp is in a small wooded valley; it is 5 miles from the Bear Valley trailhead.

Sky Camp is on the western side of Mt. Wittenberg at an elevation of 1,024 feet. It is 2.5 miles from the Bear Valley trailhead and has a view of Drakes Bay and surrounding hills.

Wildcat Camp lies in a grassy meadow near a small stream that flows into the sea. It is 6.3 miles from the Bear Valley trailhead and has easy access to Wildcat Beach.

▲ Each campground has pit toilets, a hitching rail where horses must be tied, and drinking water. Do not drink water from streams or lakes without properly filtering or treating it.

▲ Each campsite has a picnic table, a space for a tent, a food storage locker and a charcoal grill. Wood fires are prohibited; use charcoal in the grills or use a backpacking stove.

▲ Raccoons and skunks are numerous and aggressive; store food properly in the food storage lockers.

▲ The principal trailheads are Bear Valley, Palomarin, Five Brooks, and Estero; all have adequate parking. Excellent trail maps are available at any visitor center.

▲ Bicyclists and horseback riders should check at a visitor center for information about trail use and restrictions.

▲ Driftwood fires are permitted only on sandy beaches below the high tide line; put fires out with water, not sand.

▲ Drakes Beach and Limantour Beach are both protected beaches good for wading, picnicking, and sunning. The water temperature is 50 to 55°F, and there are no lifeguards.

▲ Do not go near the water at either Point Reyes Beach North or South as the hammering surf and rip currents are extremely hazardous and the entire area is subject to severe undertow; they are ideal areas for picnicking or beachcombing.

▲ Climbing on the cliffs or walking near the edge invites catastrophe; they crumble easily and your foothold may vanish.

▲ Sleeping on the beach is not only prohibited, it is also dangerous. High tide frequently comes to the base of the cliffs and can trap the unwary. Check tide tables even before walking on beaches.

▲ Weather is usually cool and often damp, with average daytime temperatures between 45 and 55°F, so warm clothes are advisable. Coastal areas can become quite foggy, especially during the summer months. Strong winds may occur at anytime. For recorded weather and information, phone: 415/663-9029.

Facilities & Activities

45 backpack campsites
7 backpack group campsites
picnicking
beachcombing
wading/swimming
surf fishing
self-guiding nature trails
over 140 miles of hiking trails
over 35 miles of bicycle trails
stables/horseback trails
food service at Drakes Beach
3 visitor centers/exhibits
ranger-led programs
guided tours on weekend year-round
replica of Coast Miwok Indian village

Richardson Grove State Park

For Information

Richardson Grove State Park
1600 U.S. Highway 101, #8
Garberville, CA 95542
707/247-3318

Location

Richardson Grove State Park is located 8 miles south of Garberville on US 101. This 1,500-acre park is a cool, dark and still forest of towering coast redwoods along the South Fork of the Eel River at an elevation of 450 feet.

Special Notes

The Eel River gives life to the great stands of redwoods that line its banks, and offers its waters to swimmers in summer and steelhead fishing enthusiasts during the fall and winter. A widely varied system of trails offers good hiking to all visitors. A lodge, constructed in 1928, and now the visitor center, contains displays about Indian life in this area. The park has 3 campgrounds: Huckleberry, Madrone, and Oak Flat. The 92-site Oak Flat Campground is closed mid-September through mid-June because the bridge over the river is removed.

Facilities* & Activities

3 campgrounds
170 developed campsites
wheelchair accessible campsites
showers
24-foot trailers; 30-foot campers
enroute campsites
1 hike/bike campsite
group camping area (40)
picnicking
swimming
fishing
windsurfing
nature & hiking trails
food service/supplies
exhibits/visitor center

*On state park reservation system.

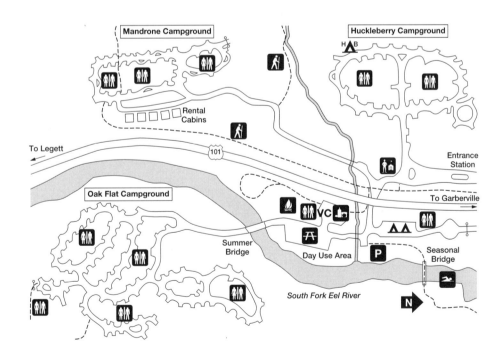

Russian Gulch State Park

For Information

Russian Gulch State Park
P.O. Box 440
Mendocino, CA 95460
707/937-4296 or 937-5804

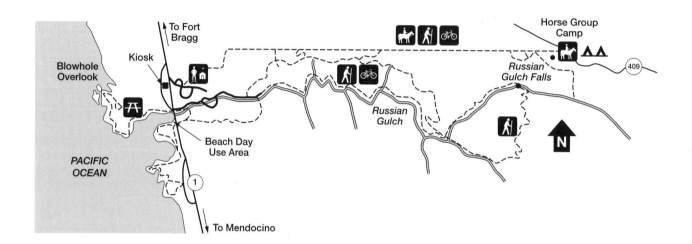

Location

This state park is located 10 miles south of Fort Bragg or 2 miles north of Mendocino on Highway 1. The 1,300-acre park, at an elevation of 100 feet, has narrow roads. The campground is closed November through March and is subject to early closure due to the rainy season.

Facilities* & Activities

30 developed campsites
wheelchair accessible campsites
showers
24-foot trailers; 27-foot campers
1 hike/bike campsite
group camping area (40)
equestrian camping† (16)
picnicking
fishing
designated underwater area
hiking & bicycle trails
summer programs

---

*On state park reservation system.
†Phone park for reservations.

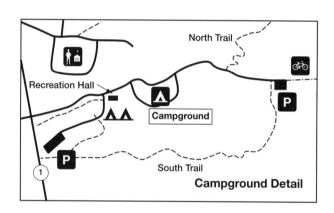

Campground Detail

Special Notes

The Devil's Punch Bowl—a 200-foot-long sea-cut tunnel that collapsed at its inland end to form a "blowhole"—is a headland feature. Inland, the park includes nearly 3 miles of the heavily forested Russian Gulch Creek Canyon. A scenic 3-mile paved bicycle trail makes it easy to see the lower part of the canyon, and a hiking trail continues inland past a beautiful 36-foot-high waterfall and up onto the surrounding ridges. The beach is suitable for swimming and sunbathing, although the water is cold; it is also used as an entry point for scuba divers and snorkelers.

Salt Point State Park

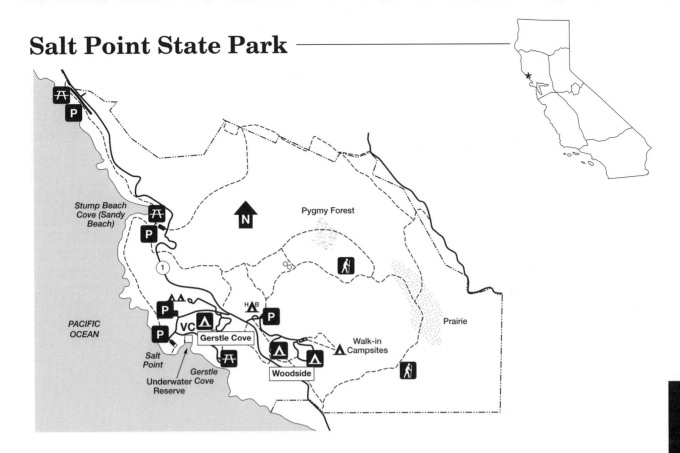

For Information

Salt Point State Park
25050 Coast Highway 1
Jenner, CA 95450
707/847-3286 or 865-2391

Location

Salt Point State Park is located 20 miles north of Jenner on Highway 1. It is on the rugged northern California coastline about 90 miles north of San Francisco. The shoreline within the 5,970-acre park features rocky promontories, such as Salt Point, which jut out into the Pacific Ocean. Elevation is 100 feet above sea level. The park has 2 campgrounds: Woodside and Gerstle Cove.

Special Notes

The 4-mile coastline varies dramatically from protected, sandy beach coves to sharp bluffs and sheer sandstone cliffs that plunge straight into the sea. At the top of the coastal ridge there is a large open "prairie" and a pygmy forest where stands of cypress, pine, and even the normally gigantic redwood grow in profusion—all of them stunted. Many miles of hiking and equestrian trails traverse the park. Salt Point is one of the first underwater parks to be established in California. January through April is whale-watching time at the park.

Facilities* & Activities

30 developed campsites at Gerstle Cove
80 developed campsites at Woodside
27-foot trailers; 31-foot campers
trailer sanitation station
enroute campsites
20 walk-in campsites
10 hike/bike campsites
5 environmental campsites
group camping area (40)
picnicking
fishing
designated underwater area
hiking & horseback riding trails
visitor center

*On state park reservation system.

Samuel P. Taylor State Park

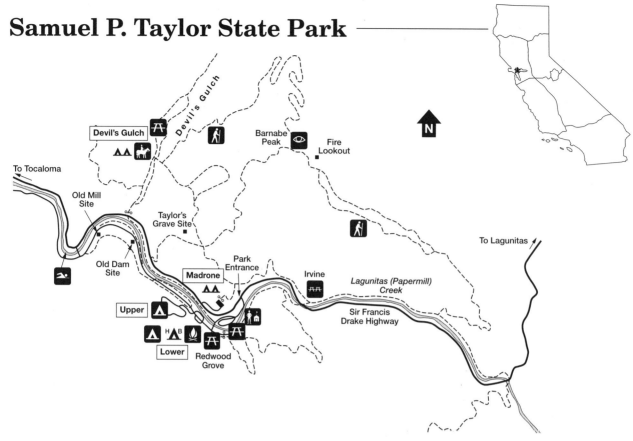

For Information

Samuel P. Taylor State Park
P.O. Box 251
Lagunitas, CA 94938
415/488-9897

Location

Located 15 miles west of San Rafael on Sir Frances Drake Highway, this park features 2,708 acres of beautifully wooded countryside in steep, rolling hills; elevation ranges from 150 feet to 1,466 feet.

Special Notes

Open hillsides are laced with hiking, mountain biking, and equestrian trails, rushing creeks, and cool canyons where redwoods thrive. This area is most enjoyable during the spring until early summer when temperatures are moderate and California's grasslands are still lush and green. It's a fairly easy walk to the top of Mount Barnabe. A paved bike trail runs about 3 miles through the park near the entrance west of Tocoloma.

Facilities* & Activities

85 developed campsites
wheelchair accessible campsites
showers
24-foot trailers; 28-feet campers
60 enroute campsites
30-foot trailers; 30-foot campers
1 hike/bike campsite
2 group camping areas (25 & 50)
equestrian camping† (15)
picnicking
group picnic area† (100)
swimming
nature trails
hiking & horseback riding trails
paved bicycle trail
exhibits
state historic landmark

*On state park reservation system.
†Phone park for reservations.

Sinkyone Wilderness State Park

For Information

Sinkyone Wilderness State Park
P.O. Box 245
Whitethorn, CA 95589
707/986-7711 or 247-3318

Location

Sinkyone Wilderness State Park is on California's Lost Coast—an area of unstable earth. The famed San Andreas fault lies just offshore of the wilderness. The wilderness park is 7,312 acres; elevations range from 0 to 1,900 feet. Access to the northern section of the park at Needle Rock is via County Road 435 (Briceland Road) west from Redway for 36 miles. The last 9 miles are rugged and unpaved. Access to the southern section of the park at Usal Beach is from Milepost 90.8 on Highway 1 about 3 miles north of Rockport; turn west on County Road 431 for 6 miles of rugged and unpaved road. The access roads are passable for passenger cars in summer; in winter, 4-wheel drive may be required. Campers, RVs, and trailers are not recommended.

REGION 2

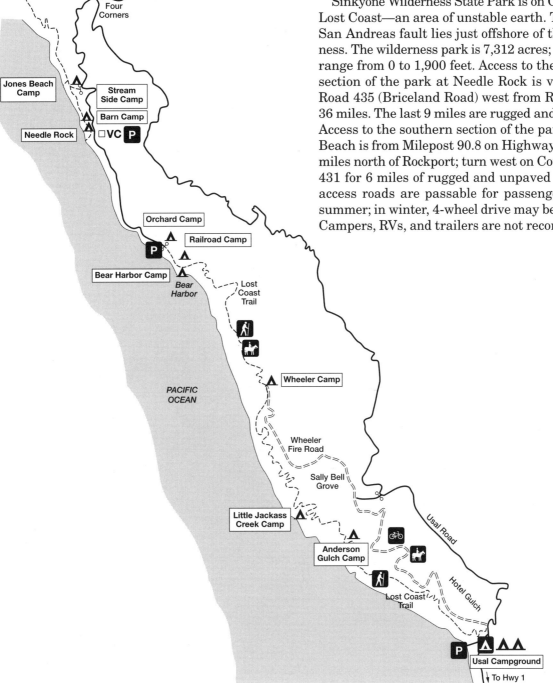

Sinkyone Wilderness State Park
(continued)

Special Notes

The principal recreation here is ocean related, such as abalone diving, surf fishing, tide pooling, or walking the bluffs or beach. The park is characterized by rugged terrain—deep canyons and steep slopes rising to a north-south trending ridge some 2,000 feet above the sea. Along the shoreline, narrow black sand beaches lie at the base of nearly vertical 200-foot-high coastal bluffs. The downstairs portion of the turn-of-the-century Needle Rock Ranch House serves as a visitor center; volunteers provide information and handle campsite registration. Visitors at Usal Beach self-register.

All campsites are available on a first-come, first-served basis. Three trail camps, located in the center portion, are reached via the 16.7-mile Lost Coast Trail. This trail is designed for the hardy backpacker; 3 days and 2 nights are recommended due to the physical stress and numerous points of interest. There is no developed water supply so bring your own or be prepared to purify. Six secluded hike-in primitive camps, with 15 campsites, are located in the northern section. Treated water is available at Needle Rock. Car camping is permitted at Usal Campground; drinking water is not available.

Horses are allowed the entire length of the trail; at the south end they use the Wheeler Fire Road but not the hiking trail. Horse camping is permit-ted at Usal Campground, Needle Rock, and Wheeler. Bicycles may use a 6-mile portion of the Hotel Gulch Fire Road northwest from Usal Beach; they are not permitted on trails or the last 4 miles of the fire road.

The climate in this area is cool and moist. Spring and fall are usually clear and pleasant. During the summer, particularly in July and August, fog banks tend to move in from the sea. The fog is usually high, which makes beach use pleasant. The rainy season begins in late October and about two-thirds of the average annual total occurs by March.

Facilities & Activities

15-unit drive-in primitive campground at Usal Beach
    tables, fire rings, pit toilets
group camping at Usal Beach
3 sites for horse camping
6 secluded hike-in primitive camps (17 sites) in northern section
3 trail camps (10 sites) along the Lost Coast Trail
treated water available at Needle Rock
no trailers or RVs
picnicking
fishing
25 miles of hiking trails
30 miles of equestrian trails
12-mile round-trip mountain bike trail
visitor center
state historic landmark

Roosevelt elk browse in the area of the turn-of-the-century Needle Rock Ranch House. The downstairs portion of the house serves as a visitor center.

Sonoma Coast State Beach

For Information

Sonoma Coast State Beach
3095 Highway 1
Bodega Bay, CA 94923
707/875-3483

Location

Sonoma Coast State Beach, actually a series of beaches separated by rocky bluffs, extends 13 miles between Bodega Head and the Meyers Gulch. The 5,000-acre state beach is accessible from more than a dozen points along coast Highway 1. There are 2 family campgrounds: Bodega Dunes and Wrights Beach. Bodega Dunes is ½ mile north of Bodega Bay on Highway 1 and Wrights Beach is 6 miles north of Bodega Bay on Highway 1. Environmental campsites are at 2 locations: Willow Creek and Pomo Canyon. Both are located on Willow Creek Road; travel 9 miles north of Bodega Bay on Highway 1, then turn east. Travel ½ mile to the Willow Creek Campground and an additional 1½ miles to the Pomo Canyon Campground.

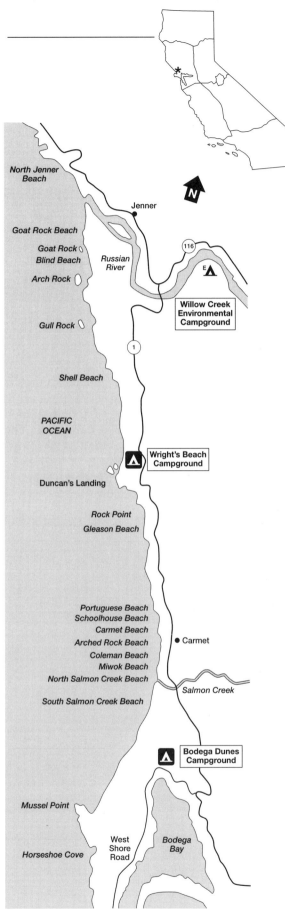

Hikers enjoy the view of the ocean from the Pomo Canyon and Russian River area; the park extends for 13 miles along the coast. (Photo: Lillian Morava)

Sonoma Coast State Beach
(continued)

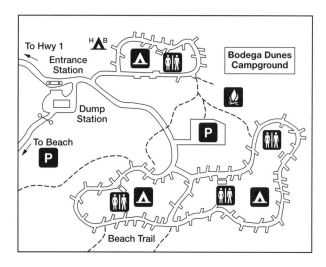

Special Notes

Like most north coast beaches, Sonoma Coast is not for swimming, and lifeguard service is not provided. Strong undertow, heavy surf, and sudden ground swells make even surf play dangerous. The individual beaches have their unique attractions, such as Shell Beach being a favorite of the beachcomber. December through April is the season for whale watching at Bodega Head.

Goat Rock is located at the north end of the park near Jenner. A large seal rookery is farther north near the mouth of the Russian River. (Photo: Lillian Morava)

Facilities* & Activities

98 developed campsites at Bodega Dunes
　　wheelchair accessible campsites
　　hot showers
　　31-foot trailers; 31-foot campers
　　trailer sanitation station
　　15 enroute campsites
30 developed campsites at Wrights Beach
　　27-foot trailers; 27-foot campers
　　20 enroute campsites
6 hike/bike campsites at Bodega Dunes
11 environmental campsites at Willow Creek
　　no water, pit toilets, self-register
20 environmental campsites at Pomo Canyon
　　water, pit toilets, self-register
picnicking
fishing
designated underwater area
hiking & horseback riding trails
harbor seal/whale watching
exhibits

*On state park reservation system.

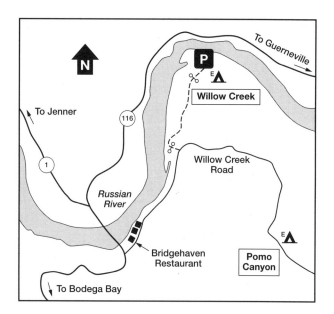

Standish-Hickey State Recreation Area

To Garberville

101

Gordon Creek

Mill Creek

South Fork Eel River

Grove Trail

Page and Gates Road

Landslide Area

Mill Creek Loop

Capt. Miles Standish Tree

Big Tree Trail

Hickey

Rock Creek

101

P

Redwood

South Fork Eel River

Page and Gates Road

Lookout Trail

Page and Gates Road

1

To Fort Bragg

To Leggett

For Information

Standish-Hickey State Recreation Area
Box 208
Leggett, CA 95585
707/925-6482 or 247-3318

Location

At the gateway to the "tall tree country," Standish-Hickey State Recreation Area is located 2 miles north of Leggett on US 101. The 1,070-acre park is situated along the South Fork of the Eel River for almost 2 miles and is at 800 feet elevation.

Special Notes

The river winds through second-growth redwoods, and steep trails line the river canyon. A scenic feature is the Captain Miles Standish tree, a 225-foot redwood, 40 feet in circumference, with an estimated age of 1,200 years. The 15- to 20-foot-deep swimming holes carved in the river's bed are the most popular places in the park on a hot summer day. Steelhead and salmon spawn in the fall and winter.

The park has 3 campgrounds: Hickey, Rock Creek, and Redwood. Hickey and Rock Creek,

located high on bluffs overlooking the river, are open year-round and are popular in winter with fishermen and kayaking groups. The bridge to Redwood Campground is removed after each summer season, thus, the campground is not open year-round.

Facilities* & Activities

3 campgrounds
162 developed campsites
wheelchair accessible campsites
pay showers
24-foot trailers; 27-foot campers
no trailers at Redwood
3 hike/bike campsites
picnicking
fishing
swimming
9 miles of hiking trails
summer nature programs/activities

*On state park reservation system.

Standish-Hickey State Recreation Area   **119**

Sugarloaf Ridge State Park

For Information

Sugarloaf Ridge State Park
2605 Adobe Canyon Road
Kenwood, CA 95452
707/833-5712 or 938-1519

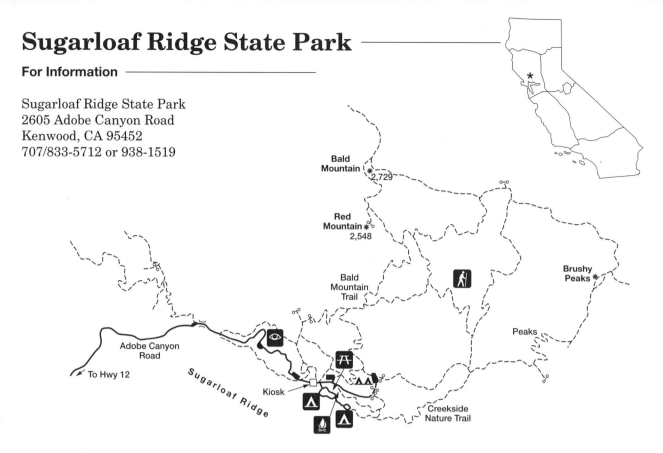

Location

Sugarloaf Ridge State Park is located 7 miles east of Santa Rosa on Highway 12, then north on Adobe Canyon Road for 3 miles. This 2,700-acre park varies in elevation from 600 feet at the entrance to 2,729 feet at the top of Bald Mountain. The entrance road includes 1 mile of steep, narrow, winding road.

Special Notes

Sonoma Creek begins in the park and runs for 3 miles through its southern portion. It's too shallow for swimming, and often dries up by late summer—so fishing for steelhead and trout is best in late spring. Summers at Sugarloaf Ridge are hot and dry, and fog sometimes penetrates this far inland. Many people enjoy the area most in the spring and fall. In spring, the park comes alive with wildflowers.

Facilities* & Activities

50 developed campsites
24-foot trailers; 27-foot campers
group camping (50)
picnicking
group picnic area† (40)
nature & hiking trails
horseback riding trail
exhibits/visitor center

---

*On state park reservation system.
†Phone park for reservations.

Horseback riding is popular at the park; a riding concession operates year-round. (Photo: Marsha Elmore)

Tomales Bay State Park

For Information

Tomales Bay State Park
Star Route
Inverness, CA 94937
415/669-1140

| H△B Hike/Bike Campsites Only

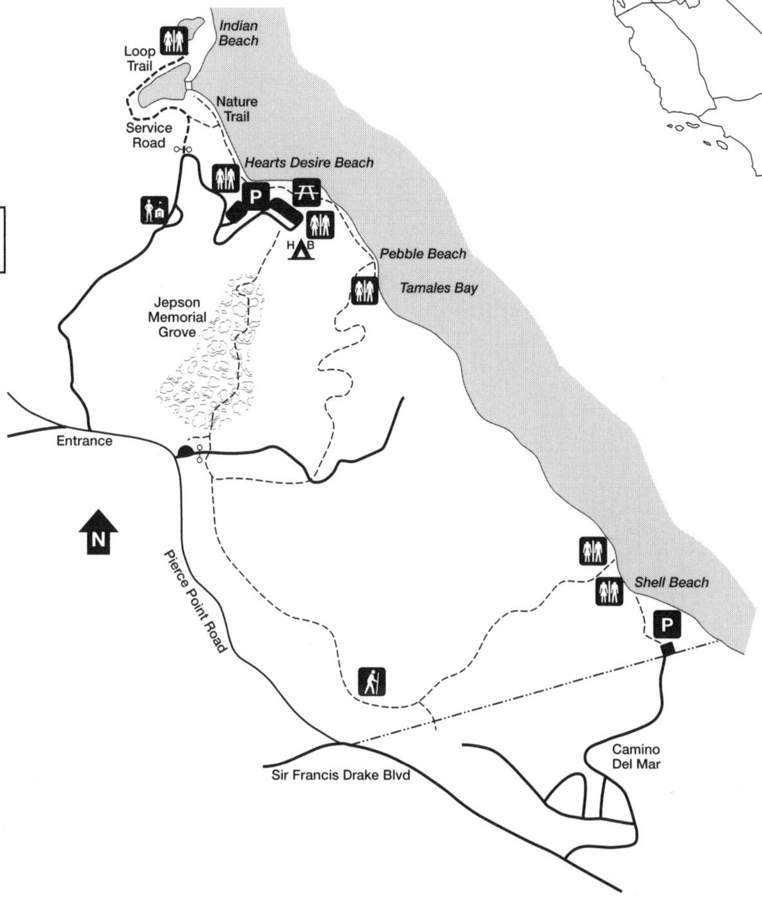

Indian Beach

Loop Trail

Nature Trail

Service Road

Hearts Desire Beach

P

Jepson Memorial Grove

H△B

Pebble Beach

Tamales Bay

Entrance

N

Pierce Point Road

Shell Beach

P

Camino Del Mar

Sir Francis Drake Blvd

Location

This 2,001-acre park is located on the eastern edge of the Point Reyes Peninsula and is adjacent to Point Reyes National Seashore. It is on the west side of Tomales Bay, 8 miles from Highway 1, and 4 miles north of Inverness via Sir Francis Drake Blvd. and Pierce Point Road. Its elevation is 86 feet above sea level.

Special Notes

The park is a lush wilderness of forests, beaches, fields, hills, meadows, and marshes, each with its own plant life. The beaches and east-facing slopes of this area are especially pleasant because they are protected from the prevailing winds by Inverness Ridge—the high backbone of the Point Reyes Penin-

sula. Four gently sloping, surf-free beaches are the primary recreational attraction within the park. There are no boat-launching facilities, but hand-carried boats may be put in the water away from the swimming areas.

Facilities & Activities

10 hike/bike campsites
cold showers
picnicking
4 swimming beaches
fishing
kayaking
windsurfing
nature/hiking trails
exhibits

Van Damme State Park

Gordon Lane

Highland Meadow

Fern Canyon
Scenic Trail

Little River

N

Beach

PACIFIC
OCEAN

Little River
Airport Road

To Comptche

Pygmy
Forest

Mendocino
County Airport

P

To Albion

For Information

Van Damme State Park
P.O. Box 440
Mendocino, CA 95460
707/937-5804

Location

This state park is located 3 miles south of Mendocino on Highway 1. It consists of 2,163 acres of beach and uplands on the Mendocino Coast. The elevation is 15 feet.

Facilities* & Activities

74 developed campsites
pay showers
27-foot trailers; 27-foot campers
30 enroute campsites during busy season
1 hike/bike campsite
10 environmental campsites
group camping area (50)
picnicking
fishing
designated underwater area
nature & hiking trails
bike trails
visitor center
summer programs

—————
*On state park reservation system.

Special Notes

One of the park's features is the lush Fern Canyon Scenic Trail. The walls of the canyon are covered with millions of ferns, dominated by the western sword fern. Bicyclists can use part of the scenic trail, but no motor vehicles of any type are allowed. Other features include the Pygmy Forest, where mature, cone-bearing cypress and pine trees stand 6 inches to 8 feet tall, and the bog or Cabbage Patch, where skunk cabbage grows in abundance. Swimming is not recommended because of the cold water.

The walls of Fern Canyon are covered with millions of ferns, dominated by the western sword fern.

Westport-Union Landing State Beach

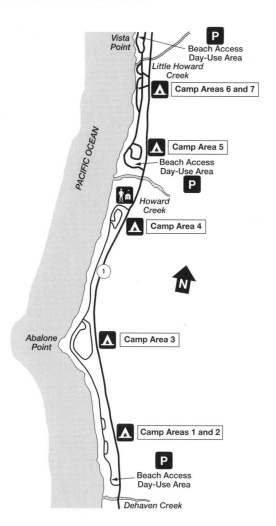

For Information

Westport-Union Landing State Beach
P.O. Box 440
Mendocino, CA 95460
707/937-5804

Location

Westport-Union Landing State Beach is located 2 miles north of the village of Westport and 19 miles north of Fort Bragg on Highway 1. Visitors have the opportunity to experience the scenic and rugged Mendocino coastline at this 41-acre state beach.

Special Notes

The park is a narrow 2-mile-long strip where 7 camping areas sit on coastal bluffs with a splendid view of the ocean and coastal hills. The park is popular with visitors who enjoy exploring its sandy beaches and rocky tidal areas. The beaches are not suitable for swimming but during the spring and summer months, the coarse black sand beaches experience spawning runs of surf smelt, which are eagerly sought by fishermen using A-frame dip nets or throw nets. A little farther from shore, diving for abalone or spear fishing are both challenging activities for visitors.

Facilities & Activities

7 camping areas
130 primitive camping sites
   picnic tables, fire rings
   pit toilets, water nearby
enroute campsites
2 picnic areas with day-use parking and beach access
fishing
scuba diving/snorkeling

Primitive camping sites sit on coastal bluffs with a splendid view of the ocean and coastal hills.

REGION 2

Woodson Bridge State Recreation Area

For Information

Woodson Bridge State Recreation Area
25340 South Avenue
Corning, CA 96021-0616
916/839-2112

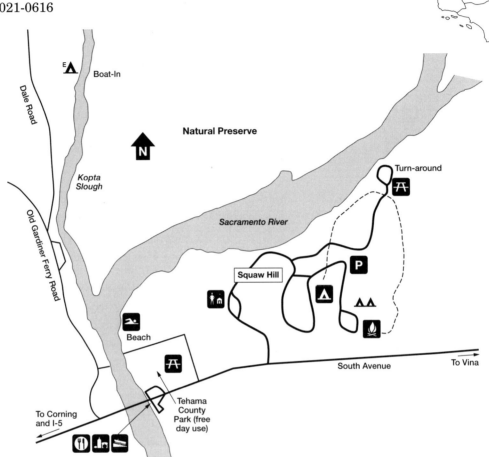

Location

Woodson Bridge State Recreation Area is located 6 miles east of Corning and I-5 on South Avenue and 3 miles west of Highway 99 at Vina. The 428-acre recreation area has a 200-foot elevation.

Special Notes

Nestled in oak woods on the Sacramento River, fishing is superb here with 3 distinct runs of king salmon and plenty of steelhead, striped bass, catfish, and bluegill. Because the park is on the main flyway between Mexico and Canada, it is a bird-watcher's delight. Spring and fall are favored seasons at Woodson Bridge, but summer camping can also be delightful.

Facilities* & Activities

46 developed campsites
wheelchair accessible campsites
showers
31-foot trailers; 31-foot campers
5 enroute campsites
group camping area (40)
boat-in camping
picnicking
fishing
swimming
nature trail

_____
*On state park reservation system.

Region 3

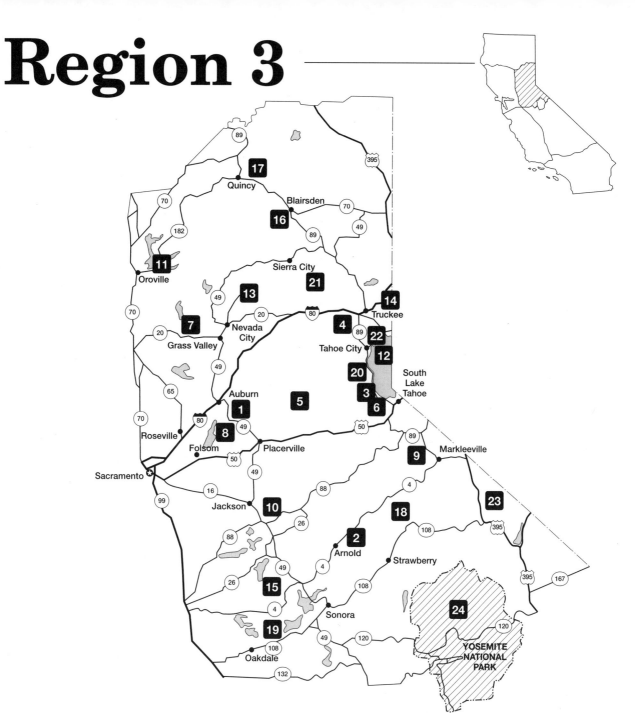

Auburn State Recreation Area

For Information

Auburn State Recreation Area
P.O. Box 3266
Auburn, CA 95604-3266
916/885-4527 or 916/988-0205

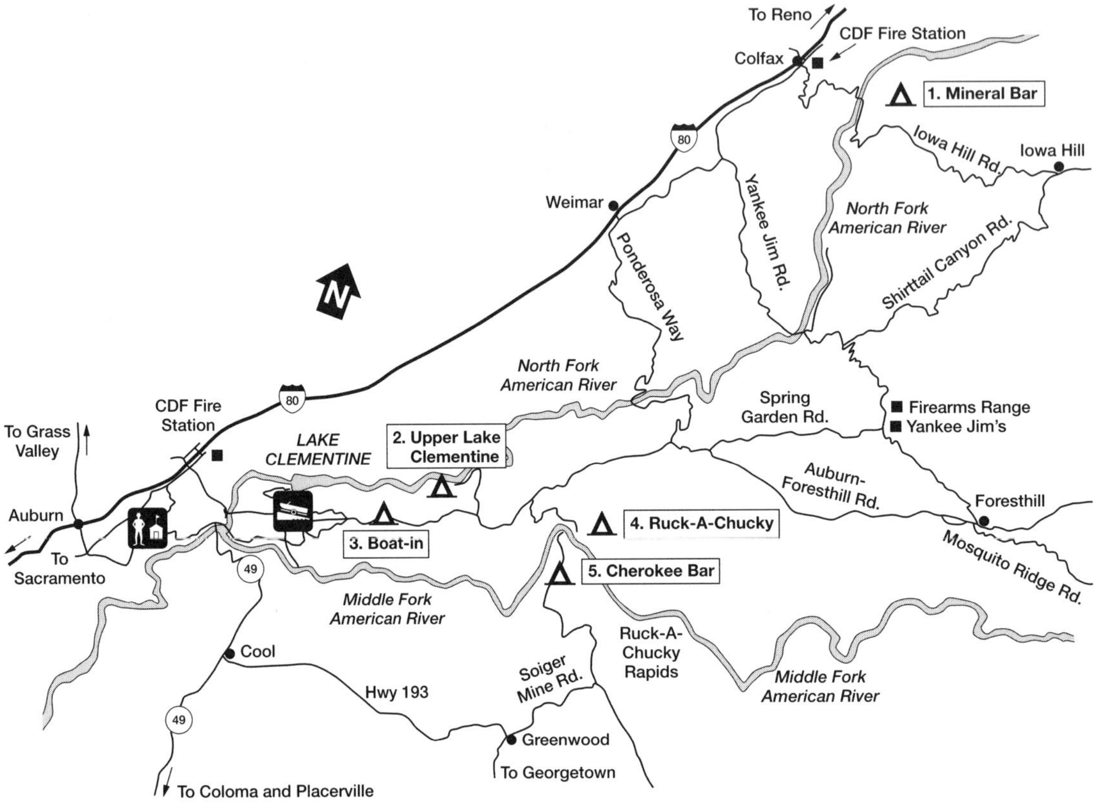

Location

Auburn State Recreation Area is located 1 mile south of Auburn on Highway 49. The 42,000-acre park is located along more than 30 miles of the North and Middle Forks of the American River. These rivers provide boaters with a challenging wilderness experience that requires a sound background in technical white-water skills; they are not for beginners. Elevations range from 500 feet to 1,200 feet.

Primitive Camping Areas

Site #1: Mineral Bar—Camping (17 sites) is permitted on the east side of the river, upstream from the old bridge on Colfax Iowa Hill Road. Camping is limited to 15 continuous days.

Site #2: Upper end of Lake Clementine—Camping (14 sites) is permitted on the south side of the river; access is from the Foresthill Road. Generally closed from October to May. Camping is limited to 7 continuous days.

Site #3: Boat-in camping—Camping (22 sites) at Lake Clementine; no vehicle access. Open Memorial Day to the end of September; camping is limited to 14 continuous days. On state reservation system.

Site #4: Ruck-a-Chucky—Camping (10 sites) is permitted on the north side of the river; access is from Drivers Flat Road off of Foresthill Road. Check with the office before driving to this area, as the road is closed during inclement weather. Camping is limited to 15 continuous days.

Site #5: Cherokee Bar—Camping is permitted on the south side of the river; access is from Sliger Mine Road. Camping is limited to 15 continuous days.

Auburn State Recreation Area
(continued)

Special Notes

Scenic Highway 49 winds through the park—an historic placer mining area—and offers a glimpse of the sharp canyons and rugged countryside of the Sierra foothills. There are over 50 miles of hiking and riding trails in the American River Canyon. Early in the season, trout fishing is good. Camping is permitted in areas other than those listed under "campground specifics" on a permit basis. Information and permits are available at the park office, 1 mile south of Auburn on Highway 49.

Facilities & Activities

5 primitive camping areas
no drinking water
river-trail camps*
boat-in group camp[†] (20)
picnicking
gold panning & rockhounding
fishing
swimming
launch ramp/marina at Lake Clementine
water skiing
white-water rafting/kayaking
hiking & horseback riding trails
40+ miles of mountain bike trails
1,000-acre area for off-road motorcycles & ATVs

---

*Information and permits for camping in some areas outside of the designated campgrounds are available at ranger station.
[†]On state park reservation system.

Calaveras Big Trees State Park

For Information

Calaveras Big Trees State Park
P.O. Box 120
Arnold, CA 95223
209/795-2334

Location

Calaveras Big Trees State Park is located 4 miles northeast of Arnold on Highway 4 on the western slope of the Sierra Nevada. The 6,075-acre park is on both sides of the Stanislaus River and Beaver Creek watersheds at an elevation of 4,700 feet. The park has 2 campgrounds: North Grove and Oak Hollow.

Special Notes

The park features 2 magnificent groves of giant sequoia (North and South Groves) and is open all year. An increasing number of park visitors enjoy this area most of all when the ground is covered with snow. Contact the park for winter camping information as there are opportunities for winter snowshoeing and cross-country skiing; there are self-guiding trails in both groves.

Facilities* & Activities

129 developed campsites
wheelchair accessible campsites at North Grove
pay showers
27-foot trailers; 27-foot campers
trailer sanitation station
group camping area (100)
picnicking
group picnic area[†] (250)
fishing
swimming
nature & hiking trails
snowshoeing/cross-country skiing
guided hikes/campfire talks
exhibits
visitor center (open during peak periods)

---

*On state park reservation system.
[†]Phone park for reservations.

REGION 3

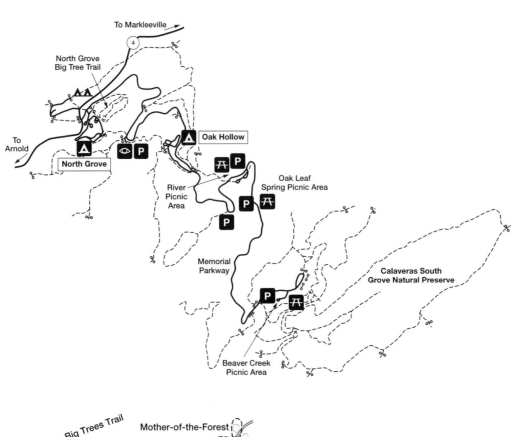

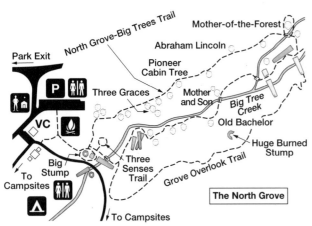

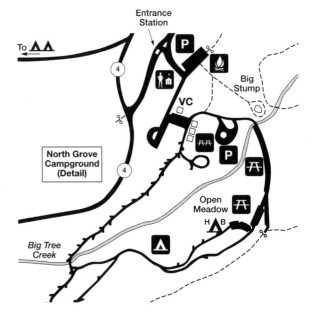

D. L. Bliss State Park

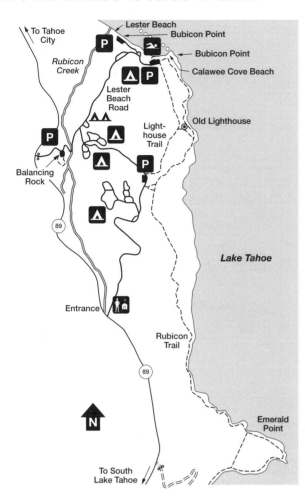

For Information

D. L. Bliss State Park
P.O. Box 266
Tahoma, CA 96142-0266
916/525-7277 (seasonal) or 525-7982

Location

Located 17 miles south of Tahoe City on Highway 89, this 1,237-acre park is at an elevation of 6,920 feet. The park is north of and adjacent to Emerald Bay State Park; it is usually closed to camping from October through Memorial Day.

Special Notes

The park features the popular Old Lighthouse and the Balancing Rock Nature trails. D. L. Bliss State Park and the adjacent Emerald Bay State Park include some 6 miles of magnificent Lake Tahoe shoreline. The hiking trail from Calawee Beach to the Vikingsholm at Emerald Bay is 4½ miles.

Facilities* & Activities

168 developed campsites
showers
15-foot trailers; 21-foot campers
group camping area (50)
picnicking
fishing
swimming
scuba diving underwater area
nature & hiking trails

---

*On state park reservation system.

D. L. Bliss State Park and Emerald Bay State Park offer magnificent panoramas of Lake Tahoe, which to the Indians meant "lake in the sky."

Donner Memorial State Park

For Information

Donner Memorial State Park
12593 Donner Pass Road
Truckee, CA 96161
916/582-7892

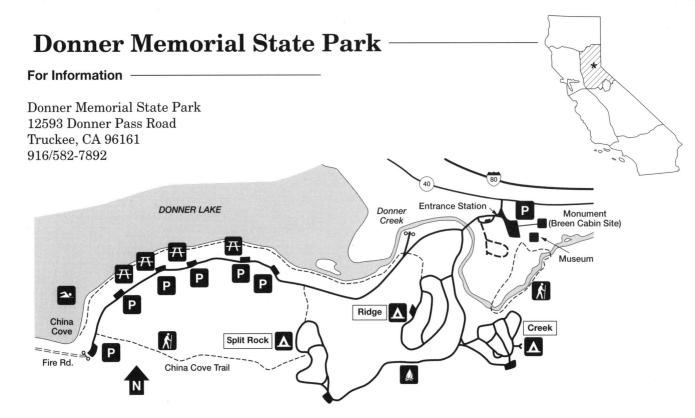

Location

Donner Memorial State Park is located in the beautiful Sierra Nevada on Donner Pass Road, 2 miles west of Truckee. This 353-acre park on Donner Lake is a geological wonderland; elevation is 5,950 feet.

Special Notes

In and around the park you can see some of the Sierra Nevada's geologic history, and the Sierra's steep eastern face. The park has more than 3 miles of frontage on Donner Lake and Creek. The Emigrant Trail Museum recounts the tragic story of the Donner Party trapped there in the savage winter of 1846–47.

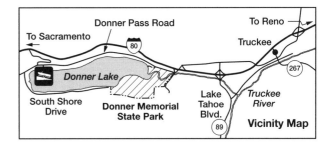

Windsurfing is popular at the mile-high Donner Memorial State Park.

Facilities* & Activities

154 developed campsites
wheelchair accessible campsites
showers
24-foot trailers; 28-foot campers
10 enroute campsites
picnicking
fishing
swimming
windsurfing
nature & hiking trails
cross country ski trail
museum (open 10–4:00)
exhibits/visitor center
state historic landmark

———
*On state park reservation system.

Eldorado National Forest

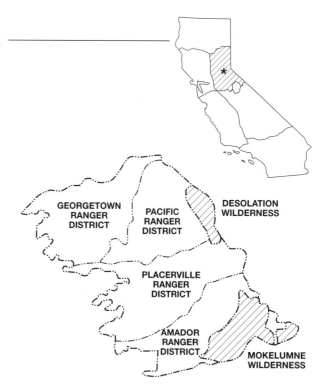

For Information

Supervisor's Office
Eldorado National Forest
100 Forni Road
Placerville, CA 95667
916/622-5061

Eldorado Information Center
3070 Camino Heights Drive
Camino, CA 95709
916/644-6048

Location

Eldorado National Forest lies east of Sacramento and southwest of Lake Tahoe. One-fourth of the lands within the boundaries of this 884,688-acre forest are privately owned. The area contains some of the most productive timber-growing soils in the West, and timber harvesting is an activity you are likely to see in the spring, summer, and fall months.

Special Notes

Although spring and summer are the most popular recreation seasons, winter has its share of activities. Four down-hill ski areas are located on national forest land—Sundown and Kirkwood along Highway 88, and Sierra Ski Ranch and Ski Echo-Tahoe along US 50. Cross-country skiing and snowmobiling are popular activities through the forest, but the main play areas are at sites along Highways 50 and 88.

By late November winter has set in, and it's time for the cross-country skiers to make tracks for another season.

Elevations range from about 3,000 to 10,000 feet. At the 5,000-foot elevation, summer usually comes to an end with a series of minor storms in late September or October, and by late November winter has set in. Because of the weather, most of the dirt roads on the forest are closed to vehicle travel between October and April. Many of the recreation areas are accessible by mid-April.

Wilderness Areas

The **Mokelumne Wilderness** is characterized by massive granite formations and deep canyon. The 100,600-acres of designated wilderness is located between Highways 4 and 88, and takes in portions of the Eldorado, Stanislaus, and Toiyabe national forests. The elevations range from 4,000 feet near Salt Springs Reservoir to higher than 10,000 feet at Round Top. A wilderness permit is required between May 25 and September 15.

Characterized by many small lakes, the 63,500-acre **Desolation Wilderness** varies in elevation from 6,500 feet to 10,000 feet. Primary use season is June through September; snow packs sometimes close higher passes until July. Because of its beauty and accessibility, Desolation Wilderness is one of the most heavily-used wilderness areas in the U.S. Entry quotas have been established for overnight users from June 15 through Labor Day, but campers may reserve permits up to 60 days in advance for that period. Wilderness permits are required year-round.

REGION 3

Eldorado National Forest (continued)

Amador Ranger District

For Information

Amador Ranger District
26820 Silver Drive
Pioneer, CA 95666
209/295-4251

Campgrounds*	Elevation (feet)	# of Units	Drinking Water	Toilets Vault/Pit	Trailer Space	Camping Fee
Bear River Group**	6,000	3	•	V		•
Caples Lake	7,800	35	•	V	•	•
Kirkwood	7,600	12	•	V		•
Lower Blue Lake	8,100	16	•	V	•	•
Lumberyard	6,200	5		V	•	
Middle Creek†	8,200	5	•	V	•	•
Mokelumne	3,200	8	Str.	V		
Moore Creek	3,200	8	Str.	V		
Pi Pi††	4,100	51	•	V	•	•
Silver Lake East††¶	7,200	62	•	V	•	•
Silver Lake West¶	7,200	35	•	V	•	•
South Shore	5,900	22	•	V	•	•
Sugar Pine Point	6,000	10		P		•
Upper Blue Lake†	8,200	32	•	•	•	•
Upper Blue Lake Dam†	8,200	25	•	V	•	•
White Azalea	3,500	6	Str.	V		
Winton	6,000	10		P		•
Woods Lake	8,200	25	•	V		•

Notes:
* Campgrounds at lower elevations open as early as May and close in mid-Novermber; those at higher elevations open in June or July and close in mid-October.
** Capacity for Bear River Group Campground: 2 units for 25 persons, 1 unit for 50. Reservations are required. Phone 209/295-4512.
† Upper & Lower Blue Lake, Upper Blue Lake Dam, and Middle Creek are Pacific Gas & Electric (PG&E) campgrounds.
†† Reservations are available. Phone 1-800-280-CAMP.
¶ Silver Lake East & West are cooperative campgrounds with PG&E.

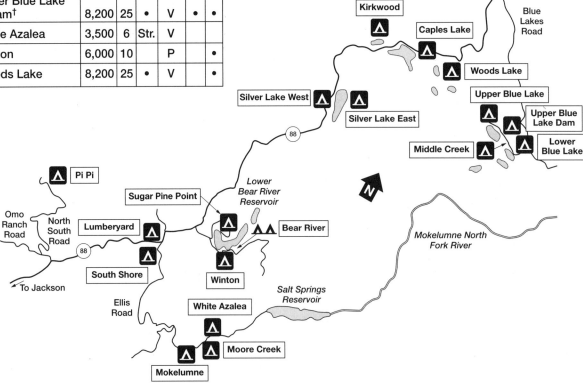

Eldorado National Forest *(continued)*

Placerville Ranger District

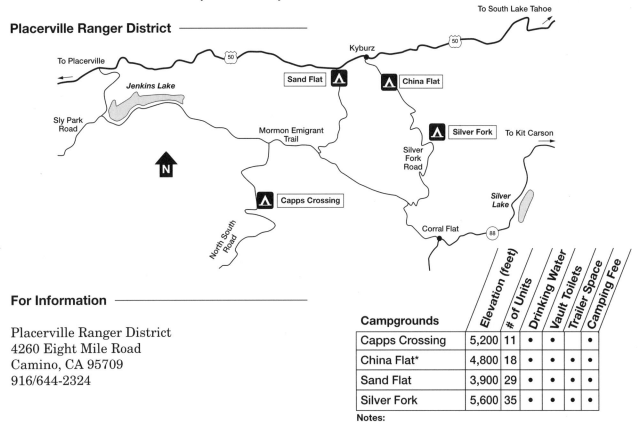

For Information

Placerville Ranger District
4260 Eight Mile Road
Camino, CA 95709
916/644-2324

Campgrounds	Elevation (feet)	# of Units	Drinking Water	Vault Toilets	Trailer Space	Camping Fee
Capps Crossing	5,200	11	•	•		•
China Flat*	4,800	18	•	•	•	•
Sand Flat	3,900	29	•	•	•	•
Silver Fork	5,600	35	•	•	•	•

Notes:
*Campsites at China Flat include 8 walk-in tent units.

Georgetown Ranger District

Campgrounds	Elevation (feet)	# of Units	Drinking Water	Toilets Vault/Pit	Trailer Space	Camping Fee
Big Meadows	5,300	54	•	V	•	•
Black Oak Group* (Site #1, 3, 4)	4,400	3	•	V		•
(Site #2)	4,400	1			•	•
Hell Hole (walk-in tent)	5,200	10	•	V		•
Middle Meadows Group**	5,000	2	•	V	•	•
Stumpy Meadows†	4,400	40	•	V	•	•
Upper Hell Hole	4,600	15	Str.	P		

Notes:
* Capacity at Black Oak Group Campground: 25 max. at Site #4; 50 max. at Sites #1 & 3; 75 max. at Site #2. Black Oak Group Site #2 is for self-contained vehicles only.
** Capacity at Middle Meadows Group Campground: 25 & 50 max.
† Reservations are available for Stumpy Meadows; they are required for the group campgrounds. Phone 1-800-280-CAMP.

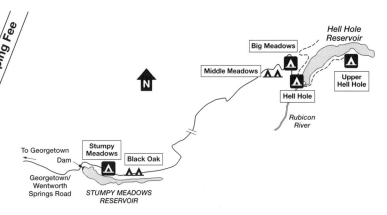

For Information

Georgetown Ranger District
7600 Wentworth Springs Road
Georgetown, CA 95634
916/333-4312

Eldorado National Forest (continued)

Pacific Ranger District

Campgrounds	Elevation (feet)	# of Units	Drinking Water	Toilets Flush/Vault	Trailer Space	Camping Fee
Fashoda Tent (walk-in)	4,900	30	•	V		•
Gerle Creek*	5,300	50	•	V	•	•
Ice House*	5,500	83	•	V	•	•
Jones Fork	4,900	10		V		
Loon Lake*	6,500	53	•	V	•	•
Loon Lake Boat Ramp	6,500	15		V	•	•
Loon Lake Equestrian*	6,500	9	•	V		•
Loon Lake Equestrian Group**	6,500	5	•	V		•
Loon Lake Group #1** (walk-in tent)	6,500	10	•	V		•
Loon Lake Group #2**	6,500	6	•	V		•
Northshore RV	6,500	15		V	•	
Northwind	5,500	10		V	•	
Pleasant (boat/trail access)	6,500	10	Str.	V		
Red Fir Group**	6,500	1	•	V		•
Silver Creek	5,200	11	Str.	V		
South Fork	5,200	17	Str.	V	•	
Strawberry Point	5,500	10		V	•	
Sunset*	4,900	131	•	V	•	•
Wench Creek	4,900	100	•	F/V	•	•
Wench Creek Group*	4,900	2	•	F/V	•	•
Wentworth Springs	6,000	8	Str.	V		
Wolf Creek	4,900	42		V	•	
Wrights Lake**	7,000	71	•	V	•	•
Yellowjacket	4,900	40	•	F/V	•	•

Notes:

* Reservations are available. Phone 1-800-280-CAMP.

** Reservations are required. Phone 1-800-280-CAMP.

Access to Wentworth Springs Campground recommended for motorcycles and 4-WD vehicles only.

Camping at Loon Lake Boat Ramp is for self-contained vehicles only.

Three other campgrounds are for self-contained vehicles (Northshore RV, Northwind, & Strawberry Point) although tents are o.k.

Capacity for group campgrounds: Loon Lake Equestrian (25), Loon Lake #1 (50), Loon Lake #2 (25), Red Fir (25), & Wench Creek (100).

For Information

Pacific Ranger District
7887 Highway 50
Pollock Pines, CA 95726-9602
916/644-2349

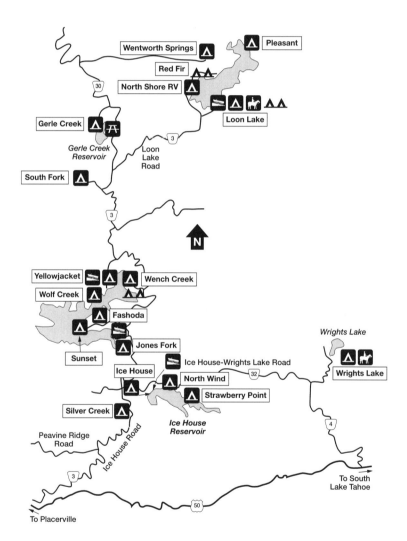

Emerald Bay State Park

For Information

Emerald Bay State Park
P.O. Box 266
Tahoma, CA 96142-0266
916/541-3030 (seasonal) or 525-7982

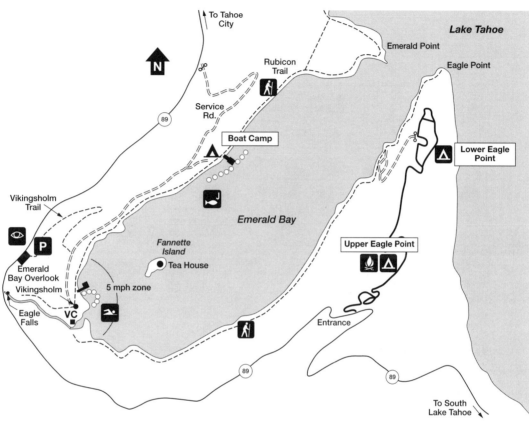

Location

Emerald Bay State Park is located 22 miles south of Tahoe City on Highway 89. The 593-acre park is 6,800 feet above sea level and is south of and adjacent to D. L. Bliss State Park; it is closed from mid-September until mid-June.

Special Notes

Emerald Bay State Park offers a panoramic view of Lake Tahoe from Eagle Falls and a spectacular 38-room mansion, an exact replica of an A.D. 800 Norse fortress known as Vikingsholm. Open July 1 to Labor Day, there is a guided tour for a nominal fee. The building is about a mile down by trail from the parking lot at the Emerald Bay Overlook. From Vikingsholm, another trail leads to Eagle Falls.

Facilities* & Activities

100 developed campsites
showers
21-foot trailers; 24-foot campers
boat-in camping (20 primitive)
picnicking
fishing
swimming
scuba diving
hiking trails
boating/boat mooring
exhibits/visitor center

*On state park reservation system.

REGION 3

Englebright Lake

For Information

Englebright Lake
P.O. Box 6
Smartville, CA 95977-0006
916/639-2342

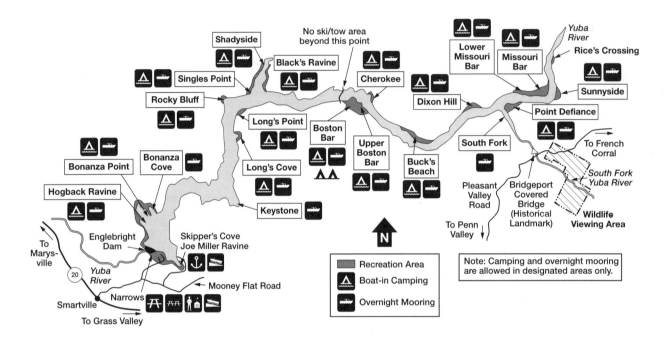

Boat-in Campsites only

Shadyside
Black's Ravine
No ski/tow area beyond this point
Cherokee
Yuba River
Rice's Crossing
Lower Missouri Bar
Missouri Bar
Singles Point
Sunnyside
Rocky Bluff
Dixon Hill
Long's Point
Point Defiance
Boston Bar
Bonanza Point
Bonanza Cove
Upper Boston Bar
South Fork
To French Corral
Long's Cove
Buck's Beach
South Fork Yuba River
Hogback Ravine
Pleasant Valley Road
Bridgeport Covered Bridge (Historical Landmark)
Wildlife Viewing Area
Keystone
To Marys-ville
Englebright Dam
Skipper's Cove
Joe Miller Ravine
To Penn Valley
Yuba River
Mooney Flat Road
20
Narrows
Smartville
To Grass Valley

N

Recreation Area
Boat-in Camping
Overnight Mooring

Note: Camping and overnight mooring are allowed in designated areas only.

Englebright Lake is narrow and long—nine miles long to be exact; boaters can travel a long time when using a trolling motor.

Englebright Lake (continued)

The upper half of Englebright Lake is closed to waterskiers, but the sport is quite popular on the lower half.

Recreation Areas	Number of Campsites	Overnight Mooring	Boat-In Camping	Toilets Vault/Flush	Paved Launch Ramp	Hiking Trail	Fishing Access
Narrows*				F	•	•	•
Joe Miller Ravine**				F	•	•	•
Hogback Ravine	8	•	•	V			
Bonanza Point	3	•	•	V			
Bonanza Cove		•		V			
Keystone		•					
Long's Cove	8	•		V			
Long's Point	5	•		V			
Rocky Bluff	4	•	•	V			
Singles Point	3	•	•	V			
Shadyside	4	•	•	V			
Black's Ravine	1	•	•	V			
Boston Bar†	12	•	•	V	•		
Upper Boston Bar	6	•	•	V			
Cherokee	3	•	•	V			
Buck's Beach	5	•	•	V			
Dixon Hill	2	•	•	V			
South Fork		•					
Point Defiance	8	•	•	V			
Lower Missouri Bar	4	•	•	V			
Missouri Bar	15	•	•	V			
Sunnyside	2	•	•	V			
Rice's Crossing			•	V			•

Notes:
*Narrows day-use area has 11 picnic sites and 1 group picnic area.
**Joe Miller Ravine has a marina that offers boat rentals and mooring, gas, vessel pump-out, and store facilities.
†Boston Bar has a group camp; it can accommodate 30; phone the park office for reservations.
Drinking water is provided near each of the 2 launch ramps.

Location

Englebright Lake is located on the historic Yuba River, 20 miles east of Marysville, and just north of Highway 20. Constructed in the steep Yuba River gorge known as the Narrows, the lake offers a narrow corridor of clear, cool water. Two power plants are located below the dam for the generation of hydroelectric power. The upper half of the lake is closed to waterskiers.

Camping at Englebright Lake is unique as all campsites are boat-in only. All campgrounds are located along the lake's 24 miles of shoreline. Each campsite consists of a table, a fire grill, and a level spot for your tent. Portable restrooms and refuse cans are centrally located near to all the campsites. All individual campsites are on a first-come, first-served basis with a 14-day limit; there are no fees for camping.

Lake Statistics

779-acre surface area
9 miles long
24 miles of shoreline

Folsom Lake State Recreation Area

For Information

Folsom Lake State Recreation Area
l7806 Folsom-Auburn Road
Folsom, CA 95630-1797
916/988-0205

Location

Folsom Lake State Recreation Area is set in the Sierra-Nevada foothills 25 miles east of Sacramento, via US 50 or I-80. The 17,718-acre lake and recreation area has an elevation of 456 feet. The park has 3 campgrounds: Peninsula, Beals Point, and Negro Bar.

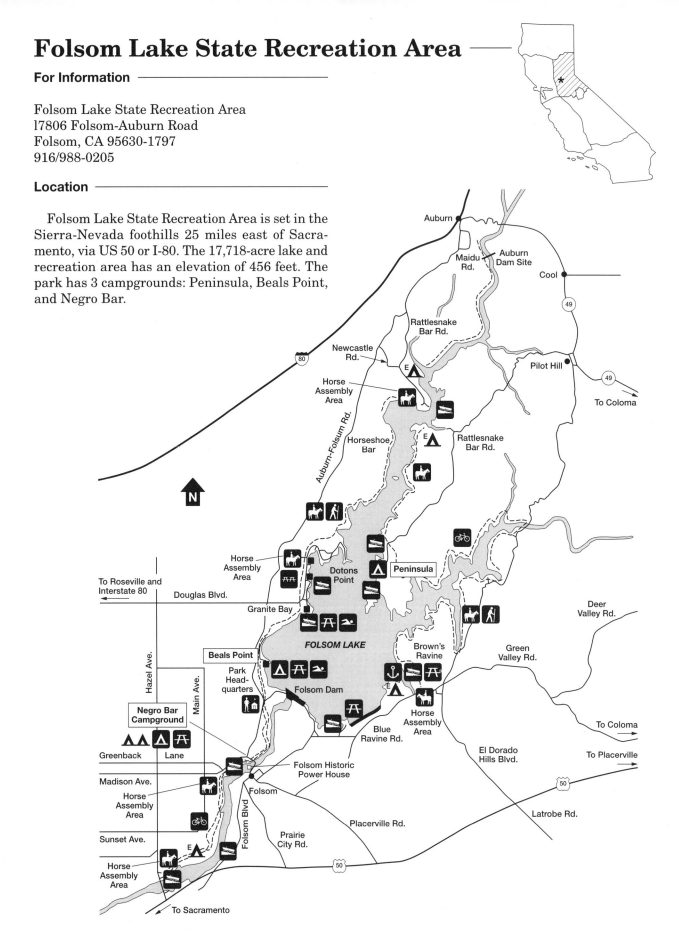

Folsom Lake State Recreation Area *(continued)*

Special Notes

Folsom Lake has 75 miles of shoreline, and extends for 15 miles up the canyon of the American River's North Fork. Level of the lake varies from a high of 466 feet elevation in early summer to as low as 426 feet in early winter. This recreation area offers numerous opportunities to the outdoor enthusiast, but the most popular pastime is probably fishing. Bicycling is also popular and horses may be rented.

Facilities* & Activities

100 developed campsites at Peninsula
    31-foot trailers; 31-foot campers
48 developed campsites at Beals Point
    wheelchair accessible campsites
    solar-heated showers
    31-foot trailers; 31-foot campers
    trailer sanitation station

20 developed campsites at Negro Bar
    cold showers
    31-foot trailers; 31-foot campers
    trailer sanitation station
environmental campsites
3 group camping areas at Negro Bar (125)
boat-in (on-board) camping
picnicking
group picnic area at Granite Bay[†] (400)
fishing
swimming
windsurfing
boating/rentals
launch ramp/boat mooring
seasonal marina
water skiing
nature trails
60 miles of hiking & horseback riding trails
10 miles of bicycle trails
food service
state historic landmark

*On state park reservation system.
[†]Phone park for reservations.

The recreation area at Folsom Lake has 10 miles of bicycle trails and 60 miles of hiking and horseback riding trails; horses may be rented.

Grover Hot Springs State Park

For Information

Grover Hot Springs State Park
P.O. Box 188
Markleeville, CA 96120
916/694-2248

Old Irrigation Ditch

Burnside Lake Trail

Buck Creek

"Transition Walk" Nature Trail

Sawmill Creek Trail

Hot Springs Trail

N

P

Toiyabe

Quaking Aspen

Hot Springs Creek

Shay Creek

To Markleeville

P

Location

Grover Hot Springs State Park is located 3 miles west of Markleeville on Hot Springs Road. Mountains rise abruptly on three sides of this 700-acre park; its altitude is 5,840 feet above sea level. The park has 2 campgrounds: Quaking Aspen and Toiyabe.

Special Notes

The water from the park's hot springs contains very little sulfur. One of the concrete pools is fed by the run-off from six mineral springs. The temperature remains between 102 and 105°F in the hot pool. The pool is open all year; hours depend on the season, so phone the park before you visit. Excess water and overflow from the pools are diverted into nearby Hot Springs Creek, a year-round stream that flows through the middle of the park's large meadow.

In winter, visitors enjoy cross-country skiing and snowshoeing as well as soaking in the hot pools. From early October to May, when the campground is closed, camping is allowed in the picnic area adjacent to the park entrance; there is piped water and restrooms, but no showers then. In the summer months, visitors can fish the creek for trout.

Facilities* & Activities

76 developed campsites
wheelchair accessible campsites
showers
24-foot trailers; 27-foot campers
10 enroute campsites
picnicking
fishing
swimming
nature & hiking trails

*On state park reservation system.

In winter, park visitors enjoy snowshoeing and cross-country skiing, as well as soaking in the hot pools that are fed by the run-off from mineral springs.

Indian Grinding Rock State Historic Park

For Information

Indian Grinding Rock State Historic Park
14881 Pine Grove-Volcano Road
Pine Grove, CA 95665
209/296-7488

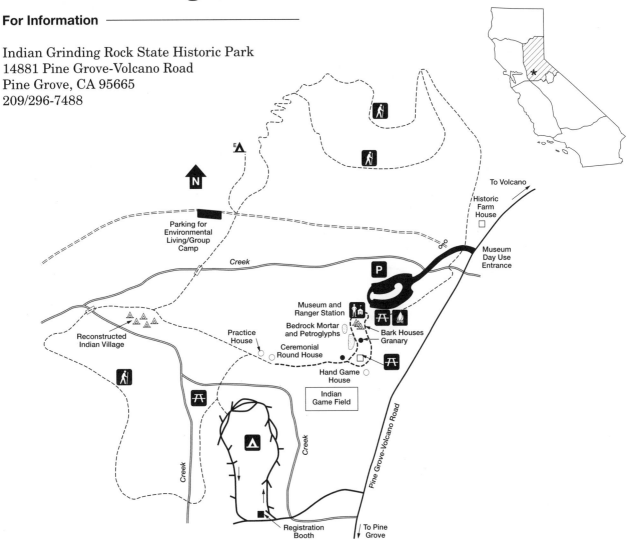

Location

Indian Grinding Rock State Historic Park is located 11 miles northeast of Jackson and 1.4 miles from Highway 88 on Pine Grove-Volcano Road. This 136-acre park has an elevation of 2,418 feet.

Special Notes

The park is the site of the Northern Miwok Indian "grinding rock," where acorns were ground into a fine meal of flour, a staple in the Indian's diet. The main grinding rock is a limestone outcropping measuring 173 feet by 82 feet. It is covered with 363 petroglyphs, or rock carvings, and 1,185 mortar cups used to pulverize the acorns and other seeds. Also at the site are a round-house, a bark conical dwelling, and an Indian football field.

Facilities & Activities

23 developed campsites
pay showers
27-foot trailers; 27-foot campers
group environment campsite* (5 teepees, 30 campers)
picnicking
nature & hiking trails
reconstructed Miwok village
interpretive talks for groups*
exhibits/cultural center
state historic landmark

*Phone park for reservations.

REGION 3

Lake Oroville State Recreation Area

For Information

Lake Oroville State Recreation Area
400 Glen Drive
Oroville, CA 95966-9222
916/538-2200

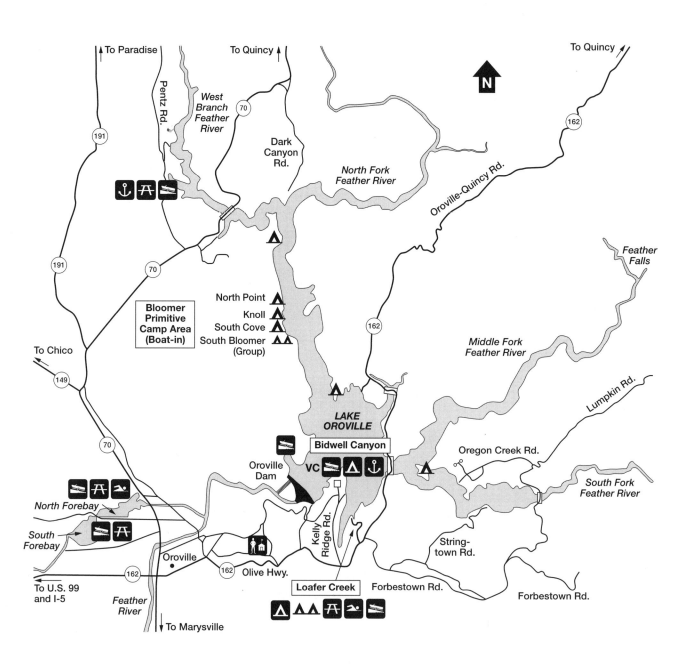

Lake Oroville State Recreation Area
(continued)

Location

This state recreation area is 7 miles east of Oroville via Highway 162. It consists of 16,100 acres and 15,500 acres of lake surface at an elevation of 900 feet. The lake was created by the Oroville Dam on the Feather River—the highest earth-filled dam in the United States. When the lake is at its maximum elevation, it includes 167 miles of shoreline. There are 2 campgrounds: Loafer Creek Campground is on Highway 162, and Bidwell Canyon Campground is 1½ miles north of Highway 162 on Kelly Ridge Road.

Special Notes

More than a million fish have been planted in Lake Oroville in the past few years, so both shore and boat fishing are popular. Loafer Creek and the North Forebay are the only designated swimming areas. The lake level fluctuates daily through the year—in the summer and fall the level is down; in winter and spring there is a rise. Feather Falls, a 640-foot-high waterfall on the Fall River, is a scenic highlight of the area and well worth a trip up the Middle Fork of the Feather River; it is especially beautiful during the spring run-off. When the lake is at its maximum elevation, you can boat within a quarter of a mile of the falls.

Facilities* & Activities

137 developed campsites at Loafer Creek
   wheelchair accessible campsites
   showers
   31-foot trailers; 40-foot campers
   trailer sanitation station
   closed in winter
70 campsites with full hookups at Bidwell Canyon
   showers
   31-foot trailers; 40-foot campers
   trailer sanitation station
   open year-round
40 enroute campsites
7 group camping areas (150)
1 boat-in group campsite (25)
93 boat-in campsites
on-board boat-camping
picnicking
fishing
swimming
windsurfing
nature & hiking trails
horseback riding trails
boating/rentals
launch ramp/boat mooring
2 full-service marinas
waterskiing
supplies
exhibits/visitor center
state historic landmark

*On state park reservation system.

This recreation area can handle large camping trailers and motor homes. Bidwell Canyon has 70 campsites with full hookups, and Loafer Creek has 137 developed campsites.

Lake Tahoe Basin Management Unit

For Information

Supervisor's Office
870 Emerald Bay Road, Suite 1
South Lake Tahoe, CA 96150
916/573-2600

Location

The Lake Tahoe Basin Management Unit is located in the states of California and Nevada surrounding Lake Tahoe. It is an administrative unit established by the Forest Service in 1973 to manage all national forest lands in the Lake Tahoe Basin. Prior to April 1973, three national forest supervisors' offices administered the national forest lands through four district offices.

Special Notes

The clarity and purity of Lake Tahoe's water is world renowned. Its size (22 miles long, 12 miles wide, and 71 miles around), its great depth (1,645 feet), and the altitude of the surface of the lake (6,223 feet above sea level), make Lake Tahoe the highest, largest clear-water lake in the world. The lake is surrounded by mountains, some reaching almost 11,000 feet, forming a picturesque basin. More than 100 smaller alpine lakes and many miles of streams provide an abundance of fishing waters for all types of fishing enthusiasts.

The Taylor Creek Visitor Center is located 3 miles west of South Lake Tahoe on the lake side of Highway 89. The visitor center is open throughout the summer and into October; it offers a wide range of maps, brochures, and interpretive programs, and is the site for five self-guided trails and the Lake of the Sky Amphitheater. The Stream Profile Chamber, an underground viewing chamber that allows visitors to watch trout, Kokanee salmon,

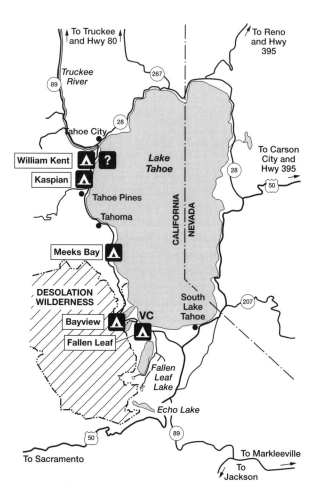

Desolation Wilderness is the most heavily used wilderness area per acre in the United States. Overnight users must obtain a free wilderness permit year-round.

Lake Tahoe Basin Management Unit
(continued)

and other aquatic life in Taylor Creek, is also located at the Taylor Creek Visitor Center. Another national forest information center is located two miles south of Tahoe City on Highway 89 at the entrance to William Kent Campground.

The Lake Tahoe Basin offers the boating enthusiast a variety of boating opportunities at three lakes—Lake Tahoe, Echo Lake, and Fallen Leaf Lake. Two very popular areas for canoeing, kayaking, and rafting in the Lake Tahoe Basin are the Upper Truckee River flowing into Lake Tahoe on the South Shore, and the Lower Truckee River flowing out of Lake Tahoe at Tahoe City on the North Shore.

The Lake Tahoe Basin boasts many activities appealing to winter visitors. Three downhill ski areas are located on Forest Service land in California—Heavenly Valley, Homewood, and Tahoe Ski bowl. Several areas are ideal for cross-country skiing and snowmobiling. Inquire at the Forest Service office.

Wilderness Area

Desolation Wilderness lies on both sides of the Sierra Nevadas, west of Lake Tahoe in both Eldorado National Forest and Lake Tahoe Basin. The most heavily used wilderness area per acre in the United States, it contains 63,475 acres of subalpine forests, glacial lakes and valleys, and granite peaks. A portion of the Pacific Crest National Scenic Trail/Tahoe Rim Trail passes through the area. All persons entering Desolation must obtain a free wilderness permit year-round. Day hikers may self-register at the trailheads, but overnight users must obtain the permit in person. From June 15 through Labor Day, a wilderness permit quota system is in place for overnight campers.

Campgrounds*	# of Units	Drinking Water	Flush Toilets	Max. RV Length	Camping Fee
Bayview**	10	•			
Fallen Leaf	205	•	•	40′	•
Kaspian	10	•	•	20′	•
Meeks Bay	40	•	•	20′	•
William Kent†	95	•	•	24′	•

Notes:
 *All campgrounds are open from Memorial Day through Labor Day.
** Bayview has a 48-hour camping limit.
 † William Kent Campground has a trailer sanitary station.

Lake Tahoe is the highest and largest clear-water lake in the world. All national forest lands in the Lake Tahoe Basin are managed by one administrative unit. (Photo: California Office of Tourism)

Malakoff Diggins
State Historic Park

For Information

Malakoff Diggins State Historic Park
23579 North Bloomfield Road
Nevada City, CA 95959
916/265-2740

(Map of Malakoff Diggins State Historic Park showing Cruzon Grade Rd., Rim Trail, Chute Hill, Diggins Loop Trail, Diggins Pond, BLAIR LAKE, North Bloomfield, Crystal Hill Mine, Diggins Overlook, Hiller Tunnel, Humbug Creek, Lake City Road, North Bloomfield/Graniteville Rd., To Tyler Foote Crossing Rd., Relief Hill Rd., Marten Ranch, and a parking area marked P)

Vicinity Map showing Cherokee, North Columbia, Backbone Road, Cruzon Grade Rd., Malakoff Diggins S.H.P., Graniteville Rd., North Bloomfield, Lake City Road, Lake City, Relief Hill Rd., Relief Hill, Tyler-Foote Crossing, North Broomfield/Graniteville Rd., Nevada City, Highway 49, Highway 20

Location

Malakoff Diggins State Historic Park is a 3,000-acre park and has an altitude of 3,300 feet. Via North Bloomfield Road—a very steep and gravel road—the park is 16 miles northeast from Nevada City. Motor homes and trailers should use Tyler-Foote Crossing Road—a road that heads west off of Highway 49 from 11 miles north of Nevada City; the distance is then 27 miles. The last 8 miles to the park is on a road named Cruzon Grade.

Special Notes

This was California's largest "hydraulic" mine. Today you can see the huge cliffs carved by the great streams of water, and examine the 7,847-foot bedrock tunnel that served as a drain. Visitor center exhibits also feature life in the old mining town of North Bloomfield. Tours are conducted during the summer.

Facilities & Activities

30 developed campsites
wheelchair accessible campsites
18-foot trailers; 24-foot motor homes
5 environmental campsites
3 rustic cabins*
group camping area** (50)
picnicking
fishing
swimming
hiking & bicycle trails
horseback riding trails
supplies
interpretive talks for groups*
guided tours in summer
museum exhibits on hydraulic mining
state historic landmark

*Phone park for reservations.
**On state park reservation system.

Martis Creek Lake

For Information

Martis Creek Lake
P.O. Box 6
Smartville, CA 95977-0006
916/639-2342

Location

Martis Creek Lake is located on Martis Creek about 2 miles above where it meets with the Truckee River, and about 5 miles southeast of Truckee on Highway 267. It nestles in the high Sierra, close to Lake Tahoe's north shore. The lake is kept at minimum pool to provide space for flood protection in the Truckee River Basin. The Martis Creek area features exciting trout fishing in the lake and surrounding streams.

Lake Statistics

71-acre surface area
2 miles long
3 miles of shoreline

Special Notes

Martis Creek Lake is the only lake in the California Fish and Game Commission designated "wild trout" management program. Impoundment of water inundated a stream system that was an important spawning area for Lahontan Cutthroat from the Truckee River. The watershed has been chemically treated and replanted with Lahontan Cutthroat. A 1,050-acre wildlife management area has been set aside to preserve as much land as possible in its natural state for wildlife study and appreciation.

Facilities & Activities

25 campsites at Alpine Meadow
  2 wheelchair accessible campsites*
  flush toilets/showers
  amphitheater
day-use area at Sierra View
  6 picnic sites
  no drinking water/vault toilets
day-use Wildlife Area
  picnicking
  no drinking water/vault toilets
swimming
fishing (catch & release in lake)
boating (non-motorized)
no boat-launching ramp
hiking trail at Wildlife Management Area
cross-country skiing

---

*May be reserved.

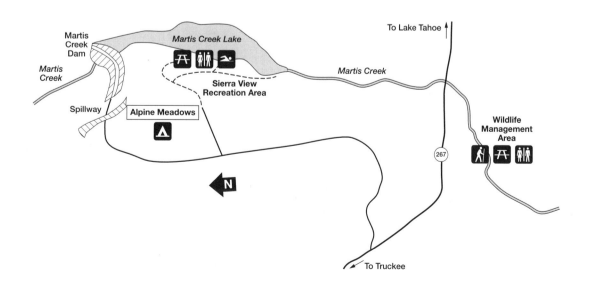

REGION 3

New Hogan Lake

For Information

New Hogan Lake
2713 Hogan Dam Road
Valley Springs, CA 95252-9510
209/772-1343

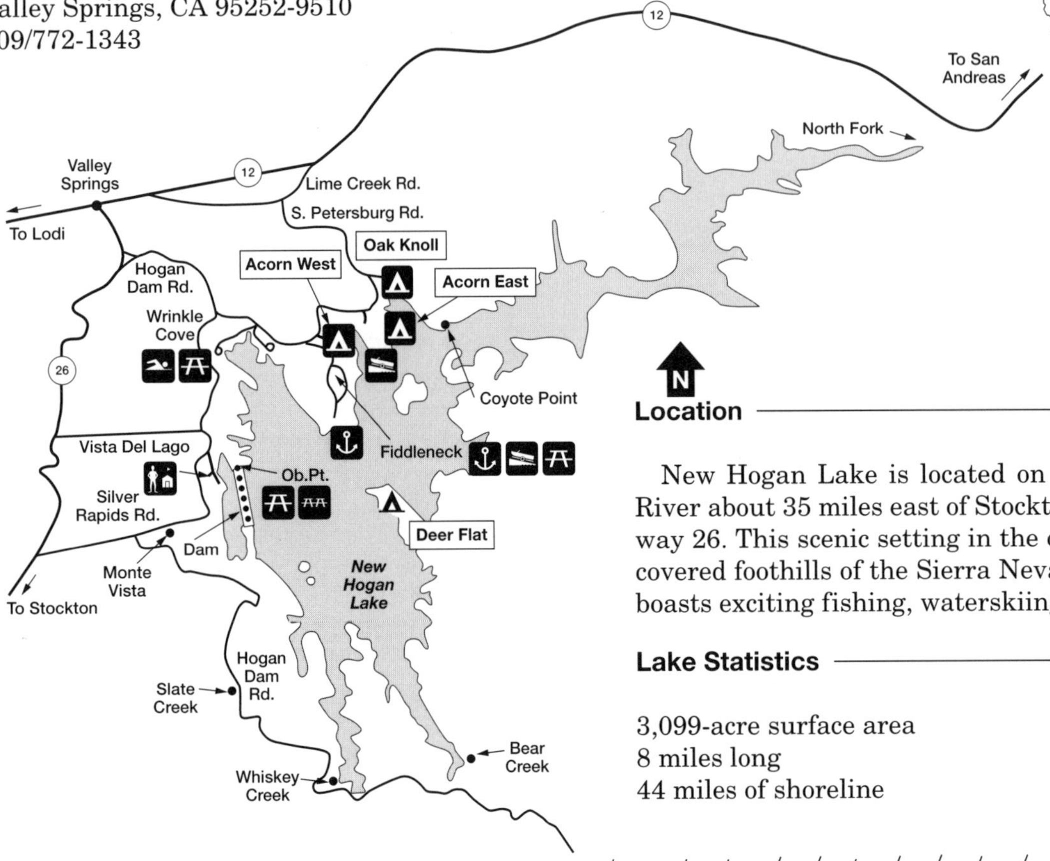

Location

New Hogan Lake is located on the Calaveras River about 35 miles east of Stockton, off of Highway 26. This scenic setting in the oak and brush-covered foothills of the Sierra Nevada Mountains boasts exciting fishing, waterskiing, and hiking.

Lake Statistics

3,099-acre surface area
8 miles long
44 miles of shoreline

Recreation Areas	Total Number of Campsites	Group Camping Area	Toilets (Flush/Vault)	Showers	Trailer Dump Station	Picnic Sites	Group Picnic Areas	Boat Launching Ramp	Swimming Area/Beach	Fishing Access	Hiking Trails
Acorn (East & West)	129		F	•	•			•		•	
Deer Flat* (Boat-in)	30		V								
Fiddleneck†			F/V			•		•		•	•
Oak Knoll	50	•	V		•					•	
Observation Point			F			•	•			•	
Wrinkle Cove			V			•			•	•	

Notes:
*Deer Flat Campground (boat-in) is open May–Sept.; register at Acorn West.
†Fiddleneck has a marina.
Monte Vista is the staging area for an 8-mile equestrian trail.
Bear Creek, Monte Vista, North Fork, & Whiskey Creek have fishing access.
North Fork & Monte Vista have hiking trails.

Plumas-Eureka State Park

For Information

Plumas-Eureka State Park
310 Johnsville Road
Blairsden, CA 96103
916/836-2380

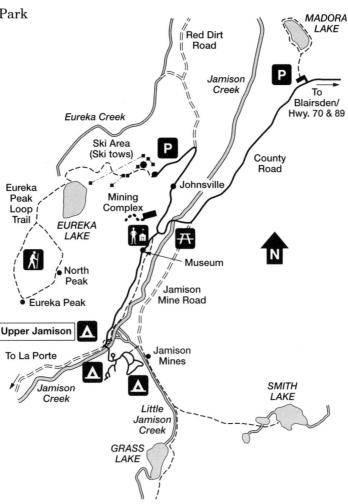

Location

Five miles west of Blairsden on County Road A-14, Plumas-Eureka State Park is high on the east slopes of the Sierra Nevada 80 miles north of Lake Tahoe. The 6,749-acre park sits amid spectacular mountain scenery in the headwaters country of the Yuba and Feather rivers. The elevation is 5,175 feet.

Special Notes

The park's high mountain location means lots of cold and snow during the winter; it is an early winter sports center—a delightful place for family snow-play and skiing. A ski-lift is operated in the Eureka Bowl. The campground is closed after about October 1. However, the park's headquarters and mining history museum remain open throughout the year; pioneer life in this hardrock mining area is displayed. Reservations can be made for interpretive talks for groups.

Facilities & Activities

67 developed campsites
wheelchair accessible campsites
showers
24-foot trailers; 30-foot campers
picnicking
fishing
nature & hiking trails
cross country/downhill skiing
interpretive talks for groups*
museum on mining & pioneer life
visitor center
state historic landmark

---

*Phone park for reservations.

REGION 3

Plumas National Forest

For Information

Supervisor's Office
Plumas National Forest
159 Lawrence Street
P.O. Box 11500
Quincy, CA 95971
916/283-2050

Location

Plumas National Forest, with a total acreage of 1,146,900 acres, is situated in the area where the Sierra Nevada and the Cascade ranges blend together and encompasses nearly all of the Feather River drainage system. The terrain is mountainous, rugged, and exceedingly steep in some places. The forest, ranging in elevation from 1,000 feet to 8,372 feet, is cut by deep canyons, with large grassy valleys interspersed in the rugged terrain.

Special Notes

Areas of interest in the Plumas National Forest include the Middle Fork of the Feather River, designated a part of the National Wild and Scenic River System; Feather Falls, the sixth highest waterfall in the continental United States, located in the Feather Falls Scenic Area; and Lakes Basin, containing over 50 jewel-like lakes tucked away in granite pockets—a favorite hiking area in the forest.

Five large reservoirs offer camping, swimming, waterskiing, boating, and fishing. Generally, fee campgrounds are open from April through October. Those at higher elevations open in mid to late May. Fees are charged at campgrounds having a developed water system, maintained restrooms, and garbage collection. Water from springs, lakes, ponds, and streams should be properly treated before drinking.

The Middle Fork of the Feather River consists of two Wild River Zones, two Scenic River Zones, and a Recreational River Zone. The Wild Zones are extremely treacherous and are not for the inexperienced. These contain a deep canyon with numerous large boulders, narrow steep canyon walls, and some impassable waterfalls. Rafting and canoeing are feasible in some of the Scenic and Recreation Zones in the spring. By early July, flows are low enough so that innertubes are the usual mode for short float trips in these areas. The Feather River, below Oroville, and the Sacramento River do provide opportunities for extended trips. Obtain specific information on the zones from the Forest Service.

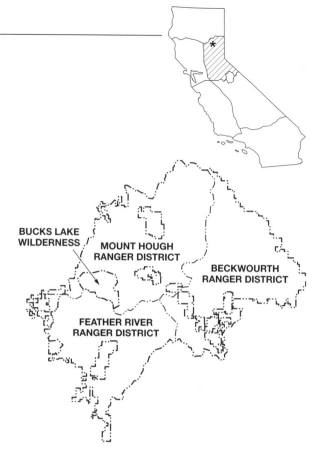

Wilderness Area

Located in the northwestern portion of the forest, the 21,000-acre **Bucks Lake Wilderness** is an area of broad diversity of vegetation and topography. Elevation ranges from 2,000 feet in the Feather River Canyon to the 7,017-foot Spanish Peak and includes areas of gentle slopes, steep canyons, and sheer cliffs. The Pacific Crest Trail traverses the top of the escarpment; Mt. Lassen is visible on clear days.

Five large reservoirs in the Plumas National Forest offer camping, so campsites near the water are plentiful.

Plumas National Forest *(continued)*

Feather River Ranger District

For Information

Feather River Ranger District
875 Mitchell Ave.
Oroville, CA 95965-4699
916/532-1210

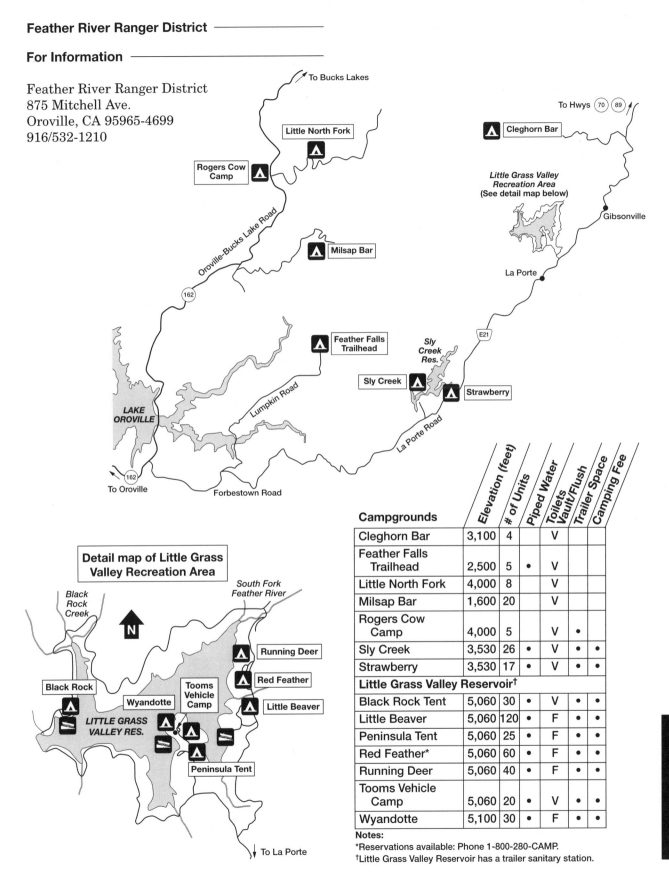

Campgrounds	Elevation (feet)	# of Units	Piped Water	Toilets Vault/Flush	Trailer Space	Camping Fee
Cleghorn Bar	3,100	4		V		
Feather Falls Trailhead	2,500	5	•	V		
Little North Fork	4,000	8		V		
Milsap Bar	1,600	20		V		
Rogers Cow Camp	4,000	5		V	•	
Sly Creek	3,530	26	•	V	•	•
Strawberry	3,530	17	•	V	•	•
Little Grass Valley Reservoir[†]						
Black Rock Tent	5,060	30	•	V	•	•
Little Beaver	5,060	120	•	F	•	•
Peninsula Tent	5,060	25	•	F	•	•
Red Feather*	5,060	60	•	F	•	•
Running Deer	5,060	40	•	F	•	•
Tooms Vehicle Camp	5,060	20	•	V	•	•
Wyandotte	5,100	30	•	F	•	•

Notes:
*Reservations available: Phone 1-800-280-CAMP.
[†]Little Grass Valley Reservoir has a trailer sanitary station.

REGION 3

Plumas National Forest *(continued)*

Beckwourth Ranger District ————————————

For Information ————————————

Beckwourth Ranger District
23 Mohawk Highway Rd.
P.O. Box 7
Blairsden, CA 96103
916/836-2575

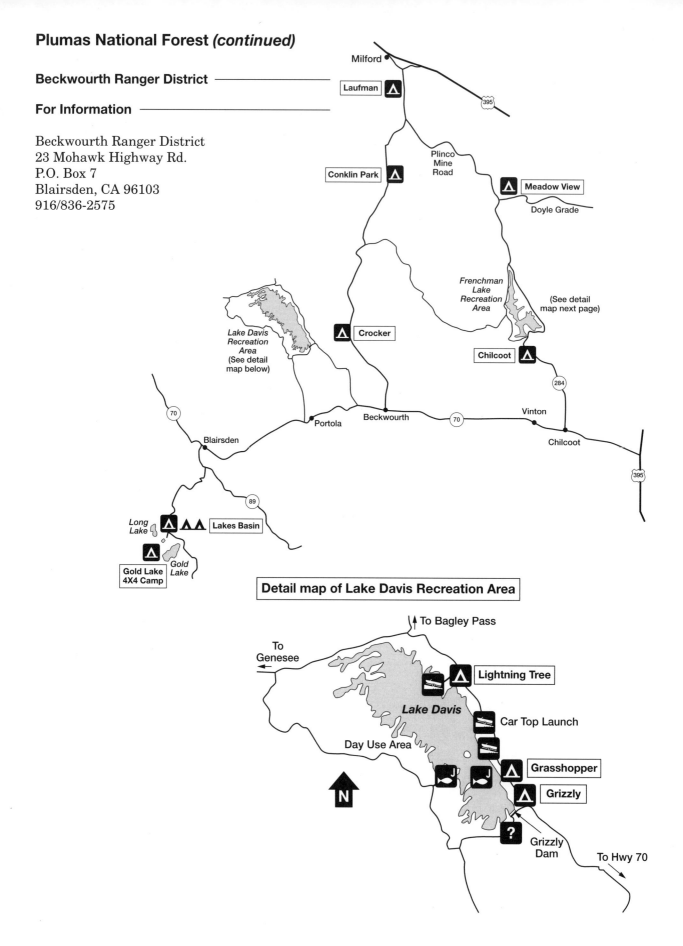

Milford

Laufman

395

Plinco
Mine
Road

Conklin Park

Meadow View

Doyle Grade

*Frenchman
Lake
Recreation
Area*

(See detail
map next page)

*Lake Davis
Recreation
Area*
(See detail
map below)

Crocker

Chilcoot

284

70

Blairsden

Portola

Beckwourth

70

Vinton

Chilcoot

395

89

*Long
Lake*

Lakes Basin

Gold Lake
4X4 Camp

*Gold
Lake*

Detail map of Lake Davis Recreation Area

↑ To Bagley Pass

To
Genesee

Lightning Tree

Lake Davis

Car Top Launch

Day Use Area

Grasshopper

N

Grizzly

?

Grizzly
Dam

To Hwy 70

Plumas National Forest (continued)

Water activities are plentiful in the Plumas National Forest. In addition to fishing, boating, and waterskiing on the lakes, the Middle Fork of the Feather River is designated a part of the National Wild and Scenic River system.

Campgrounds	Elevation (feet)	# of Units	Piped Water	Toilets Vault/Flush	Trailer Space	Camping Fee
Chilcoot*	5,400	40	•	F	•	•
Conklin Park	5,900	9		V	•	
Crocker	5,800	10		V	•	
Gold Lake 4x4 Camp	6,250	6		V		
Lakes Basin*	6,400	24	•	V	•	•
Lakes Basin Group*†	6,400	1	•	V		•
Laufman	5,100	6		V	•	
Meadow View	6,100	6		V	•	
Frenchman Lake Recreation Area*						
Big Cove	5,700	38	•	F	•	•
Cottonwood Springs	5,700	20	•	F	•	•
Cottonwood Group*†	5,700	2	•	F	•	•
Frenchman	5,700	38	•	V	•	•
Spring Creek	5,700	35	•	V	•	•
Lake Davis Recreation Area*						
Grasshopper Flat	5,800	70	•	F	•	•
Grizzly	5,800	55	•	F	•	•
Lightning Tree**	5,800	38		V	•	

Notes:

*Reservations are available. Phone: 1-800-280-CAMP. Five of the campsites at Chilcoot are walk-in for tent camps only.

†Lakes Basin Group & Cottonwood Group are available by reservation only. Capacity for group camps: Cottonwood—25 & 50; Lakes Basin—20.

**Lightning Tree is a self-contained RV campground.

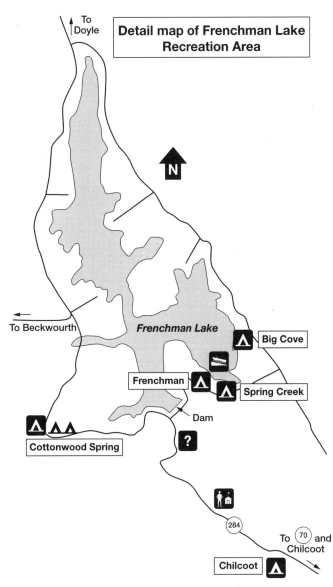

Detail map of Frenchman Lake Recreation Area

To Doyle

N

To Beckwourth

Frenchman Lake

Big Cove

Frenchman

Spring Creek

Dam

Cottonwood Spring

284

To 70 and Chilcoot

Chilcoot

Mount Hough Ranger District

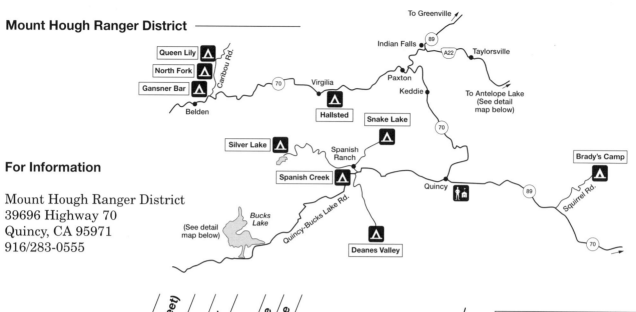

For Information

Mount Hough Ranger District
39696 Highway 70
Quincy, CA 95971
916/283-0555

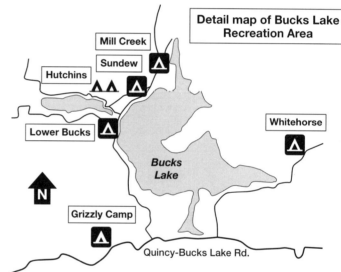

Detail map of Bucks Lake Recreation Area

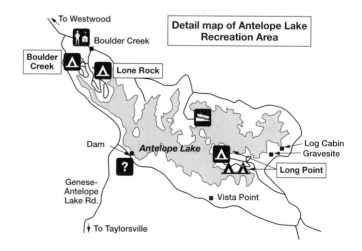

Detail map of Antelope Lake Recreation Area

Campgrounds	Elevation (feet)	# of Units	Piped Water	Toilets Vault/Flush	Trailer Space	Camping Fee
Antelope Lake Recreation Area*						
Boulder Creek	5,000	70	•	V	•	•
Lone Rock	5,000	86	•	V	•	•
Long Point	5,000	38	•	V	•	•
Long Point Group*	5,000	4	•	V	•	
Bucks Lake Recreation Area						
Grizzly Creek	5,400	8		V	•	•
Hutchins Group Camp*†	5,100	3	•	V	•	•
Lower Bucks**	5,000	6			•	•
Mill Creek	5,100	10	•	V	•	•
Sundew	5,100	19	•	V	•	•
Whitehorse	5,200	20	•	V	•	•
Campgrounds Off of State Highway 70						
Brady's Camp	7,200	4		V		
Deanes Valley	4,400	7		V	•	
Gansner Bar	2,300	14	•	F	•	•
Hallsted*	2,800	7	•	F	•	•
North Fork	2,600	20	•	F	•	•
Queen Lily	2,600	12	•	F	•	•
Silver Lake	5,800	8		V		
Snake Lake	4,200	7		V		
Spanish Creek	3,200	19		V	•	

Notes:

*Reservations required for Long Point Group; reservations available for others. Phone: 1-800-280-CAMP.

†Hutchins Group Camp has a 25-person/8-vehicle max. per site.

**Lower Bucks is for self-contained RVs only.

Stanislaus National Forest

For Information

Supervisor's Office
Stanislaus National Forest
19777 Greenley Road
Sonora, CA 95370
209/532-3671

Location

The Stanislaus National Forest, located in the high Sierra Nevada mountain country of central California, contains 1,090,039 acres located between the Mokelumne and Merced rivers. The forest is located in Gold Rush Country and is rich in early California history; it was named for the Stanislaus River, whose headwaters rise within its boundaries. Elevation ranges from 1,100 to 11,675 feet.

Special Notes

The Stanislaus National Forest has deep canyons cut by the Merced, Tuolumne, Stanislaus, and Mokelumne rivers. Portions of the Merced and Tuolumne rivers are designated as "wild and scenic." Rafting season usually extends May through October. Good fishing exists along the 810 miles of streams and on the 7,000 surface acres of lakes.

Most developed campgrounds offer running water. However, remote sites without water will require visitors to bring their own. Water taken from nearby rivers and streams should be boiled prior to consumption. Most campgrounds are operated on a first-come, first-served basis; however, a few reservation campgrounds are available. Many of the campgrounds are operated by a concessionaire; they are indicated with an asterisk (*) on the facility charts.

The forest has almost 1,000 miles of trails; about 400 miles are suitable for horseback riding. There is an off-road vehicle plan to allow 4-wheel-drive vehicles, motorcycles, and snowmobiles in designated areas. There are two ski resorts in the forest: Mt. Reba/Bear Valley, via Highway 4 on the Calaveras Ranger District, and Dodge Ridge, via Highway 108 on the Summit Ranger District. Cross-country ski trails of varying difficulty are near Pinecrest on the Summit District and near Bear Valley. Snowmobiling is also popular at several locations along Highways 4 and 108.

Wilderness Areas

Permits are required for all travel into the wilderness from May 25 through September 15. Permits are free and may be obtained from the appropriate ranger district office: Calaveras Ranger District for Mokelumne south side entry, and Carson-Iceberg wilderness areas; and Summit Ranger District for Carson-Iceberg west side entry, and Emigrant wilderness areas. The best travel times are usually mid-June through October.

The **Emigrant Wilderness** spans 112,277 acres, with broad expanses of glaciated granite, towering lava-capped peaks, numerous alpine lakes, and deep granite-walled canyons. The area is usually snow free from July through September. Elevations range from 5,200 feet near Cherry Bluffs to 11,570 feet at the top of Leavitt Peak.

The **Carson-Iceberg Wilderness** is primarily sandwiched between Highways 4 and 108; it contains 158,900 acres, of which 77,993 acres are situated on the Stanislaus. The other portion is located on the Toiyabe National Forest. The topography is varied, with 12 prominent peaks exceeding 12,000 feet elevation and many more exceeding 9,000 feet. Rugged granite peaks and boulders, steep ridges and narrow valleys are typical. There are about 100 miles of trails within the wilder-

Stanislaus National Forest *(continued)*

ness area, including a 22-mile section of the Pacific Crest National Scenic Trail.

The **Mokelumne Wilderness** contains, 100,600 acres, of which 22,267 acres are situated on the Stanislaus. The other portions are on the Eldorado and Toiyabe national forests. Mokelumne River bisects this rugged remote area. Elevations range from 4,000 feet in the west to 10,000 feet in the east. Mokelumne River Canyon is extremely rugged. The Pacific Crest Trail and the Emigrant Summit National Trail cross the area. Water may be scarce late in the summer.

Calaveras Ranger District

For Information

Calaveras Ranger District
P.O. Box 500
Hathaway Pines, CA 95233
209/795-1381

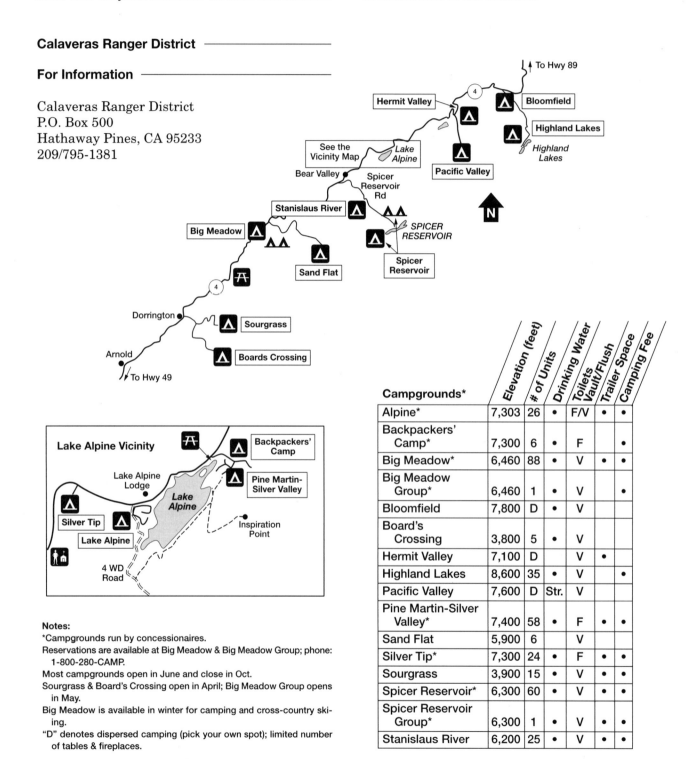

Notes:

*Campgrounds run by concessionaires.

Reservations are available at Big Meadow & Big Meadow Group; phone: 1-800-280-CAMP.

Most campgrounds open in June and close in Oct.

Sourgrass & Board's Crossing open in April; Big Meadow Group opens in May.

Big Meadow is available in winter for camping and cross-country skiing.

"D" denotes dispersed camping (pick your own spot); limited number of tables & fireplaces.

Campgrounds*	Elevation (feet)	# of Units	Drinking Water	Toilets Vault/Flush	Trailer Space	Camping Fee
Alpine*	7,303	26	•	F/V	•	•
Backpackers' Camp*	7,300	6	•	F		•
Big Meadow*	6,460	88	•	V	•	•
Big Meadow Group*	6,460	1	•	V	•	•
Bloomfield	7,800	D	•	V		
Board's Crossing	3,800	5	•	V		
Hermit Valley	7,100	D		V	•	
Highland Lakes	8,600	35	•	V		•
Pacific Valley	7,600	D	Str.	V		
Pine Martin-Silver Valley*	7,400	58	•	F	•	•
Sand Flat	5,900	6		V		
Silver Tip*	7,300	24	•	F	•	•
Sourgrass	3,900	15	•	V	•	•
Spicer Reservoir*	6,300	60	•	V	•	•
Spicer Reservoir Group*	6,300	1	•	V	•	•
Stanislaus River	6,200	25	•	V	•	•

Stanislaus National Forest *(continued)*

Groveland Ranger District

For Information

Groveland Ranger District
24545 Old Highway 120
Groveland, CA 95321
209/962-7825

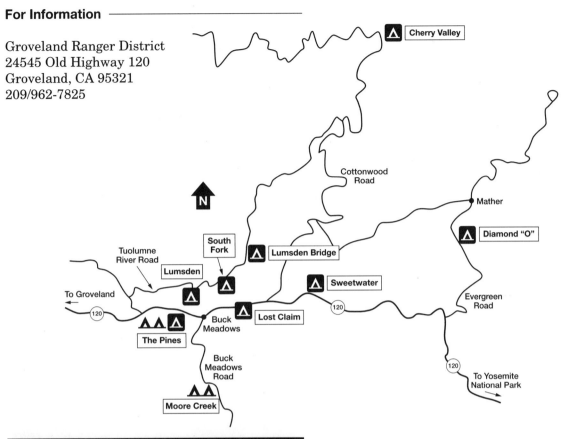

Lake Alpine, which is about a mile long, is but one of many lakes and reservoirs in the Stanislaus National Forest. (Photo: California Office of Tourism)

Campgrounds	Elevation (feet)	# of Units	Drinking Water	Vault Toilets	Trailer Space	Camping Fee
Cherry Valley*	4,700	46	•	•	•	•
Diamond "O"	4,400	38	•	•	•	•
Lost Claim*	3,100	10	•	•	•	•
Lumsden	1,500	11		•		
Lumsden Bridge	1,500	9		•		
Moore Creek Group	2,800	1		•		
South Fork	1,500	8		•		
Sweetwater*	4,700	13	•	•	•	•
The Pines*	3,200	12	•	•	•	•
The Pines Group*	3,200	1	•	•	•	•

Notes:
*Campgrounds run by concessionaires.
Campgrounds open in April/May and close in Oct./Nov.
Lumsden Campground is open year-round.
Reservations for Moore Creek Group are available through Groveland R.D. office; capacity is 75.

REGION 3

Stanislaus National Forest *(continued)*

Mi-Wok and Summit Ranger Districts

For Information

Mi-Wok Ranger District
P.O. Box 100
Mi-Wuk Village, CA 95346
209/586-3234

Summit Ranger District
No. 1 Pinecrest Lake Road
Pinecrest, CA 95364
209/965-3372

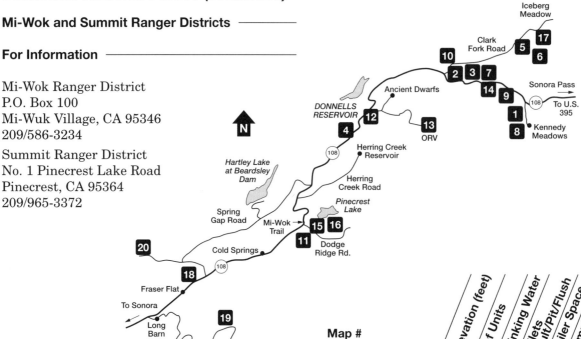

Map # Campgrounds	Elevation (feet)	# of Units	Drinking Water	Toilets Vault/Pit/Flush	Trailer Space	Camping Fee
Summit Ranger District						
1—Baker*	6,200	44	•	V	•	•
2—Boulder Flat*	5,600	23	•	V	•	•
3—Brightman Flat*	5,600	30		V	•	•
4—Cascade Creek	6,000	12		V	•	
5—Clark Fork*	6,200	88	•	V/F	•	•
6—Clark Fork Horse Camp	6,200	12		P	•	•
7—Dardanelle*	5,600	28	•	V	•	•
8—Deadman*	6,200	17	•	V/F	•	•
9—Eureka Valley*	6,100	27		V	•	•
10—Fence Creek	6,100	30		P	•	
11—Meadowview*	5,600	100	•	F		•
12—Mill Creek	6,200	17		V	•	•
13—Niagara Creek	6,600	7		V	•	•
13—Niagara OHV	6,600	10		V	•	
14—Pigeon Flat (walk-in)*	6,000	7		V		•
15—Pinecrest*	5,600	200	•	F	•	•
16—Pioneer Trail Group*	5,700	3	•	V		•
17—Sand Flat*	6,200	53	•	V	•	•
Mi-Wok Ranger District						
18—Fraser Flat*	4,800	38	•	V	•	•
19—Hull Creek	5,600	16	•	V	•	•
20—Sand Bar Flat	3,000	10	•	V		•

Notes:
*Campgrounds run by concessionaires.
Campgrounds open in May and close in Sept. or Oct.
Winter camping is permitted at Hull Creek.
Reservations are available at Pinecrest, Pioneer Trail Group, &
    Dardanelle; phone: 1-800-280-CAMP.

*There are two ski resorts in the forest: Mt. Reba/Bear
Valley, via Highway 4, and Dodge Ridge, via Highway 108.
Start 'em young . . . they love it! (Photo: California Office
of Tourism)*

Stanislaus River Parks

For Information

Stanislaus River Parks
P.O. Box 1229
Oakdale, CA 95361-1229
209/881-3517

Location

The Stanislaus River is located in central California and crosses Highway 99 six miles north of Modesto. The lower Stanislaus runs from Goodwin Dam to the San Joaquin River, a distance of about 59 miles. Highways 108 from Sonora and 120 from Yosemite National Park run alongside the river for quite a distance. The river passes through steep canyons near Goodwin Dam into rolling foothills at Knights Ferry; then the river widens and slows into the flatlands of the San Joaquin Valley.

Special Notes

Stanislaus River Parks comprise a unique system of river parks providing boat-in camping and picnicking facilities to rafters and canoeists traveling on the lower Stanislaus River. The 4 miles of rapids between Goodwin Dam and Knights Ferry are classified for expert rafters and kayakers only. Canoeists should stick to the river below Knights Ferry to where the Stanislaus meets the San Joaquin River; this section is a mixture of mild rapids and placid waters that offer a more leisurely ride.

There are 7 developed parks and 9 parks with little or no development along this 59-mile stretch of the river. Boat-in camping is permitted in designated campgrounds at 3 recreation areas: Horseshoe Road, Valley Oak, and McHenry Avenue. Free permits are required and may be obtained by mail or picked up in person at the Knights Ferry Information Center. Phone reservations are taken. No drinking water is available at Horseshoe Road. Individual sites are available on a first-come, first-served basis. Each boat-in camping area has 1 group site with a maximum capacity of 25; phone the park to reserve them.

The U.S. Army Corps of Engineers also welcomes you to its information center in Knights Ferry. The town boasts one of the few remaining historic covered bridges in California. At 330 feet, it is the longest covered bridge west of the Mississippi River. Exhibits at the information center near the bridge describe the Stanislaus River and its history; a short film introduces you to the Stanislaus River Parks.

Stanislaus River Parks comprise a unique system of parks providing boat-in camping and picnicking to rafters and canoeists. (Photo: California Office of Tourism)

Stanislaus River Parks *(continued)*

Recreation Areas	Parking	Picnicking/Grills	Group Picnic Area	Drinking Water	Restroom	Boat Access/Camping	Group Camping Areas	Kayaking	Canoe Put-In/Take-Out	Hiking	Park Office/Information Center
1—Goodwin Dam	No Facilities Available										
2—Two-Mile Bar	•				•			•		•	
3—Knights Ferry	•	•	•	•	•			•	•	•	•
4—Lover's Leap	No Facilities Available										
5—Horseshoe Road	•				•	16	1		•	•	
6—Honolulu Bar	•	•			•				•	•	
7—Buttonbush	No Facilities Available										
8—Orange Blossom	•	•	•	•	•				•	•	
9—Valley Oak	•	•		•	•	10	1		•	•	
10—Oakdale	•				•				•	•	
11—Riverbank	No Facilities Available										
12—Jacob Meyers	•									•	
13—McHenry Avenue	•	•	•	•	•	19	1		•	•	

Notes: All recreation areas provide fishing access.

The four miles of rapids between Goodwin Dam and Knights Ferry are classified for expert rafters and kayakers only. (Photo: California Office of Tourism)

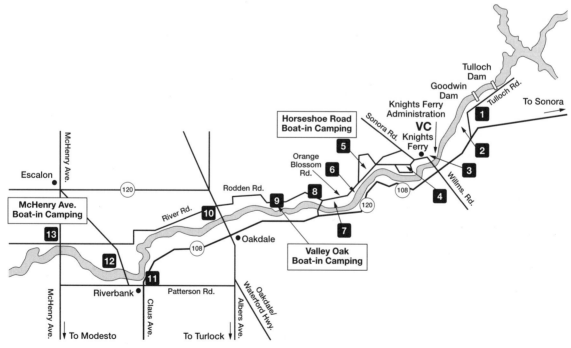

Sugar Pine Point State Park

For Information

Sugar Pine Point State Park
P.O. Box 266
Tahoma, CA 96142-0266
916/525-7982

Location

Sugar Pine Point, a gently sloping, beautifully forested promontory on the western side of Lake Tahoe, is located 10 miles south of Tahoe City on Highway 89; it has an elevation of 6,250 feet. The 2,011-acre park extends 3½ miles into the General Creek watershed to the west and includes 1¾ miles of frontage on Lake Tahoe.

Facilities* & Activities

175 developed campsites
showers in summer only
24-foot trailers; 30-foot campers
trailer sanitation station
30 enroute campsites
10 group camps (400)
picnicking
fishing
swimming
nature & hiking trails
bicycle trails
cross country ski trail
nature center open in summer (noon to 4:00)
exhibits/visitor center
state historic landmark

*On state park reservation system.

Special Notes

This park is the only state park in the lake basin that keeps its campground open year-round. Considerable forethought and good camping equipment are important during the winter because conditions include frequent snow storms and deep snow pack. The park is a popular jumping-off place for the High Sierra backcountry west of Lake Tahoe, including the northerly part of the Desolation Wilderness Area.

The park's half-mile sandy beach and central pier are popular places; due to space limitations, boats may not be moored or beached overnight. In the developed area south of General Creek are several historic buildings including a pioneer-built, hand-hewn log cabin and an elegant summer home, the Ehrman Mansion.

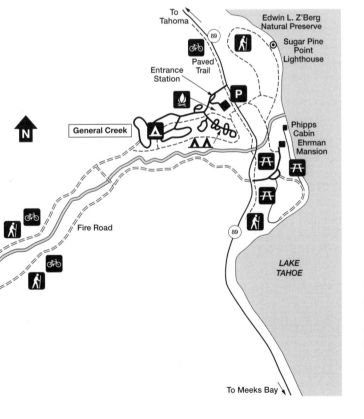

Tahoe National Forest

For Information

Supervisor's Office
Tahoe National Forest
631 Coyote Street
P.O. Box 6003
Nevada City, CA 95959
916/265-4531

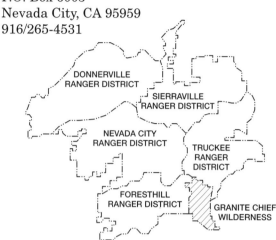

Location

The Tahoe National Forest is located northeast of Sacramento in the central portion of the Sierra Nevada Mountains and extends from Lake Tahoe to north of the prominent Sierra Buttes. Elevations vary from about 1,500 feet in the foothills to more than 9,000 feet at the Sierra Crest within a relatively short distance. Within the boundaries of the Tahoe National Forest, roughly 800,000 acres are public lands and 400,000 acres are privately owned.

Special Notes

The Tahoe National Forest offers a unique combination of scenic beauty and attractive climate that has made it an outstanding outdoor recreation area. The climate on the eastern side of the forest reflects the desert influence and is subject to seasonal extremes in temperature. There is a more moderate climate on the Pacific slope.

The forest has about 550 miles of trails for hiking, horseback riding, trail biking, cross-country skiing, and 4-WD vehicles; an additional 250 miles of trails are provided for snowmobiling. There are four winter sports sites available on forest land—Alpine Meadows, Boreal Ridge, Powder Bowl, and

The Tahoe National Forest has about 550 miles of trails for hiking, horseback riding, and trail biking. These same trails are available in the winter for cross-country skiing.

Sugar Bowl—and twice as many private ski areas, such as Squaw Valley and Soda Springs.

The main camping season is from Memorial Day to Labor Day. Although some campgrounds remain open after the regular season, water systems are shut down to prevent freeze damage. Many of the campgrounds use river, stream, or lake water; campers should remember to purify the water before drinking.

Wilderness Areas

Granite Chief Wilderness is a remote alpine area characterized by steep, rugged ridges and barren peaks. Below these towering landforms lie picturesque glaciated valleys. Elevations range from 5,000-foot valleys to 9,000-foot peaks. Many streams and a few lakes are scattered through the area; water is usually available year-round in the major creeks. The Pacific Crest Trail runs north and south through the area near its eastern border. This 25,700-acre wilderness is shared with Eldorado National Forest, and Lake Tahoe Basin Management Unit.

Tahoe National Forest *(continued)*

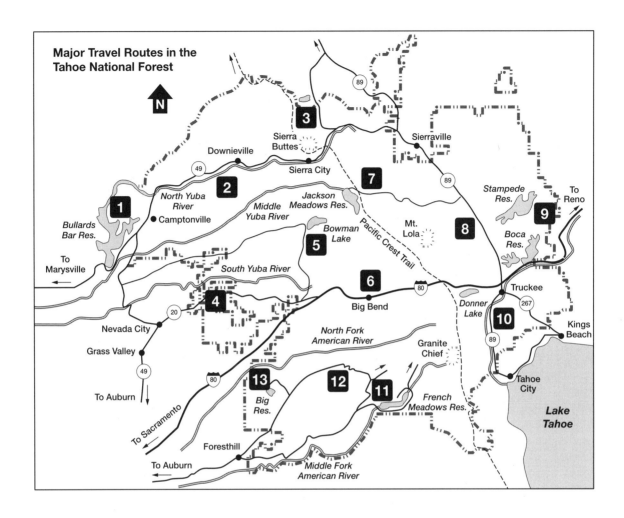

Major Travel Routes in the Tahoe National Forest

Ranger Districts

Downieville Ranger District
Map #1—Bullards Bar Reservoir Area
Map #2—Highway 49 (Middle Yuba & North
    Yuba Rivers)
Map #3—Sierra Buttes-Gold Lake Highway

Nevada City Ranger District
Map #4—Highway 20 (South Yuba River)
Map #5—Bowman Road Area (Grouse Ridge-
    Bowman Lake)
Map #6—Interstate 80 Area

Sierraville Ranger District
Map #7—Jackson Meadow Reservoir Area

Sierraville & Truckee Ranger Districts
Map #8—Highway 89 (Sierraville to Truckee)

Truckee Ranger District
Map #9— Stampede and Boca Reservoir Area
Map #10—Truckee River Corridor

Foresthill Ranger District
Map #11—French Meadows Reservoir Area
Map #12—Foresthill Divide-Big Reservoir Area
Map #13—Sugar Pine Reservoir Area

Tahoe National Forest (continued)

Downieville Ranger District

For Information

Downieville Ranger District
North Yuba Ranger Station
15924 Highway 49
Camptonville, CA 95922-9707
916/478-6253

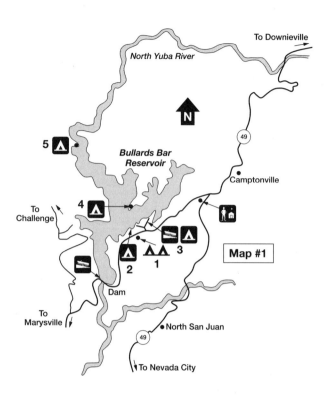

Map #1

Campgrounds	Elevation (feet)	# of Units	Drinking Water	Toilets Vault/Flush	Trailer Space	Camping Fee
Map #1—Bullards Bar Reservoir Area						
1—Hornswoggle Group*	2,200	5	•	F/V		•
2—Schoolhouse*	2,200	67	•	F	•	•
3—Dark Day* (tent only)	2,000	16	•	V		•
4—Garden Point (boat access only)	2,000	16	Lake	V		•
5—Madrone Cove (boat access only)	2,000	10	Lake	V		•
Map #2—Highway 49 (Middle Yuba & North Yuba Rivers)						
6—Carlton Flat	1,500	30	•	V		•
7—Cal-Ida	2,200	20	•	V		•
8—Fiddle Creek (tent only)	2,200	13	•	V		•
9—Indian Valley	2,200	17	•	V	•	•
10—Rocky Rest	2,200	10	•	V		•
11—Ramshorn	2,600	16	•	V		•
12—Union Flat	3,400	14	•	V		•
13—Loganville	4,200	20	•	V	•	
14—Wild Plum	4,400	47	•	V	•	•
15—Sierra	5,600	16	Rvr.	V	•	
16—Chapman Creek	6,000	29	•	V	•	•
17—Yuba Pass	6,700	20	•	V		
Map #3—Sierra Buttes - Gold Lake Highway						
18—Sardine	5,800	29	•	V	•	•
19—Salmon Creek	5,800	31	•	V	•	•
20—Snag Lake	6,600	16	Lake	V	•	
21—Berger	5,900	10	Str.	V	•	
22—Diablo	5,800		Str.	V	•	
23—Packsaddle	6,000		Str.	V	•	

Notes:

*Reservations required for Hornswoggle Group; reservations
   available for Schoolhouse & Dark Day through Emerald
   Cove Marina. Phone: 916/692-3200.

Hornswoggle has four 25-person, & one 50-person group
   campsites.

Map #2

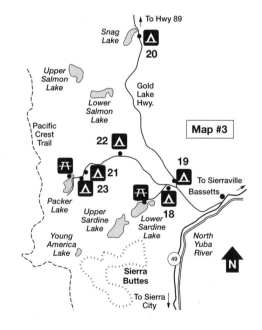

Map #3

Tahoe National Forest *(continued)*

Nevada City Ranger District ────────────────

For Information ────────────────────────

Nevada City Ranger District
631 Coyote Street
P.O. Box 6003
Nevada City, CA 95959
916/265-4531

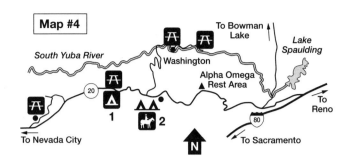

Map #4

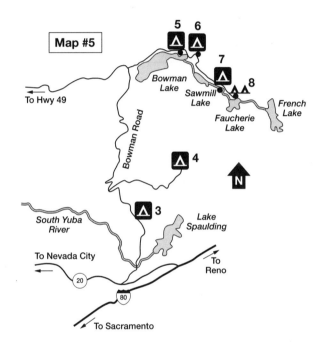

Map #5

Campgrounds	Elevation (feet)	# of Units	Drinking Water	Toilets Vault/Flush	Trailer Space	Camping Fee
Map #4—Highway 20 (South Yuba River)						
1—White Cloud	4,200	46	•	F/V	•	•
2—Skillman Group Equestrian*	4,400	1	•	V	•	•
Map #5—Bowman Road Area						
3—Fuller Lake walk-in, tent only	5,600	9	Lake	V		
4—Grouse Ridge	7,400	9		V	•	
5—Bowman Lake	5,565	7	Lake	V		
6—Jackson Creek	5,600	14	Str.	V		
7—Canyon Creek	6,000	20	Str.	V	•	
8—Faucherie Group*	6,000	1	Lake	V	•	•
Map #6—Interstate 80 Area						
9—North Fork	4,400	17	•	V	•	•
10—Tunnel Mill Group*	4,400	2	Str.	V		•
11—Indian Springs	5,600	35	•	V	•	•
12—Woodchuck (tent only)	6,300	8	Str.	V		
13—Lake Sterling	7,000	6	Lake	V		
14—Big Bend	5,900	15	•	V	•	•
15—Hampshire Rocks	5,800	31	•	V	•	•

Notes:
*Reservations required. Skillman: 209/295-4512; Faucherie & Tunnel Mill: 1-800-280-CAMP.
Group camp accommodations: Skillman, 16; Faucherie, 25; Tunnel Mill, 30 each site.

Map #6

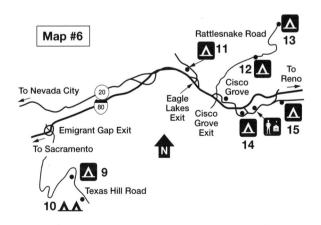

REGION 3

Tahoe National Forest (continued)

Sierraville Ranger District

For Information

Sierraville Ranger District
Highway 89
P.O. Box 95
Sierraville, CA 96126
916/994-3401

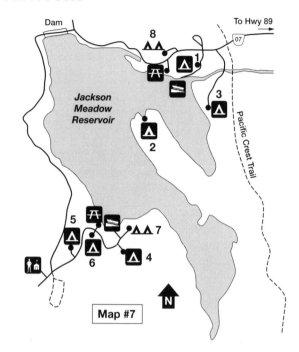

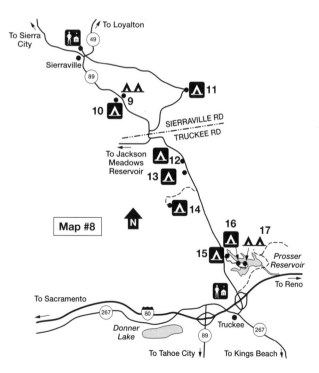

Campgrounds	Elevation (feet)	# of Units	Drinking Water	Toilets Vault/Flush	Trailer Space	Camping Fee
Map #7—Jackson Meadow Reservoir Area						
1—Pass Creek	6,100	30	•	V	•	•
2—Jackson Point (boat access only)	6,100	10	Lake	V		
3—East Meadow	6,100	48	•	F	•	•
4—Woodcamp	6,100	20	•	F	•	•
5—Findley	6,200	14	•	F	•	•
6—Fir Top	6,200	12	•	F		•
7—Silver Tip Group*	6,100	2	•	V		•
8—Aspen Group*	6,100	3	•	V		•
Map #8—Highway 89 (Sierraville to Truckee)						
9—Cottonwood Group*	5,800	1	•	V	•	•
10—Cold Creek	5,800	13	•	V	•	•
11—Bear Valley	6,700	10	•	V		•
12—Upper Little Truckee*	6,100	26	•	V	•	•
13—Lower Little Truckee*	6,000	15	•	V	•	•
14—Sagehen	6,500	10	Str.	V		
15—Lakeside	5,700	30	Lake	V	•	
16—Prosser	5,800	29	•	V		•
17—Prosser Group*	5,800	1	•	V	•	•

Notes:

*Reservations required. Cottonwood, Prosser, & Aspen:
1-800-280-CAMP; Silver Tip: 916/544-5994.

Reservations available at Upper Little Truckee & Lower Little
Truckee: 1-800-280-CAMP.

Capacity for group camps: Silver Tip, two 25-person; Aspen,
two 25-person, one 50-person; Cottonwood, 125; Prosser,
50.

Tahoe National Forest *(continued)*

Truckee Ranger District

For Information

Truckee Ranger District
10342 Highway 89 North
Truckee, CA 96161
916/478-6257

Campgrounds	Elevation (feet)	# of Units	Drinking Water	Toilets Vault/Flush	Trailer Space	Camping Fee
Map #9—Stampede and Boca Reservoir Area						
1—Boca	5,600	20	Lake	V	•	•
2—Boca Rest	5,700	25	•	V		•
3—Boca Spring	5,700	17	•	V		•
4—Boyington Mill	5,700	12	River	V	•	•
5—Emigrant Group*	6,000	4	•	V	•	•
6—Logger*	6,000	252	•	V	•	•
7—Davies Creek	6,000	7	Lake	V		
Map #10—Truckee River Corridor						
8—Granite Flat	5,800	75	•	V	•	•
9—Goose Meadows	5,800	25	•	V		•
10—Silver Creek	5,800	25	•	V	•	•

Notes:

*Reservations required for Emigrant Group Camp & available for Logger. Phone: 1-800-280-CAMP.

Emigrant Group Campground has two 25-person & two 50-person campsites.

Granite Flat & Silver Creek each have 7 walk-in campsites.

These backpackers are headed to the Granite Chief Wilderness—-a remote alpine area characterized by steep, rugged ridges and barren peaks.

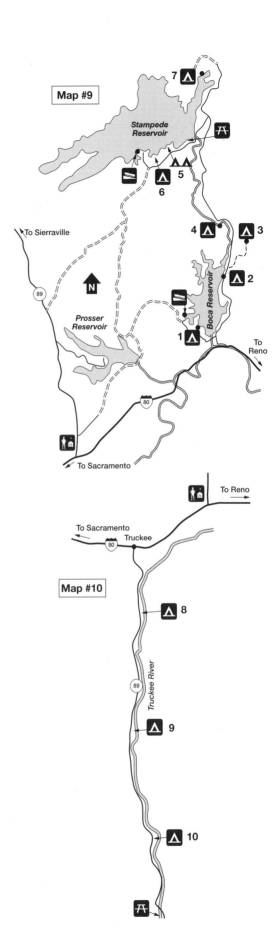

REGION 3

Tahoe National Forest   167

Tahoe National Forest *(continued)*

Foresthill Ranger District

For Information

Foresthill Ranger District
22830 Foresthill Road
Foresthill, CA 95631
916/367-2226

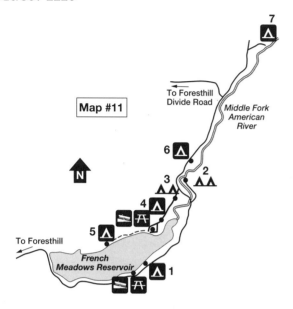

Campgrounds	Elevation (feet)	# of Units	Drinking Water	Toilets Vault/Flush	Trailer Space	Camping Fee
Map #11—French Meadows Reservoir Area						
1—French Meadows	5,300	75	•	F		•
2—Gates Group*	5,300	3	•	V		•
3—Coyote Group*	5,300	4	•	V/F		•
4—Lewis	5,300	40	•	F		•
5—Poppy	5,300	12	Lake	V		
6—Ahart	5,300	12	River	V		
7—Talbot	5,600	5	River	V		
Map #12—Foresthill Divide-Big Reservoir Area						
8—Big Reservoir	4,000	100	•	V	•	•
9—Secret House	5,400	2		V		
10—Robinson Flat	6,800	5	Str.	V		
Map #13—Sugar Pine Reservoir Area						
11—Forbes Creek Group*	3,500	2	•	V	•	•
12—Giant Gap	3,500	30	•	V	•	•
13—Shirttail Creek	3,500	30	•	V	•	•

Notes:

*Reservations required for Gates, Coyote & Forbes Creek Group. Phone 1-800-280-CAMP.

Capacity for group campgrounds: Gates, two 25-person, one 75-person; Coyote, three 25-person, one 50-person; Forbes, two 50-person.

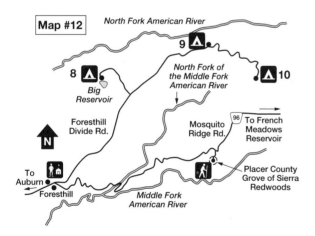

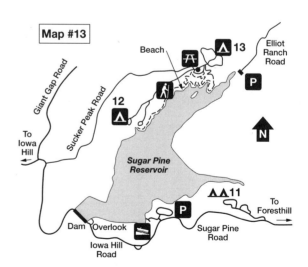

Tahoe State Recreation Area

For Information

Tahoe State Recreation Area
P.O. Box 266
Tahoma, CA 96142-0266
916/583-3074 (seasonal) or 525-7982

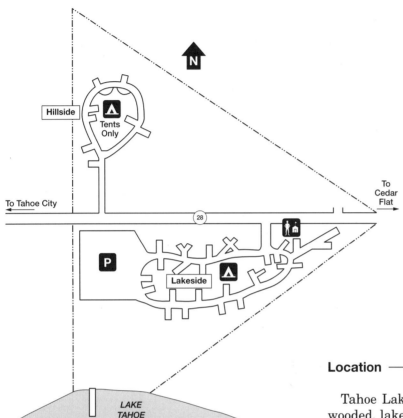

This recreation area is a small, wooded, lakeside campground located on the shore of Lake Tahoe.

Location

Tahoe Lake State Recreation Area is a small, wooded, lakeside, 57-acre campground located ¼-mile northeast of Tahoe City on Highway 28. On the shore of beautiful Lake Tahoe, the recreation area is 6,250 feet above sea level. The recreation area provides a lake frontage view and groves of ponderosa and Jeffrey pine. The 2 campgrounds—Lakeside and Hillside—are closed to camping October to mid-May.

Facilities* & Activities

28 developed campsites at Lakeside
   showers
   15-foot trailers; 21-foot campers
11 developed campsites at Hillside
   showers/tents only
picnicking
fishing
swimming
boating/boat mooring

*On state park reservation system.

Toiyabe National Forest

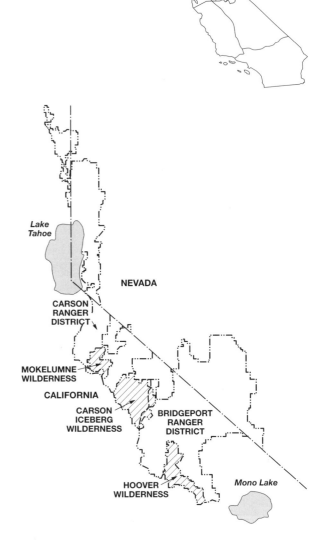

For Information

Supervisor's Office
1200 Franklin Way
Sparks, NV 89431
702/331-6444

Location

The Toiyabe National Forest has the largest land area of any national forest in the lower 48 states. It is scattered across central, south, and western Nevada in three distinct divisions. The Sierra Division stretches along the steep eastern slope of the Sierra Nevada Mountains, generally lying west of US 395 along the Nevada-California border. The acres of the forest within California, said to be approximately one million acres, are under the jurisdiction of two ranger districts—Carson and Bridgeport.

Special Notes

The Carson Ranger District straddles the border of California and Nevada in a strip about 15 miles wide and 96 miles long. The 45-mile section of the Pacific Crest National Scenic Trail, the Carson-Iceberg Wilderness and the Mokelumne Wilderness offer outstanding primitive recreational opportunities.

On the Bridgeport Ranger District you can sample the splendor of the High Sierra Mountains and the vastness of the Great Basin Area ranges. Camping opportunities vary from the popular developed sites to the solitude of the High Sierra wilderness and the undeveloped desert areas.

Wilderness Areas

The 80,971 acres of the **Carson-Iceberg Wilderness** on the Toiyabe National Forest is contiguous with another 78,000 acres of the wilderness on the Stanislaus National Forest. The Toiyabe portion of the wilderness is located on the east side of the Sierra Nevada Range between Highways 4 and 108. Elevations range from 6,500 feet along the East Carson River to numerous peaks in excess of 10,000 feet. Wilderness permits are required from May 25 through September 15.

The **Mokelumne Wilderness** consists of 100,600 acres in three National Forests—Eldorado, Stanislaus, and Toiyabe. The Mokelumne River bisects this rugged remote area, with eleva-

tions from 4,000 feet in the west to 10,000 feet in the east. East side entry into the wilderness is from Toiyabe National Forest; permits are required between May 25 and September 15. Water may be scarce late in the summer.

The **Hoover Wilderness** has more than 39,000 acres of the total 48,600-acre wilderness area in the Toiyabe National Forest. The area is extremely rugged with elevations from 8,000 to 14,000 feet. The best time to travel is July through September. South side entry is from Inyo National Forest and east side entry is from Toiyabe. Wilderness permits are required; quotas are in effect from the last Friday in June through September 15.

Toiyabe National Forest *(continued)*

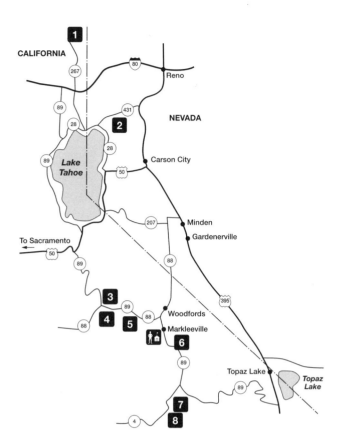

Bridgeport Ranger District

Bridgeport Ranger District
P.O. Box 595
Bridgeport, CA 93517
619/932-7070

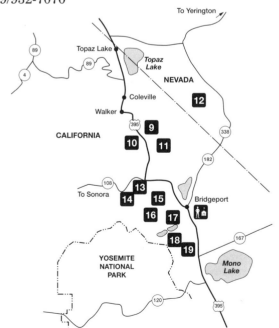

Carson Ranger District ——————

Carson Ranger District
1536 South Carson Street
Carson City, NV 89701
702/882-2766

	Campgrounds	Elevation (feet)	# of Units	Drinking Water	Toilets Vault/Flush	Trailer Space	Camping Fee
Carson Ranger District	1—Lookout	6,700	22	•	V	•	•
	1—Lookout Group	6,700	1	•	V		•
	1—Hunting Camp #2	6,200			V	•	
	1—Hunting Camp #4	6,400			V	•	
	2—Mt. Rose*	8,900	24	•	F	•	•
	3—Kit Carson	6,900	12	•	V	•	•
	4—Snowshoe Springs	6,600	13	•	V		•
	5—Crystal Springs	6,000	22	•	V	•	•
	6—Markleeville	5,500	10	•	V	•	•
	7—Silver Creek*	6,800	22	•	V	•	•
	8—Hope Valley*	7,300	20	•	V	•	•
	8—Hope Valley Group*	7,300	1			•	
Bridgeport Ranger District	9—Shingle Mill	6,500	90	•	V	•	•
	10—Bootleg*	6,600	63	•	F	•	•
	11—Chris Flat	6,600	15	•	V	•	•
	12—Desert Creek	6,300	13		V		
	13—Sonora Bridge*	6,800	23	•	V	•	•
	14—Leavitt Meadow	7,000	16	•	V	•	•
	15—Obsidian	7,800	14		V	•	•
	16—Buckeye	7,000	65	•	F	•	•
	16—Buckeye Group*	7,000	1	•	F	•	•
	17—Honeymoon Flat*	7,000	45	•	V	•	•
	17—Robinson Creek*	7,000	54	•	F	•	•
	17—Paha*	7,000	22	•	F	•	•
	17—Crags	7,000	27		F	•	•
	17—Lower Twin*	7,000	15	•	F	•	•
	18—Green Creek	7,500	11	•	V	•	•
	18—Green Creek Group*	7,500	2	•	V	•	•
	19—Trumbull Lake*	9,500	45	•	V	•	•

Notes:
*On reservation system. Phone: 1-800-280-CAMP.
Opening dates range from mid-April to mid-May; closing dates range from Oct. 1 to late Nov.; check with the ranger district office.

REGION 3

Yosemite National Park

For Information

Yosemite National Park
P.O. Box 577
Yosemite National Park, CA 95389
209/372-0200 for 24-hour recorded message
1-900/454-YOSE for live operator, Mon.–Fri.

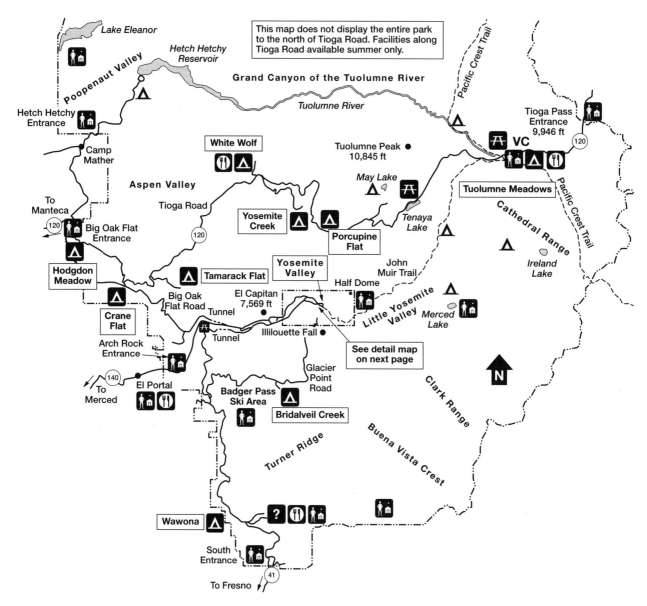

This map does not display the entire park to the north of Tioga Road. Facilities along Tioga Road available summer only.

Lake Eleanor

Poopenaut Valley

Hetch Hetchy Reservoir

Grand Canyon of the Tuolumne River

Tuolumne River

Pacific Crest Trail

Hetch Hetchy Entrance

Camp Mather

White Wolf

Tuolumne Peak 10,845 ft

Tioga Pass Entrance 9,946 ft

VC

To Manteca

Aspen Valley

Tioga Road

May Lake

Tuolumne Meadows

Big Oak Flat Entrance

Yosemite Creek

Porcupine Flat

Tenaya Lake

Cathedral Range

Hodgdon Meadow

Tamarack Flat

Yosemite Valley

John Muir Trail

Ireland Lake

Crane Flat

Big Oak Flat Road

El Capitan 7,569 ft

Half Dome

Little Yosemite Valley

Merced Lake

Tunnel

Arch Rock Entrance

Tunnel

Illilouette Fall

See detail map on next page

Clark Range

N

To Merced

El Portal

Glacier Point Road

Badger Pass Ski Area

Bridalveil Creek

Turner Ridge

Buena Vista Crest

Wawona

South Entrance

To Fresno

Location

Yosemite National Park embraces a vast track of scenic wildlands set aside in 1890 to preserve a portion of the Sierra Nevada Mountains. More than 94% of the 748,542-acre park is designated as wilderness. The park ranges from 2,000 feet to more than 13,000 feet above sea level and offers 3 major features: alpine wilderness, groves of giant sequoias, and Yosemite Valley. Access to Yosemite is via Highway 140 and 120 eastbound from Merced and Manteca; Highway 41 northbound from Fresno; and Highway 120 westbound from Lee Vining (closed in winter).

Yosemite National Park *(continued)*

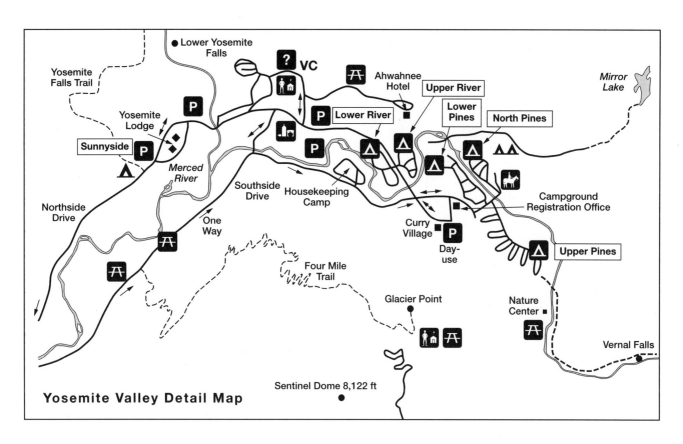

Yosemite Valley Detail Map

Labels on the map:
- Lower Yosemite Falls
- Yosemite Falls Trail
- VC
- Ahwahnee Hotel
- Upper River
- Mirror Lake
- Yosemite Lodge
- P
- Lower River
- Lower Pines
- North Pines
- Sunnyside
- P
- Merced River
- Northside Drive
- Southside Drive
- Housekeeping Camp
- Campground Registration Office
- One Way
- Curry Village
- Day-use
- Upper Pines
- Four Mile Trail
- Glacier Point
- Nature Center
- Vernal Falls
- Sentinel Dome 8,122 ft

Points of Interest

▲ Yosemite Valley is world famous for its impressive waterfalls, cliffs, and unusual rock formations.

▲ Yosemite, Bridalveil, Vernal, Nevada, and Illilouette are the most prominent of the waterfalls around the valley's perimeter, reaching their maximum flow in May and June and lowest from mid-August through early fall.

▲ Glacier Point offers what may be Yosemite's finest view of Yosemite Valley, Half Dome, the panoramic expanse of the High Sierra, and the 2,425-foot drop of Yosemite Falls.

▲ Tioga Road crosses the Tuolumne Meadows (at 8,600 feet) section of Yosemite with scenic turnouts that offer superb views of sparkling lakes, fragile meadows, domes, and lofty peaks.

▲ At Tioga Pass the road crosses the Sierra's crest at 9,945 feet, the highest automobile pass in California.

▲ Open-air tram rides through Mariposa Grove, the largest of three sequoia groves in Yosemite, are available from May until October; Tuolumne, and Merced Groves are off of the Big Oak Flat Road, near Crane Flat.

Glacier Point offers what may be Yosemite's finest view of Yosemite Valley, Half Dome, and the panoramic expanse of the High Sierra. The Badger Pass ski area is located on the road to Glacier Point. (Photo: California Office of Tourism)

REGION 3

Yosemite National Park *(continued)*

The Merced River enters Yosemite Valley via Illilouette Fall, Nevada Fall, and Vernal Fall, and flows the length of the valley.

General Information

▲ An entry fee is charged and is valid for 7 consecutive days. Camping fees are charged at all of the campgrounds.

▲ There are 4 visitor centers:

Valley Visitor Center, located in Yosemite Valley, is open year-round.

Tuolumne Meadows Visitor Center near the Tioga Pass entrance is closed in winter, and generally open June through September.

Big Oak Flat Information Station on Highway 120 at the western edge of the park, is open spring through fall.

Wawona Information Station, near the park's south entrance on Highway 41 is also open on a more limited basis.

▲ The visitor centers offer general park information, a self-help backcountry information counter, free wilderness permits, an orientation slide show, displays and exhibits; books, maps, and postcards are for sale.

▲ A variety of ranger-led walks, talks, and evening programs are scheduled throughout the season. Check the activity schedule in the free *Yosemite Guide* for programs offered in Yosemite Valley, Wawona, Mariposa Grove, Glacier Point, Tuolumne Meadows, and Crane Flat/Big Oak Flat.

▲ Camping is permitted only in designated campgrounds. Four campgrounds are open year-round: Lower Pines, Sunnyside Walk-In, Wawona, and Hodgdon Meadow. The season of operation differs for the others (see chart). For general campground information, call 209/372-0200.

Yosemite Valley is world-famous for its impressive waterfalls, cliffs, and unusual rock formations. Bridalveil Fall is located near the entrance to the valley. (Photo: Lillian Morava)

Yosemite National Park *(continued)*

▲ Between May 1 and September 15, the camping limit for all campgrounds in Yosemite Valley is 7 days; the remainder of the year the limit is 30 days. Maximum length for RVs is 40 feet.

▲ Outside of Yosemite Valley, the camping limit is 14 days between May 1 and September 15, except for Wawona which is limited to 7 days; the remainder of the year the limit is 30 days. Maximum length for RVs is 35 feet.

▲ Reservations are required for campsites in Yosemite Valley's auto campground year-round, for Hodgdon Meadow and Crane Flat campgrounds, and for one-half of Tuolumne Meadows Campground from summer through fall. All other campgrounds, except group campgrounds, are operated on a first-come, first-served basis. Reservations may be made through the national park reservation system.

▲ There are 5 group campgrounds. Reservations may be made through the national park reservation system for the group camps in Yosemite Valley, Hodgdon Meadow, and Tuolumne Meadows. Reservations for Bridalveil Creek and Wawona may be made through the Wawona Ranger Office (209/375-6592). All groups must include 10–30 persons; a group can reserve a maximum of 2 campsites.

▲ To protect Yosemite's wilderness, there are quotas for overnight use. Free wilderness permits are required and are available from ranger stations and visitor centers; phone 209/372-0310 for current hours of operation. At least 50% of each trailhead quota is available on a first-come, first-served basis no earlier than the morning of the day before you wish to begin your hike. Maximum group size is 25 for trail travel, or 8 or less for off-trail travel.

▲ For information on reservations for High Sierra Camps, phone: 209/454-2002.

▲ To avoid the parking problem in Yosemite Valley, visitors are encouraged to park at Curry Village and take the free shuttle bus; they operate daily at 10-minute intervals except during early morning or late evening hours, when intervals may be 20 minutes. The shuttle buses serve 19 stops, including campgrounds, hotels, the visitor center, Yosemite Village stores, and restaurants.

▲ Complimentary shuttle bus service is provided in the summer from Wawona to Mariposa Grove, and from Tioga Pass to Tenaya Lake. Hikers buses run daily to Glacier Point late spring through autumn and to Tuolumne Meadows late

The Mariposa Grove, 35 miles south of Yosemite Valley, is the largest of three sequoia groves in Yosemite. (Photo: Lillian Morava)

June through Labor Day. Call 209/372-1240 for hikers' bus fee, schedule, and reservations.

▲ Road and trail conditions and available services may change with the weather; for current conditions and general information call 209/372-0200.

▲ A self-guiding auto tour is available with the aid of a guide book or a cassette tape sold at visitor centers.

▲ Sightseeing tours on an open-air tram or bus are available. These narrated tours by informed guides operate daily to most points of interest in the park including Yosemite Valley (year-round), Tuolumne Meadows (summer), Glacier Point, Wawona, and Mariposa Grove of giant sequoias (spring through fall). For reservations and information, call 209/372-1240.

▲ More than 8 miles of surfaced bicycle paths wind through the eastern end of Yosemite Valley. Bikes are allowed only on paved bikeways and roads open to private vehicles; all bikes are prohibited from pedestrian and hiking trails. Rental bikes are available at Yosemite Lodge and Curry Village, conditions permitting.

▲ Horseback riding is available spring into autumn with two-hour, half-day, and full-day rides

The Tioga Road, State Route 120, crosses the Tuolumne Meadows and the high country. The road passes through an area of sparkling lakes, fragile meadows, domes, and lofty peaks. The road is closed November to May.

departing daily from stables in Yosemite Valley, Wawona, and in summer, from Tuolumne Meadows. For information, phone: 209/372-8348.

▲ Rock climbing classes, for beginner through advanced, are offered in Yosemite Valley in the spring and fall, and in Tuolumne Meadows each summer by the Yosemite Mountaineering School and Guide Service. For information, phone: 209/372-8435.

▲ Rafting on the Merced River in Yosemite Valley is open to any type of non-motorized vessel between Clark's Bridge and Cathedral Beach Picnic area from 10 a.m. to 6 p.m. daily. In addition, the South Fork of the Merced River in Wawona is open for rafting from 10 a.m. to 6 p.m. daily between Swinging Bridge and Wawona Campground. Raft rentals are available in season at Curry Village. Phone: 209/372-8341.

▲ Swimming is permitted at all lakes and streams except where posted. During the summer the pools at Yosemite Lodge and Curry Village are open from 10 a.m. to 5 p.m.

▲ Reservations for all overnight lodging in Yosemite may be made by calling 209/252-4848. Lodging in Yosemite Valley includes Curry Village, Housekeeping Camp, Yosemite Lodge, and The Ahwahnee Hotel; lodging outside Yosemite Valley includes the Wawona Hotel and Tuolumne Meadows Lodge.

▲ Eating facilities and stores are available in Yosemite Valley and Wawona year-round and at Tuolumne Meadows and White Wolf during the summer season.

▲ Hot showers and laundry facilities are available year-round in Yosemite Valley; hot showers are available seasonally at Tuolumne Meadows and White Wolf. Service stations are located at Yosemite Valley, Crane Flat, Tuolumne Meadows, and Wawona.

▲ Fishing is permitted with a California license, which can be purchased at the Village Store Sport Shop or Wawona Store (summer) or Curry Village Mountain Shop (winter). State rules apply on season and catch. Local regulations may apply in Yosemite Valley.

▲ For visitors with disabilities, an accessibility brochure and vehicle wheelchair-emblem placards for special driving privileges are available at park entrance stations and visitor centers. Wheelchair rentals are available at Yosemite Medical Clinic. Phone: 209/372-4637.

▲ Black bears inhabit the park; they are attracted to human food. Store food in an ice chest, then lock it in a trunk or recreational vehicle. In campgrounds, use food storage lockers or store properly in vehicles. In the backcountry, use the bear-resistant portable food canisters; they are available for rental or purchase. Information on bears and precautions are available at park entrances and campgrounds.

Group Campgrounds	Total Units	Drinking Water	Flush Toilets	Limit of Stay	Season (Approx.)
Bridalveil Creek** (walk-in)	1	•	•	14	June–Sept.
Hodgdon Meadow* (walk-in)	4	•	•	14	all year
Tuolumne Meadows* (walk-in)	8	•	•	14	July–Labor Day
Wawona** (walk-in)	1	•	•	14	mid-May– Sept.
Yosemite Valley* (walk-in)	11	•	•	7	mid-May– Sept.

Notes:
*Reservations required through DESTINET.
**Reservations required through Ranger Station District Office.

Yosemite National Park *(continued)*

General Location	Campgrounds	Elevation (feet)	Total Sites	RV Space	Drinking Water-Stream (boil it)	Toilets Flush/Pit	Sanitary Dump Station	Season (Approx.)
Yosemite Valley	North Pines*	4,000	85	•	•	F		April–Oct.
	Upper Pines*	4,000	238	•	•	F	•	April–Nov.
	Lower Pines*	4,000	172	•	•	F		all year
	Upper River*	4,000	124		•	F		late April–Oct.
	Lower River*	4,000	126	•	•	F	•	early April–Nov.
	Sunnyside Walk-In	4,000	35		•	F		all year
Along Hwy.41	Wawona	4,000	100	•	•	F	•	all year
	Bridalveil Creek	7,200	110	•	•	F		June–Sept.
Along Highway 120	Hodgdon Meadow* (near Big Oak Flat)	4,872	105	•	•	F		all year
	Crane Flat* (near the Tioga Road turnoff)	6,191	166	•	•	F		June-Oct.
	Tamarack Flat	6,315	52		Str.	P		July–early Sept.
	White Wolf	8,000	87	•	•	F		July–early Sept.
	Yosemite Creek	7,659	75		Str.	P		July-early Sept.
	Porcupine Flat	8,100	52	•	Str.	P		July–early Sept.
	Tuolumne Meadows**	8,600	314	•	•	F	•	mid-June–Sept.

Notes:

*Reservations available through DESTINET.

**Tuolumne Meadows has 25 walk-in spaces available for backpackers/visitors without vehicles.

Facilities & Activities

865 RV and tent campsites at 6 campgrounds in Yosemite Valley

210 RV and tent campsites at 2 campgrounds at Glacier Point/Wawona

851 RV and tent campsites at 7 campgrounds along the Big Oak Flat and Tioga Roads

5 group campgrounds

backcountry camping; permit required

self-guiding nature trails

over 800 miles of hiking/backpacking trails

35 miles of trails in Yosemite Valley

picnicking

8 miles of bikeway in Yosemite Valley/rentals

horseback riding/guided trail rides/rentals

guided backpacking trips

swimming

fishing

rafting/floating in any non-motorized vessel/rentals

rock climbing/rock climbing classes

ice skating

cross-country skiing/snowshoeing

downhill skiing

self-guiding auto tour

sightseeing tour on an open-air tram or bus

complimentary shuttle bus service

4 visitor centers/information stations

ranger-led walks, talks, and evening programs

commercial services

Resources for Further Information

California Department of Parks & Recreation
P.O. Box 942896
Sacramento, CA 94296-0001
916/653-6995

California Division of Tourism
P.O. Box 1499
Sacramento, CA 95812-1499
1-800-462-2543

National Park Service
Western Region Information Office
Fort Mason, Bldg. 201
(Bay and Franklin Streets)
San Francisco, CA 94123
415/556-0560

U.S. Army Corps of Engineers
Sacramento District
1325 J Street
Sacramento, CA 95814-2922
916/440-2183

U.S. Forest Service
Pacific-Southwest Region
630 Sansome St., Room 527
San Francisco, CA 94111
415/705-2874

Bureau of Land Management
California State Office
2150 Butano Drive
Sacramento, CA 95825
916/979-2800

Camping Reservation Systems

California State Parks
DESTINET
9450 Carroll Park Drive
San Diego, CA 92121
1-800-444-7275 (PARK)
1-800-695-2269 (for cancellations)

National Park Service
DESTINET
9450 Carroll Park Drive
San Diego, CA 92121-2256
1-800-365-2267 (CAMP)
1-800-388-2733 (for cancellations)

for Yosemite reservations
1-800-436-7275 (PARK)

U.S. National Forest Service
National Recreation Reservation System
P.O. Box 900
Cumberland, MD 21502-0900
1-800-280-2267 (CAMP)
FAX: 301-722-9802

For Topographical Quad Maps

U.S. Geological Survey
Western Distribution Branch
Box 25286, Federal Center
Denver, CO 80225

Quad maps can be obtained in person from USGS offices at
504 Custom House
555 Battery Street
San Francisco, CA 94111
415/705-1010

345 Middlefield Road
Building 3, Room 3128
Menlo Park, CA 94025
415/329-4309

7638 Federal Building
300 North Los Angeles Street
Los Angeles, CA 90012
213/894-2850

Information/Publications

Off-Highway Motor Vehicle Recreation Division
California Department of Parks & Recreation
P.O. Box 942896
Sacramento, CA 94296-0001
916/324-4442
("Guide to Off-Highway Vehicle Areas of California")

California State Parks Store
P.O. Box 942896
Sacramento, CA 94296-0001
916/653-4000
("Special Park Passes")
("Official Guide to California State Parks" — $2)

California Road Conditions
Caltrans 24-hour Service: On touchtone phone, press Highway Number and Pound (#) Key
Northern California: 916/445-7623
Southern California: 213/628-7623

Index